HERE'S TO YOU, JESUSA!

HERE'S TO YOU,
JESUSA!

TRANSLATED FROM THE SPANISH

BY DEANNA HEIKKINEN

Elena Poniatowska

FARRAR, STRAUS AND GIROUX

NEW YORK

Farrar, Straus and Giroux
19 Union Square West, New York 10003

Copyright © 1969 by Elena Poniatowska
Translation copyright © 2001 by Farrar, Straus and Giroux, LLC
All rights reserved
Distributed in Canada by Douglas & McIntyre Ltd.
Printed in the United States of America
Originally published in 1969 by Ediciones Era, Mexico, as
Hasta no verte Jesús mío
Published in the United States by Farrar, Straus and Giroux
First American edition, 2001

Library of Congress Cataloging-in-Publication Data
Poniatowska, Elena.
   [Hasta no verte Jesús mío. English]
   Here's to you, Jesusa! / Elena Poniatowska ; translated by Deanna
Heikkinen.— 1st ed.
      p.   cm.
   ISBN 0-374-16819-9 (alk. paper)
   I. Heikkinen, Deanna.   II. Title.

PQ7297.P63 H313   2001
863'.64—dc21

                                          00-055125
Designed by Abby Kagan

To Bell Chevigny

Introduction

 OVER THERE where Mexico City starts getting smaller, where the streets get lost and are deserted, that's where Jesusa lives. It's so warm there's no ice left in the freezers, just water, and the Victoria and Superior beers just float around. The women's hair sticks against the nape of their necks, beaten down by sweat. Sweat dampens the air, clothes, armpits, foreheads. The heat buzzes, like the flies. The air in those parts is greasy, dirty; the people live in the very frying pans where they cook *garnachas*, those thick, filled tortillas covered in chile sauce, and potato or pumpkin-flower quesadillas, the daily bread that the women heap on tables with uneven legs along the street. The dust is the only dry thing, that and a few gourds.

Jesusa is dried up, too. She's as old as the century. She's eighty-seven and the years have made her smaller, as it has the houses, bending their backbones. They say that old people get smaller so they'll take up the least possible space inside the earth when they're done living on top of it. Jesusa's eyes, with little red veins, are tired; they've gotten gritty, gray around the pupil, the brown fading a little bit at a time. Tears no longer reach her eyes and the bright red lacrimal ducts are the most intense parts of her face. There's no water under her skin either. Jesusa constantly says: "I'm turning into parchment." But the skin remains stretched over her prominent cheekbones. "Every time I move I lose scales." She lost a front tooth and she decided: "When I go out somewhere, if

I ever do go out, I'll put a Chiclet there, I'll chew it up real good and I'll stick it on."

I met her in 1964. She lived near Morazán and Ferrocarril-Cintura, a poor neighborhood in Mexico City, whose main attraction was the Penitentiary, called El Palacio Negro de Lecumberri, the Black Palace of Lecumberri. The prison was the most important place in the area; around it swarmed the women who sold quesadillas, steaming pots of chile, sweet and butter tamales, the ones who sold *sopes*, the tortillas drenched in chile sauce, and hot *garnachas*, the big-bellied attorneys with their suits, ties, beards, and briefcases, the paperboys, the buses, the relatives of the prisoners, and those bureaucrats who always flutter around misfortune, the morbid, the curious. Jesusa lived in a tenement close to the Peni. You could hear the constant humming of a typewriter. Or maybe it was several. It smelled like dampness, fermentation.

—What do you want? What business do you have with me?

—I want to talk to you.

—To me? Listen, I work. If I don't work, I don't eat. I don't have time to hang around chatting.

Irascibly, Jesusa agreed to let me visit with her on the only free day she had during the week: Wednesday from four to six. I started living from Wednesday to Wednesday. Jesusa, on the other hand, never gave up her hostile attitude. When the neighbors would yell to her from the doorway to hold the dog so I could come in, she'd say in a bad-tempered tone: "Oh, it's you." As I skirted around the dog carrying a big square tape recorder, I could feel its breath hot on my ankles. Its barks were as gruff as Jesusa's disposition.

The tenement had a main hallway and rooms on either side. The two waterless "toilets" set up in the back were filled to the top, and the dirty papers were piled up on the floor. Jesusa's place got very little sun, and the gas from the grill made your eyes water. The walls were rotting, and although the hallway was quite narrow, half a dozen bare-bottomed little ones played there and peeked into the neighbors' rooms. Jesusa would say: "Do you want a taco? . . . No? Then don't stand around begging in doorways." The rats peered in too.

Back in those days Jesusa wasn't home much because she left early for work at the printshop. She closed up her room tightly since there was no lock, her animals asphyxiating inside, her plants too. She cleaned at the printshop, swept, picked up, dusted, rinsed and drained the metal pieces. She took the workers' overalls home and often even their everyday clothes, and she labored a second shift at her washboard. In the evening she fed her cats, chickens, and rabbit, watered her plants, and tidied up the place.

The first time I asked her to tell me her life story (because I'd heard her talking on a rooftop and the language she used was extraordinary, but above all because I was drawn to her capacity for indignation) she answered: "I don't have time." She showed me the piled-up overalls, the five chickens that had to be taken out to get some sun, the dog and the cats that had to be fed, the two birds that looked like sparrows, imprisoned inside a cage that got smaller every day.

—You see what I mean? Are you going to help me?

—Yes, I answered.

—All right, then put those overalls in gasoline.

That's when I learned what overalls really were. They were hard and stiff and full of grime with big grease stains. I put them in a washbasin to soak. The liquid wouldn't cover them because they were so rigid; the overalls were an island in the middle of water, a rock. Jesusa ordered: "While they're soaking, take the chickens out to the sidewalk." So I did, but the hens started to peck the cement, looking for the improbable. Then they jumped off the sidewalk and scattered into the street. I got scared and ran back to Jesusa.

—They're going to get run over by a car!

—*Pues*, don't you know how to put chickens out? Didn't you see the little string? You had to tie them by the leg.

She quickly got her hens back inside and scolded me again:

—Who would think of letting chickens out like that?

Upset, I answered:

—What else can I help you with?

—Let the chickens out on the roof, even if it's just for a little while!

I did so but with some apprehension. The house was so low that even I—and I'm about as tall as a sitting dog—could see them ruffling their feathers. They seemed to be happy pecking at the roof. I liked it. I thought: "Well, at least I did something right." The black dog in the doorway was annoyed, and Jesusa yelled at me again:

—What happened to the overalls?

I took them out of the gasoline. When I asked her where the sink was, Jesusa pointed to a corrugated washboard that was barely twenty or twenty-five centimeters wide by fifty long:

—A sink? Like you'd find one of those around here! Scrub on that!

She took a washbasin out from under her bed and looked at me sarcastically: she knew it was impossible for me to scrub anything. The overalls were so stiff you couldn't even grab hold of them. Jesusa exclaimed:

—It's obvious that you're high-class and useless.

She pushed me aside, and then she realized that the overalls needed to soak in the gasoline overnight and she ordered:

—Let's go get meat for my animals now.

—We'll take my car.

—No, it's right here on the corner.

She walked fast, her change purse in her hand, not looking at me. In contrast to her taciturn behavior with me, she joked with the butcher, going out of her way to be pleasant, and bought a pile of wretched carcasses wrapped in paper that immediately got bloody. At her place she threw the animal parts on the floor and the cats were right on top of them, electrified, with their tails up straight. The dogs were slower. The birds chirped. Like a fool, I asked her if they ate meat too.

—What country are you from?

I plugged in my tape recorder. It looked like a navy-blue coffin with a huge dance-hall speaker. Jesusa protested: "Are you going to pay for the electricity?" Then she gave in: "Where are you going to put that animal? I'll have to move all this crap." I told her the tape recorder was on loan to me: "Why are you using something that isn't yours? Aren't you afraid?" The following Wednesday I asked her the same questions again.

—Didn't I tell you about that last week?

—Yes, but it didn't record.

—That big animal doesn't work?

—Sometimes I don't notice if it's taping or not.

—Then don't bring it anymore.

—I don't write fast and we'd waste a lot of time.

—That's it then. It'd be better if we stopped here. After all, neither you nor I have anything to gain from this.

So I started to write in a notebook and Jesusa made fun of my handwriting: "So many years of school to end up with that scribble-scrabble!" This method worked for me, for when I got home at night, I'd re-create what she'd told me. I was always afraid that on the day when I least expected it she'd cut me off like a spurned lover. She didn't like the neighbors to see me, or for me to greet them. One day when I asked about the smiling girls who had been at the door, she insisted: "Don't call them girls, call them whores, yes, little whores, that's what they are."

One Wednesday I found Jesusa wrapped in a bright red, yellow, and parrot-green serape with wide flashy stripes. She had been lying on her bed and had only gotten up to open the door for me. Then she went back to bed to lie down, with the serape covering her whole head. She usually sat in front of the radio in the dark, like a little bundle of old age and loneliness listening, attentive, alert, critical.

I looked at the big serape, which I hadn't seen before, as I sat in a little chair at the foot of the bed. Jesusa didn't say a word. Even the radio, which was always on during our conversations, was turned off. I waited something like half an hour in the dark. Every now and then I'd ask her:

—Jesusa, do you feel sick?

There was no answer.

—Jesusa, don't you want to talk?

She didn't move.

—Are you angry?

Total silence. I decided to be patient. Many times, when we started our interviews Jesusa would be in a bad mood. After a while she settled in, but she never lost her grouchiness and her ever-present scorn.

—Have you been sick? Have you been going to work?

—No.

—Why not?

—I haven't gone in two weeks.

We went back to the most absolute silence. The birds, which always made their presence known with a humble and trivial "here I am" under the rags she covered the cage with, weren't even chirping. Discouraged, I waited a long time, dusk fell, I kept waiting, the sky turned lilac. Cautiously, I returned to the task at hand:

—Aren't you going to talk to me?

She didn't answer.

—Do you want me to leave?

Then she pulled the serape down below her eyes, then under her chin, and said with annoyance:

—Listen, you've been coming here and screwing around and annoying me for two years and you still don't understand anything. So it's better if we just stop now.

I left with my notebook pressed against my chest, like a shield. In the car I thought: "My God! What a marvelous old woman she is! She doesn't have anyone in her life, I'm the only person who visits her, and she still can tell me to go to hell."

The next Wednesday I was late (perhaps I was unconsciously getting even) and she was waiting outside on the sidewalk.

She muttered:

—Well, what's wrong with you? You don't seem to understand. When you leave, I go to the stable for my milk, I go get my bread. You screw me up if you're late.

So I went to the stable with her. In the poor neighborhoods

the countryside spills over the city's boundaries, or maybe it's the other way around, even though nothing smells like fields and everything tastes like dust, like garbage, rotten. "When we poor people drink milk we get it right from the cow, not that crap in bottles and boxes that you all drink." At the bakery, Jesusa bought four rolls: "Not sweet rolls, those don't fill you up and cost more."

I came to understand poverty through Jesusa, real poverty, where water is collected in buckets and carried very carefully so it doesn't spill, where the washing is done on a metal washboard because there is no sink, where a neighbor will tap into another's electric line, where the hens lay eggs without shells, "just membrane," because a lack of sun keeps them from hardening. Jesusa was one of the millions of men and women who don't live so much as they survive. Just getting through the day is so much work, the hours and the energy lost makes life so difficult for poor people. Survival means staying afloat, breathing calmly, even if it's only for a moment in the evening when the chickens no longer cackle in their cages and the cat stretches out on the trampled earth.

On Wednesday afternoons, as the sun set and the blue sky changed to orange, in that semidark little room, in the midst of the shrieking of the children, the slamming doors, the shouting, and the radio going full blast, another life emerged—that of Jesusa Palancares, the one that she relived as she retold it. Through a tiny crack, we watched the sky, its colors, blue, then orange, and finally black. A sliver of sky. I squinted so my gaze would fit through that crack, and we would enter the other life.

Listening to Jesusa, I imagined her as young, fast, independent, severe, and I lived her rages and her pains, her legs that became numb from the cold snow up north, her hands reddened from washing. Watching her act out her story, able to make her own decisions, made my own lack of character more obvious to me. More than anything, I liked to imagine her in the ocean, her hair loose, her bare feet on the sand, sucked in by the water, her hands made into shells to taste it, to discover its saltiness, its sting. "You know, the sea is an immensity!" I also saw her running as a child, her petticoats between her legs, stuck to her strong body, her radiant face, her beautiful head, sometimes covered with a straw hat made of *soyate*, sometimes with a rebozo. Watching her fight in the marketplace was a pleasure, a right cross, hit her lower, kick her in the back, you knocked the wind out of her, a hook to the liver, don't forget her jaw, now, get it over with, hard, throw another one, good judgment, Jesusa. But the most endearing image was that of her small figure, very straight, next to the other *adelitas*, the camp followers who rode on top of the train, her cartridge belts across her chest, Captain Pedro Aguilar's wide sombrero protecting her from the sun.

As she talked, such images gave me great joy. I felt strength from all the things I hadn't lived through. When I got home I'd say: "Something is being born inside me, something new that wasn't there before," but no one ever answered me. I wanted to tell them: "I get stronger each time, I'm growing, I'm finally going to be a woman." What was growing, although it may have been there for years, was my Mexican being, my becoming Mexican; feeling Mexico inside me, the same one that was inside Jesusa. I wasn't the eight-year-old girl who had arrived on a refugee ship, the *Marqués de Comilla*, the daughter of eternally absent parents, of transatlantic travelers, the daughter of trains. Now Mexico was inside me, it was a huge animal (as Jesusa called the tape recorder), a strong animal, energetic, one that got bigger and bigger until it filled the entire space. Discovering it was like suddenly having a truth in your hands, like a lamp that shines brightly and casts its circle of light on the floor. Before, I'd only seen floating lights that got lost in the darkness, the light from the switchman's kerosene lamp that eventually disappeared. But this stable, immobile lamp gave me security, like an anchor. My grandparents and my great-grandparents always repeated a phrase in English that they thought was poetic: "I don't belong." Maybe it was their way of distinguishing themselves from the rabble, not being like the rest. One night, before sleep overcame me, after identifying strongly with Jesusa and going over all her images one by one, I could finally say to myself in a quiet voice: "*Yo sí pertenezco*," "I do belong."

Cautiously, fearfully, fondness was born little by little between us. Trying to overcome one of the oldest problems in the world, bridging the gap between love and indifference, was a healthy blow to my self-esteem. There we were, the two of us, afraid of hurting each other. That very afternoon she made me a cup of bitter tea for indigestion and she offered me one of her chickens: "Here, take it for your mother to make you some broth." Another Wednesday I fell asleep on her bed and she gave up her radio soap operas so I wouldn't be woken up. And Jesusa lives by the radio! It's her communication to the outside, her only tie with the world. She didn't ever turn it off, but she'd lower the volume when she revealed the most intimate episodes of her life. Little by little, trust was being forged, fondness, as she called it: what we never said out loud, what we never even mentioned. I think after my son Mane, Jesusa's the person I have the most respect for. Never has one human being done as much for another as Jesusa has for me. And I knew she was going to die, as she wished; that's why every Wednesday my heart tightened when I thought that she might not be there. "Someday when you come, you won't find me, you'll just find air." And my heart opened up when I saw her sitting there, shrunken in her little chair, or on her bed, her dangling legs in cotton stockings, listening to her stories, allowing me in, grumbling, her hands all twisted up from so much washing, the yellow and brown spots on her face, her thin braids, her safety-pinned sweaters. I asked God to allow me to carry her to her grave.

While I was in France for a year, working on this novel, I sent Jesusa letters, but mostly postcards. She was the first person to write back. She'd go to the scribes at the Plaza de Santo Domingo and dictate her letter and she'd send it first-class. She wrote about the things she thought I'd be most interested in, like the president of Czechoslovakia's trip to Mexico, the foreign debt, highway accidents; we never talked about the news in the papers when I was with her. Jesusa was always unpredictable. One afternoon I found her glued to the radio, a notebook on her lap, a pencil in her hand. She was writing an upside-down *U* and a three-legged *N*; and it was extremely awkward for her. She was taking writing lessons from the radio. Stupidly I asked:

—Why do you want to learn how to do that now?

—Because I want to die knowing how to read and write.

I tried to take her out on several occasions:

—Let's go to the movies, Jesusa.

—No, I don't see well . . . I used to like the serials, the Lon Chaney ones.

—Then let's take a ride.

—And the chores? Obviously you don't have anything to do.

I suggested a trip to Tehuantepec to see her homeland again, something that I thought would please her, until I realized that the hope of something better unsettled her, it made her hostile. Jesusa was so used to her condition, so ruined by loneliness and poverty that the possibility of change seemed an insult: "Get out of here. What do you understand? I said get out. Leave me alone." I understood then that there is a point when you've suffered so much that you can't stop suffering. The only break Jesusa allowed herself was the cigarette she smoked leisurely at around six in the evening, her radio always on. She unwrapped gifts and then rewrapped them carefully. "So they don't get damaged." That's how I learned about her carton of dolls, all new, untouched. "There are four. I bought them for myself. Since I never had any as a child . . ."

In her book *Soldaderas in the Mexican Military*, Elizabeth Salas states that in 1914, between January and September, at Fort Bliss and then at Fort Wingate, 3,359 officers and soldiers were incarcerated, as well as 1,256 *soldaderas* and 554 children. The *soldaderas* were called that because they welcomed the soldiers, took care of them, never hesitating to take up a rifle and shoot when their man was eating or taking care of his business. They, on the other hand, had to watch their own backs. They gave birth on the road and kept on walking. They fought in the trenches. One of Jesusa's friends had her child in a trench, another in a desert up north, but it died from lack of water. Jesusa, Captain Pedro Aguilar's wife, not only knew the rails, the steady gunfire, the arguments between the troublemaker *soldaderas*; she also experienced the glories of battle, taking out the enemy with a single shot. The bullets in the blue air exploded like little white balls, clouds of deafening smoke covered the sky and enlivened Jesusa.

Without the *soldaderas* the Revolution would not have survived. Who would have looked after the soldiers? Without them everyone would have deserted. They made hearth and home and they buried their soldier, their Juan, when the worst happened, just as God commands. They carried their children on their backs, tied up in their rebozos, and at dawn somehow they worked it so that even under the worst circumstances the camp would awaken to the fragrant smell of coffee. Many of them died from tuberculosis, peritonitis, and diarrhea, but that didn't take away their sense of adventure. Blessed *soldaderas* so maligned! They recklessly challenged death.

What an atmosphere the *soldaderas* created! Besides casseroles, chickens, piglets, pots, serapes, pans, ammunition, baby bottles, rifles, metates, and pups that they raised, they carried guitars and sang around the campfires at night. They walked for hours without tiring, stronger than the Tameme Indians, the natives that carried huge loads on their backs. If they happened to kill a steer with a stray bullet, then they had food for several days. They were maternal, they sheltered their man, they made him laugh, they entertained him. They built fires with carefully chosen stones, they ground corn, patted out thin tortillas, and still found a way to bathe and braid their tresses with colored ribbons to brighten their Juan's day. Their men could very easily have forgotten they were women, always seeing them dressed as men.

I had a dilemma when I wrote *Hasta no verte Jesús mío* in Spanish: the curse words. In a first version, Jesusa never said a bad word and I liked to think of her as modest, reserved; I was writing the story without "haughty words," but as our trust of each other grew, which happened after I returned from my year in France, Jesusa let loose. She brought me into her world, she no longer watched what she said and she'd admonish me: "Don't be such an asshole, you're the only one who believes in people, you're the only one who thinks people are good." I had to look up some of the words she used in a dictionary of Mexicanisms; others dated back to an archaic Spanish. She threw my absence in my face: "You look out for your own interests! You'll come see me as long as you can get what you want out of me, then there'll be neither hide nor hair of you. That's how it always is, everyone uses whoever they can." Like all old people, she had a long string of ailments and complaints; her rotting backside, her aching muscles, how badly the buses ran, the horrible quality of the food, the rent that was no longer affordable, the lazy and drunk neighbors. She'd repeat the same thing over and over, sitting on her bed, her legs hanging because it was set up on bricks; the water flooded the rooms during the rainy season and Doña Casimira, the owner, never bothered to have the patio drains unclogged.

Jesusa tolerated Casimira, the "rich one," like an enemy, someone who was there just to annoy her. The owner represented authority, and Jesusa believed that authority never helped the poor, they'd rather see them three feet under. She'd experienced enough with Don Venustiano Carranza, who stole her widow's pay.

Each meeting was really a long interview. When it was over I was left with a feeling of loss because I couldn't make her spirit visible, I couldn't reveal the intensity of Jesusa's character. Looking back now, I think I got caught up in the adventures, going from one anecdote to another. I liked her picaresque life. I never made her answer anything she didn't want to. I couldn't pry into her privacy. There was no way to present those moments when we were both silent, not even thinking, waiting for a miracle. We were always a little feverish, wishing for hallucinations. I heard my nanny's voice in Jesusa's, the woman who taught me Spanish, the voices of all the maids who passed through our house like air currents, their expressions, their view of life, if you could even call it that, because they lived for the day, they had no reason to hope for anything.

The voices of these other marginalized women sang a chorus to Jesusa Palancares's melody, and that's why there are words, idiomatic expressions and proverbs in the text, that come not only from Oaxaca, Jesusa's home state, but from the whole Republic, Jalisco, Veracruz, Guerrero, the sierra of Puebla. There were Wednesdays when Jesusa talked of nothing but her obsession of that day, but in the inactivity of the routine, the difficulty of everyday living, there were moments of pleasant, unexpected respite, such as when we took the chickens out of their cages and set them on the bed like little children.

I went to see Jesusa on Wednesday afternoons and when I got home I'd accompany my mother to cocktail parties at one embassy or another. I always tried to maintain a balance between the extreme poverty that I shared at Jesusa's tenement and the splendor of the receptions. My socialism was in name only. As I got into the tub of hot water, I'd remember the washbasin under the bed where Jesusa rinsed the overalls and bathed herself on Saturdays. I was ashamed: "I hope she never sees my house or how I live." When she did, she said: "I'm never coming back, I don't want you thinking I'm a beggar." But the friendship survived, the bond had been established. Jesusa and I loved each other. Never, however, did she stop judging me. "I knew from the beginning that you were high society." When I was in the hospital, she wanted to spend the night: "I'll lie down right at the foot of your bed." I've never received so much from anyone, I've never felt more guilty. I moved over a little in the bed:

"Come on, Jesusita, there's room for both of us," but she wouldn't. She left at five in the morning while I was still saying: "Ay, but there's room for both of us." She said: "No, the only bed we both fit in is mine because it's a poor person's bed."

When I'd typed up the first clean version of her life, I took it to her bound in sky-blue covers. She said: "What do I want this for? Get that piece of shit out of here. Can't you see it's in my way?" I thought she'd like it because it was so big. When it was to be published, I chose the Niño de Atocha, the little Jesus that presided over the semidarkness of her room, for the cover of the book, and when she saw it she asked me for twenty copies, which she gave to the men at the shop so they'd know about her life, the many precipices she had crossed, and so they'd have an idea of what the Revolution was really like.

Her difficult childhood, the abuse she suffered from her step-mother, Señora Evarista, and loneliness made her suspicious, proud; she was a skittish mare who avoided any expression of af-fection, of possible closeness. She never spoke of her love life.

I tried to emphasize Jesusa's personal qualities in the novel, things that differentiated her from the traditional image of the Mexican woman, her rebellion, her independence. Her essence remains, her redeeming strength, an impression of the Mexico of 1910, although her face changed. When she got close to the truth, her survival instinct distracted her and this dreaming saved her. She wrapped metaphysical meaning in her "visions" and that soft-ened the universe that was peopled by her loved ones.

Yes, Jesusa is like the earth, tired earth, unexpectedly quick to form whirlwinds. If you look, you'll find her face at demonstra-tions, at rallies, and in the constellation of protests that ring louder and louder. If you look, you'll see her coming out of the subways, you'll find her in the tangle of rails under the Nonoalco bridge, in the radiant eyes of young women who barely lean into life, in the callused hands raised to the wind of those who say yes, in the hands that carve, the ones that serve coffee in clay mugs, in the gaze of women who can lie on the fresh grass and watch the sun, without blinking. I see Jesusa in the sky, in the dirt, every-where, like God, He, the masculine.

Jesusa Palancares died at her home, 94 South, Block 8, Lot 12, Section Three B, Nuevo Paseo de San Agustín. Past the airport, past Ecatepec, on Thursday, May 28, 1987, at seven o'clock in the morning. The truth is, I called Jesusa Jose. Her real name was Jose-fina Bórquez, but when I thought about her I thought of Jesusa.

She died as she lived, rebellious, obstinate, fierce. She threw the priest out, she threw the doctor out. When I tried to take her hand she said: "Stop pawing me!" She didn't want to have any-thing to do with our voracious eyes, our avid hands, the sticky warmth of our bodies, our cheap solicitude. She wanted us to fuck off, as she sank deeper and deeper into her cot, the predecessor to her coffin. She never asked anyone for anything; she never knew self-pity. Her whole life was a challenge. Since she believed in reincarnation, she thought that she had come to Earth this time to pay her debt for her bad behavior in previous lives. She re-flected: "I must have been a really awful man who made a lot of women unhappy," because to her being a man meant behaving badly.

The day before she died she said: "Throw me out in the street so the dogs will eat me; don't spend money on me, I don't want to owe anyone anything." Now that she's in the ground and she made it to the cemetery, I'd like to rock her, take her in my arms like a little girl, blanket her with all the love she never received, exalt her, she who, like so many women, is part of the history of my country: Mexico. But Mexico doesn't welcome them, it doesn't even acknowledge them.

At 94 South, Block 8, Lot 12, Section Three B, Nuevo Paseo de San Agustín, Jesusa built her last dwelling, with sticks, bricks, pieces of cloth. In spite of the fact that she had a stove, she built a little cooking fire on the floor and she made a curtain to separate her bed from the rest of the tiny room. She had a wooden table that she used for ironing and eating, with a brick under the wob-bly leg to even it out. She stood all her saints right next to each other in one corner, they were the same ones I'd seen at her pre-vious place. The Niño de Atocha fearlessly awaited adoration, with his basket, his ostrich-feathered Three Musketeers hat, and his shell brooch. Jesusa brought the countryside to her space on the flat roof where the chickens cackled and the pigeons could mess outside rather than inside all over the dishes. She put up a railing for protection that seemed useless to me, made of some old rusted wires, a bucket without a bottom "but the metal of the sides is still good." She tied small boards, broomsticks—any old tree branch she found on the road—together real tightly to fence in her chickens on one side and her plants on the other. She had mint, lemon grass, camomile, chives, and Mexican herb tea.

The dignity of the country folk has usually dissolved by the time they end up in the shantytowns of Mexico City. They're crushed by plastic and nylon, cheaters and swindlers, while the nonbiodegradable garbage still degrades, and televisions are purchased in installments before a table or a chair. Jesusa, unlike all the rest, transported a piece of Oaxaca to her rooftop and cultivated it. Every day she traveled huge distances without complaining, two or three hours by bus to get to the Galve printshop in San Antonio Abad, two or three hours back home at sunset. Then she went out to buy meat for her cats and corn for her chickens. Once, she started hemorrhaging, spitting up blood, on the street, so she sat down on the curb. That was the beginning of the end. Someone offered to take her to a first-aid station. She wouldn't accept. She cleaned herself up the best she could, but since she was afraid of getting dizzy again on the bus and making a mess, she walked all the way home in the heat, covering herself with her rebozo, like a dying animal that just wants to get to its lair, all the way from San Antonio Abad to Ecatepec. She walked, one step at a time, an old woman. It was an immense effort, and no one realized that this tiny woman was accomplishing such an incredible feat, it was so terrible; she was like a mountain climber who pushes his body to its limit in order to reach the top of the tallest peak of the Andes. I can imagine the desperate effort that trip must have been for her. I can see her in the blazing sun, half out of her mind, and my heart aches to think that she was so humble or so proud (the two sides of the same coin) that she would not ask for help. Jesusa was never the same after that. Too much had been demanded of her human vessel, which no longer had anything to give, and it failed her. Her eighty-seven-year-old body warned her, "I can't go on anymore, you go on ahead," and as much as Jesusa spurred it on, her erratic orders found no response. Stubborn, without breath, she shut herself up in her room.

Her small frame, more emaciated all the time, was surrounded by fluttering instruments. When she regained a little strength, Jesusa ripped them out. She stopped talking, and when the doctor made an appearance, she shut her eyes tightly. She never opened them again. There was nothing left to see on this earth. She was through with us and our tricks, our hovering, our brains cracked like nuts. The self-important production we were making of her death disgusted her. She told us all to go to hell, the very place she thought she was headed.

She was barely four feet ten inches tall, and the years had made her even smaller, stooping her shoulders, pulling her beautiful hair out by the handfuls, her thick and wavy hair that had caused the young soldiers to call her Queen Xochtil. What bothered her the most were her two thin braids. When she went downtown, for bread or milk, she covered her head with her rebozo. She walked lopsided, leaning against the wall, bent over; but I liked her graying and sparse braids, her curly white hair at her temples, over her wrinkled forehead. She had big moles on her hands. She said they were from the liver; I think they were from time. With age, men and women become covered with mountain ranges and furrows, with slopes and deserts. Jesusa looked more like the earth, a walking clod of earth, a little pile of mud that time kneaded and left out to dry up in the sun. "I have four pegs left," she assured me, and pointed with her deformed and arthritic fingers at the holes between what was left of her teeth. The years tamed Jesusa. When I met her, she wouldn't even say "come in." By the time I went to see her at the Impresora Galve, she would order:

—You sit down, you're tired.
—What about you?
—Not me. Why would I be?
She made herself out to be hard.
—Don't you ever feel alone at times?
—Alone? Me? That's what I like the best.

It was true. She didn't need anyone, she could take care of herself. Her hallucinations, the product of her solitude, were enough for her. I don't think she really liked being alone that much, but she was too proud to admit it. She never asked anyone for anything. Even as she was dying, she pushed everyone away. "Don't touch me, leave me alone. Can't you see that I don't want anyone near me?" She treated herself like an outcast animal.

During the 1985 earthquake the roof of the Impresora Galve caved in. After that day Jesusa didn't go back to the shop. There was nowhere to work, and this break in her routine really hurt her. She was used to having that responsibility. "I have needs," she'd say, "you have yours, but mine aren't the same as yours." She needed to be needed, she had to accomplish something. There were no longer overalls or the workers' clothes at her place: shirts, socks, men's T-shirts. She became angry. When I told her how wonderful it was that a dead couple, locked in an embrace, their mouths joined, had been unearthed from the rubble of the Hotel Regis on Avenida Juárez after the earthquake, how fortunate that they had decided to die in each other's arms rather than to run, she yelled at me and told me to stop being an asshole.

—How can that be good? That's just disgusting.

—Why?

—We weren't born together, we were born alone, everyone in their own space. You have to live alone, go it alone.

—Don't you think it's the ultimate test of love?

—You're back to the same story! That's just filth. You said they pulled them out all covered in dirt.

Her reactions confused me. She ripped up a photograph that Héctor García had taken of her right under my nose: "I wanted one like this," she said, and pointed to a sepia-colored photograph in a wooden frame. "This isn't what I wanted," she repeated, "not this." She wanted one that was not only sepia-colored but formal and sad, where her hair was nicely combed, and she was wearing a high-collared white blouse, her eyes looking out seriously, her mouth firm, dignified, closed, her head straight. "That's the Marcel wave, with five waves. Now that's a real photograph, not those ridiculous things you brought me." She wanted to leave a serious image of herself, one of accomplishment.

To her it seemed disrespectful that Héctor García had captured her laughing on film. The gestures, the improvisation, the naturalness of everyday life were common, therefore they were not appropriate for photography. "Don't be clowning around." Having your picture taken was an event, a ceremony, something that didn't happen all the time. Nevertheless, that same day, Jesusa happily smoked a Marlboro instead of her Faritos, and agreed to have a beer with Héctor. On one other occasion she smoked with my eldest son, Mane, and with my mother once. But when I told her that some North American friends wanted to meet her, she hollered:

—Don't be bringing so many people around here, as if I had nothing else to do.

Over a period of ten years I saw her move three times (one of the constants in her life was "the rent"; the other "the landlady" of the tenement who always threatened to raise the rent). Each time she moved farther away, because the city drives out its poor, pushes them to the edges, shoving them, marginalizing them as it expands. Jesusa finally ended up on the road to Pachuca, around some hills called Aurora—Tablas de San Agustín—where there are big placards with blue arrows pointing in all directions, where they spell sewage with a *j*, water with an *h* and electricity with no *e*. No sewaje, no wahter, no lectricity.

There's not a single tree on those bald plains, not a speck of green, no grass, not a bush, except for the ones hanging on the walls in old Mobil Oil cans. The dust storms look like the Hiroshima mushroom cloud and they seem to transport all the waste of the world, absorbing the people's souls. The worst part isn't the mountain of garbage, but the stench, a sweet smell of cold grease, excrement, a refried mixture of all the awful smells on earth blended together, piling up under the sun, and as the day goes on, it becomes more intolerable.

Jesusa ranted and raved against "modernization," today's customs, the songs on the radio, frozen food, refrigerated fish, the so-called advances. Everything was better before. She didn't trust anything. Jesusa, more than anyone, lived the tragedy of our society. No one looks out for anyone else, everyone scratches their own back, there is no possibility of good, everyone is an ingrate. Loving dogs, chickens, cats, canaries is less disappointing; they aren't as unappreciative. Nevertheless, the moment would pass, and when Jose-Jesusa would forget to be angry, she'd admit, "We're all from Oaxaca here, that's why we help each other out." If they didn't help, at least they didn't hurt each other, which says a lot in a society where a daily disaster instigated by someone else is a normal occurrence.

Through Jesusa Palancares I learned about a widespread doctrine of spiritualism in Mexico: In 1963, the Department of the Interior indicated that in the Federal District alone there were more than 176 spiritualist temples. I visited several of them and met mediums in Portales, in Tepito, on Luna Street, in the poorest neighborhoods. The Catholic Church condemns spiritism as well as spiritualism, but they both incorporate a lot of the Catholic religion and ritual. Spiritualism is obviously practiced by a minority, but its followers adopt it because they receive more personalized attention, just as they do at certain banks. Jesusa belonged to the Iglesia Mexicana Patriarcal Elías, the Mexican Patriarchal Elias Church, founded by Roque Rojas, the true and last Messiah, son of the Sun, and very proudly Mexican. Roque Rojas received the last testament of the third era of humanity and founded seven churches. Iglesia Principesca de Éfeso, Iglesia Rabínica de Esmirna, Iglesia Sacerdotal de Pérgamo, Iglesia Levítica de Tiatira, Iglesia Profética de Sardes, Iglesia Guiadora de Filadelfia, and Iglesia Patriarcal de Laodicea. Their bright colors were even more suggestive than their names: the first was emerald green, the second scarlet red, the third blue, the fourth pale pink, the fifth Carmelite brown, the sixth navy blue, and the seventh milk white. They all displayed a bright sun whose interior disc had a man's face and red and yellow rays that originated from a bugle, announcing their message to the needy: "I am the God of the past, the present, and always, the God of the Sun."

The faithful of these churches call themselves, among other

names and after swearing total allegiance to Roque Rojas, "*pueblo trinitario mariano*," for the Holy Trinity and for the Virgin Mary. They never totally break with the Catholic Church, even though they stop attending because they prefer the Obra Espiritual.

The Obra Espiritual always seemed obscure to me, sometimes incomprehensible, and Jesusa would get annoyed when I asked her to repeat some basic principle. She spoke of Alain Kardec, of her Father and Protector Manuel Antonio Mesmer.

When I visited the temple under the Nonoalco bridge, the Midday Temple on Luna Street, I met the sisterhood and brotherhood and I heard a lecture on revelation and radiation. What struck me the most was to see the women in curlers and long scarlet nails, young people, girls in miniskirts, boys in T-shirts, sitting among women wearing rebozos and men in straw sombreros. The smell of the *nubes*, little clusters of white flowers, assaulted me; I never thought that the nectar of such small flowers, so white and delicate, could emit such a repelling odor. I didn't appreciate it either when the medium or priest, Ricardo Corazón de Águila, Eagle Heart Richard, gargled and later spat Seven Machos lotion in my face in order to drive away the bad spirits. Nor was Héctor García pleased when Corazón de Águila gave him a bear hug that smashed his glasses in his shirt pocket and knocked the wind out of him, and then threw his camera to the floor to free the cursed souls imprisoned in it.

Isabel Kelly, the North American anthropologist, and Sergio Mondragón, the poet, defined the difference between spiritism and spiritualism. Those interested in spiritism are sophisticated, from a higher economic level, many of them are politicians (Madero, the assassinated president, was a spiritist and the spirits told him everything, except that he would be murdered). They focus on apparitions, ectoplasm, the effects of light and sound, levitation and spiritual writing. Poverty rules spiritualism, and many of the forsaken look for Roque Rojas's seven churches and the *trinitario mariano* temples for healing and individual treatment. People can wait for hours at the state hospitals, and no one pays any attention to them, and if they do, the doctors and nurses barely even look them over. They are ushered out in a hurry, the nurses are either angry or tired and the medication costs more than they can afford. The spiritual doctors, on the other hand, tend to charge between three and five pesos, and the operations are sometimes more efficient than the ones at the hospitals. They are, of course, more suggestive, because an injection isn't the same as a cleansing with a bouquet of seven herbs, twenty-two days of cleansings, seven with branches, seven with fire, seven with white flowers, and one good rubdown with Seven Machos lotion, a massaging that ends in ecstasy.

Men and women of all ages recognize the catharsis that occurs when they are spiritually possessed by their protectors: Mesmer, Adrián Carriel or Alán Cardel (possibly Alain Kardec), Luz de Oriente, and many Mexican spirits like Pedrito Jaramillo, Rogelio Piel Roja, and others who obey Roque Rojas, otherwise known as Padre Elías. Roque Rojas (who became Padre Elías in 1866) was the founder of spiritualism. Jesus Christ pales next to him and his portentous miracles. Besides, Roque Rojas penetrates his flock. When the men and women go into a trance, they speak out loud. Eyes closed, their bodies shake with spasms; they vent their frustrations. Conflicts erupt: the husband's impotence, the hatred for the neighbor, the disappointment. The fact that they're possessed allows them to be completely extroverted. Uninhibited, they'll do anything; after all, the spirit that possessed their body made them do it. They sob, laugh, dance, act out their own drama or roguish play: they free themselves. They play the role of their life and are great performers of their own emotions. No group therapy would be as effective, no other stage more propitious or opportune. They go home feeling lighter afterward.

Most are mestizos. They belong to that monstrous city, their income is very low, jacks-of-all-trades and masters of none. They'll tell you they can do anything you need done, their bodies so thin that their guts stick to their spines. Their cultural roots have been disturbed by the television and the radio, and for them, spiritualism is more satisfying than Catholicism: the emotions are stronger, and they are treated like "people." Spiritualism makes men and women feel as if they were chosen by God from among all the whirling souls on Earth.

For forty years, the Obra Espiritual was the only thing that gave Jesusa's life meaning, and she was even baptized. Reincarnation was another consolation, to believe that she would return to Earth in a new human form that would offer her unlimited possibilities. "Before I was born, I was dead, then I was born, I lived, I died again and floated in the air, and then the Ser Supremo hooked me and I was off again, to live and return to Earth." Jesusa left the Obra Espiritual not because of her intolerance or because its objectives seemed obscure to her as they did to me, but because the other priestesses with their white nylon robes and large bunches of expensive white flowers looked down on her and they asked her to move out of the way.

Jesusa has died and left me. I'm anxiously waiting her next reincarnation. I hope it happens before I die, and if not, I hope I find her wherever she may be. I hope I see her sitting to the right of God the Father, her legs crossed comfortably on a woolly cloud. Jesusa once said that this was the third time she'd come to Earth, and she suffered now because she'd been a queen in her previous reincarnation. "I'm on Earth paying what I owe, but my life is really another one. The people living on Earth are on loan, they're only here in passing; and when the soul detaches from the skin and bones that encompass us, when they leave their matter under the dirt, that's when they start to live. We're the dead ones, it's backwards, turned around, you see. We believe we're alive, but we're not. We just come to Earth in visible flesh to fulfill a mission, and when He calls us, our material selves die. The flesh dies and is buried. The soul returns to the place where it was released from in Heaven. Like a star. We reincarnate every thirty-three years after dying." So, between one death and another, between one trip to Earth and another, Jesusa invented an anterior and interior that made her present misery tolerable.

Jesusa has died, I can no longer see her. I can't hear her, but I feel her inside me. I revive her and she keeps me company. She's the one I invoke and evoke. I quietly repeat María Sabina's incantation, those sweet words that swing from the trees the way she sang them, like a ballad, swaying in her sleeveless *huipil*, as she came down from the sierra with her hallucinogenic mushrooms and her smell of freshly cut wood and cacao beans roasted on a comal: "I'm a woman that cries, I'm a woman that speaks, I'm the woman that waits. I'm the woman that strives, I am a female spirit, I'm a woman that screams. I'm the woman moon, I'm the woman interpreter, I'm the female star, I'm the female heaven, they know me in Heaven. God acknowledges me. Listen, Moon, listen, Southern Cross Woman, listen, Morning Star. Come. How will we find rest? We're tired and the day has still not come."

MEXICO CITY, 2000

HERE'S TO YOU, JESUSA!

*T*HIS IS MY THIRD TIME back on Earth, but I've never suffered as much as I have now. I was a queen in my last reincarnation, I know, because I saw my train during a revelation. I was standing in a beauty shop and there were these huge, long mirrors that went from floor to ceiling and I saw my dress and the train. It stretched back really far, and way back there almost at the end, at the tip, there was a triangle of marbled black and yellow tiger stripes. My clothing was all white, like a bridal gown, except for that forked piece of tiger skin, like the very tip of the devil's tail. Columbine and Pierrot peered into the mirror on either side of me, both dressed in white with those black polka dots they always wear.

I told them about my revelation at the Obra Espiritual and they said that the royal white clothing was what I was supposed to wear at my final judgment hour, and that the Lord had allowed me to see what I'd been like one of the three times that I came to Earth.

—That spot on the train of your dress is all you have left to whiten, and if you don't, it will devour your innocence.

I was wearing a queen's dress with wide sleeves covered with trim. Pierrot and Columbine were my servants but they didn't attend to me as they should have; they spent the whole time fooling around with each other. Queens are always alone. I also told them at the temple that I'd seen a large valley full of spotted cows:

—It's the herd that the Lord has entrusted to you and you must return them to Him cleansed.

I have a lot of things going on right now and I don't know when I'm going to get my herd together to remove their stains, if it'll be in this lifetime or in the next, when I evolve again . . .

There are still a number of spiritually ill Christians whom I have to cure, but since I haven't, we all keep suffering. The Ojo Avisor—the watchful eye inside its divine triangle—is following me everywhere through the antennae of its eyelashes. It's the all-powerful eye of the Creator, and if I don't complete my task, there's no point in asking the saints to pray for us because I'll be forgotten at the hand of God. That's why I go through so many purifications. Why did I come back as a poor woman this time if last time I was a queen? My debt must be really heavy, for God took my parents away when I was a child and left me alone to pay for my sins like a leper. I must've been very bad, which is why the Ser Supremo, the supreme being, has left me out here so long, to purge myself of corrupting, harmful influences.

To traverse the spiritual path we have to go through many trials and tribulations and much pain and suffering. The protector who guides us reveals himself through them, but sometimes you must return to Earth several times, depending on your debt. In my first reincarnation I lived with Turks, Hungarians, and Greeks. I saw myself wrapped in a purple cloak like the Virgin of Sorrows; my head was covered in white and I wore a heavy white robe that fell to the floor. I was standing in an empty place when I counted twelve camels approaching; he was riding on the last one. He was dark-skinned, with large, curly-lashed eyes, dressed in white and wearing a turban. He reached out his hand to me and I thought it would be brown like his face, but no, it was silver. He gestured for me to climb up on the camel. I was scared and pulled back. He had to let go of me, and I started to run. I put my hands up in the sign of the cross, and it must have worked, because he couldn't catch up to me on his swift camel. I kept running, but he took out a pistol and killed me. When I woke up I heard his name: Luz de Oriente, Light of the Orient.

The following day I went to the temple and told Padre Elías, who is also known as Roque Rojas, about my revelation. He comes down to Earth the first Friday of every month. Several different beings pass through the medium's aura after they receive the light, then the interpreters explain the revelations to the people. I told him that I'd seen that silver-skinned man

on his camel. The Ser Espiritual asked me through the medium, Trinidad
Pérez de Soto, who is now my godmother:

—Don't you know who he is?

—No, I don't.

—Don't be afraid, he's your brother . . . He was your companion the
first time around.

—What do you mean?

—He was your husband back in that primitive time when you came to
Earth. You must acknowledge him; he is your third protector and is with
you wherever you go . . . He hasn't abandoned you. He continues to guide
you into the present. That's why the Lord showed him to you as he looked
in his first reincarnation.

—Oh . . .

—You mean you didn't love him?

—Yes, I loved him.

—He's your husband, and watches out for you . . .

I didn't say anything else, but later I studied my dream on my own
and I realized who he was and why he'd killed me. He is suffering now because he wasn't a good husband. He turned out to be like Pedro Aguilar,
who said that he wouldn't leave me alone and alive on Earth, so he always
took me along with him. At least he warned me:

—If I see we've lost, I'll send you on ahead and kill you . . .

God didn't let him know he was going to die; so I'm still here. When
Luz de Oriente couldn't take me, he wanted to kill me, but I was afraid of
him and that fear saved me. I lost my fear when my father and I started
traveling with the troops. At first, when I heard shots, I'd scream, and the
commanding officers would get angry because we were on the firing line
and my screaming would give our position away. My father slipped gunpowder in my water without telling me:

—Go ahead, hijita, drink this little sip of water . . .

Since I drank any kind of water, even from puddles, it didn't taste bad
to me. They didn't tell me that it was gunpowder water for bravery until
later.

Luz de Oriente is still paying. The mediums tell me that when he enters
them and possesses their body, he weeps, and tells them:

—It's my fault . . .

They say his speech is very refined; that he sends me his regards and asks me not to forget him; that he watches over me because the Lord has entrusted me to him.

How many hundreds of years must have passed and he still protects me with his whole caravan! I haven't seen him only in a revelation; there's a painting of him in the temple on Luis Moya Street, which used to be called Calle Ancha. In the painting his eyes are open wide and really black, livid, black as coal. He's wearing a turban with a shiny rhinestone in the center and a spray of feathers coming out around it.

The Ser Supremo sends us to Earth to cleanse our souls. Because He made us clean, before we can return to Him we must be as we were when we first arrived. How are we supposed to cleanse ourselves? Through pain and suffering. We may believe that He's mistaken, but we're the ones who are wrong; we don't hear, we don't understand, we don't want to recognize the true path. If people would recognize God's clean path, there wouldn't be abusive men or women who allow men to abuse them. When I'm alone at night I think: "Ay, Señor, give me strength to endure the pain that you've sent!" And now that I'm old and I take medicine, I think: "I really shouldn't be using it. The whole point is to truly feel the purification that He sends me."

In this reincarnation God didn't send me back with a silver spoon in my mouth. Now I eat if I can find something, otherwise I don't, and that's the way it is. God said: "You must fight alone. You must suffer to know what it means to love God in the land of heathens." Even though I'm ignorant, I've sorted through what has been revealed to me about my past life. I've delved so deeply that my head hurts, as though I had this calamitous world inside it. Uy, no! *I could've gone crazy! But you have to figure these things out, because they've been inside you from birth. If you think about them at the right time, they'll become clear. We all have many eyes inside our brain, like a string of stars. To be able to see clearly, you have to keep your eyes closed tight, even at night when there's no daylight. I don't have a gift for words but I can say this: I've surmounted many obstacles in my lifetime. Only God knows all that I've suffered since my mother died and what's still ahead. I have to keep walking even though my final hour is far away. My stepmother in Tehuantepec had a book that enabled one to interpret signs. Your whole life was written down there in little numbers. She was a learned and wise person. She made me close my eyes and point with my finger at the book, and then she looked up what it meant. The book said I owe one hundred and two years, so I have a long road ahead of me. At my age that means there's a big chunk left. I don't know how many times I'll be reincarnated, or in what form, but I've asked God not to send me back to Earth for a while so I can stay in space and rest. But that's like asking Him to make blind men see and hunchbacks straight. He's the only one who knows what I actually owe, but it must be a lot, because in this last reincarnation I've been quite mean, physically abusive, and a drunk. I can't say that I've been good. I really can't say anything.*

I had a friend, Sister Sebastiana, who sold tomatoes. She had a big stall at the market, but then she got sick and couldn't work it. She fell apart; she got very, very large, but I don't think it was fat, I think she just swelled up. Her feet were like sponges and she couldn't get around. God only knows what her debt was, but she suffered a lot. Then someone told her about the Obra Espiritual and she came to the temple.

—I'm so tired, beaten down, my body has forsaken me. Please cure me. The last time I was pregnant, the child turned cancerous inside me and I almost died. My insides are rotted now and the doctors don't think I can be saved.

—What's in your heart?

—Poison.

When she accepted the Obra Espiritual, she began to get better. They did spiritual surgery on her. There were no babies inside her, but they took out the rot. She began to go to classes there and one time the Lord granted her a gift; she saw it with her eyes open, without feeling the sting. The visions went back through the centuries, and hidden things were revealed to her. Sister Sebastiana saw many hands reaching for her, surrounding her:

—All these hands are threatening me!

—Don't you recognize them? the Lord asked.

—They're young women's hands . . .

—You must analyze and study what I reveal to you . . .

The Lord wanted her to realize that she'd been a man in the previous reincarnation and that the hands belonged to all the women he'd wronged; and they now wanted revenge. For a long time she did penance and gave donations to the Catholic Church, but she didn't heal. At the Obra Espiritual they explained that those rotted children belonged to the women whom she had abandoned in the past reincarnation. Then Sebastiana knelt and asked the Ser Supremo for forgiveness.

—I agree to continue suffering, but have pity on me.

About eight years ago I saw her in the plaza. She still had her stall, but she was unrecognizable. She was raising other people's children, and they all turned out bad; they never helped her, and they never loved her. Each person pays their debts a little at a time and gets credit on Earth for all the debts that the Ser Supremo has written down up there. That's why one returns so many times. It's something that those of us who are in the Obra Espiritual understand, because our protectors drill it into us. I have three protectors. The first is old man Mesmer, the second is Manuel Allende, and the last one is Luz de Oriente, who is the handsomest of the three, but I love them all the same. It's just that Luz de Oriente looks at me hungrily; with desire in his eyes all the time, which makes me wonder. They're the great ones, but the three greatest are the Eternal Father, our Father Jesus Christ, and our messenger Elías, or Roque Rojas as he's known in this world, he's the Third Person, the Holy Ghost. The Catholic Church says the Holy Ghost is a little dove, because they don't explain things there. The priests do things differently. They know the Obra Espiritual, but they don't want to go into it any further because they're selfish. They don't want the people to figure it out, because that would kill the goose that lays the golden egg; they make a lot of money saying masses and performing weddings and christenings. In the Obra Espiritual they enlighten the people, and the whole congregation supports the temple; the priestesses, the mediums, the pedestals, and the columns all work together to hold it up. They never ask for charity. They don't tell the people: "It will cost you this much for such and such." In the Catholic Church they say: "We'll say mass for you, but you'll owe us your place in the kingdom in Heaven." At funeral services they merely bring in a fake coffin, make gestures, and swing incense around. They don't even call for the poor soul who's suffering in space. I know, because I used to have a mass said for my poor mother every Day of the Dead, but when she spoke to me through the Obra Espiritual I realized that she was totally blind and didn't know me. When she received the light she was glad that I'd finally remembered her, but I had remembered her many times before that. The priests had simply pocketed the centavos I paid them for the masses, but they didn't say them for her or for my father. And like a fool I kept paying them three pesos a crack. They probably didn't even say masses for their own mothers.

My mother hardly remembered that she had children. They took me back to when I was very young right there in the temple of Chimalpopoca. They put her spiritual hand on my face so she'd recognize me: "Awaken from your drowsiness—they told her—and remember your daughter." She let out a long sigh and said:

—Praise be to God. You have enlightened me and reminded me that I had a child.

—You didn't just have one. You had five and they're all there with you. Jesusa is the only one left on Earth.

Then her eyes were opened and she went to round up my brothers and sisters from among the dead souls that wander around in space. She called their names, but only two came forward from the celestial rows: Petra and Emiliano. Efrén, the eldest, didn't appear, and finally they assumed that he must have been reincarnated again. I don't know if the dead newborn baby had ever been baptized. I was glad to see Emiliano because he was always so good to me. He took care of me for years when I was a drunk and hung out in dives. He'd appear in other people's minds or in some other man's body and say to me:

—Let's go.

I'd stare at him:

—Pues let's go, I would answer very obediently.

We'd leave the cantinas, and while we were walking he'd disappear in the crowd and I'd look around for him. When he revealed himself at the Obra Espiritual, Emiliano asked me:

—Do you remember when I took you out of the Tranvia? Remember when I left you on Mesones Street?

I didn't say anything. "Ay, my poor little brother, how he suffered protecting me!" I was a black sheep who didn't want to get on the right path. My sister Petra didn't say a word to me in the revelation. She spoke even less in space than she did on Earth, she was always a little slow. She fi-

nally accepted the little bit of light that she could. Emiliano still follows me, though I don't see him; sometimes I can sense when he's in the room, and sometimes I can't. When I close my eyes I can see his face.

My mother started crying:

—God bless you, God bless you, child, for calling me after so many years. I'd lost my family but we've finally found each other.

Her children in space calmed her down. They told her to say goodbye to me. She kept insisting:

—Thank you, child, for remembering me . . .

There are many left in the darkness and they stay buried there until a charitable soul calls for them.

MY MOTHER had a very simple funeral. I don't know if it was because we were poor or because that's the way they did it in those days. They wrapped her in a *petate*, a straw mat, tossed her body in a hole, and threw dirt on top of her. I watched, moving closer to my father, who was talking and drinking with the people who came to the funeral. He didn't notice when I jumped into the hole and covered my mother's head with my dress so the dirt wouldn't fall on her face. No one did. Suddenly, he remembered I'd been with him and he called out for me. I answered him from below. He asked them to stop shoveling. I didn't want to get out. I wanted them to cover me up in there with my mother.

I was all covered with dirt and crying when they pulled me out. Ever since then, whenever it's windy, my eyes sting. They say it's because I breathed in cemetery air and that's why my eyes turn red.

The neighbors made a cross out of corn and planted it in a box in the atrium of the church in Mixtequilla. They said the novena for the nine days it takes the soul to cross through space. When the corn got tall and began to sprout they took it to my mother's grave at the cemetery, where it remained as a sign of her life on Earth.

––––––––

Either my mother died of fright or death came after her. She had a dream that two little dogs were biting her leg, I heard her tell my father when she woke up:

—Ay, what a nightmare I had! These dogs were biting my leg, so I wrung their necks and left them lying on the floor!

My father asked:

—What dogs? On what floor? You must have been dreaming.

—It was a dream. Come on, get up and take me out to pee.

The village had no plumbing facilities, so my parents used the patio. The neighbors would meet there in the evening to talk. There was a house across the street on the corner that had an elongated stone in front that was big enough for a person to lie on. One moon-filled night when you could see everything clearly, my mother said to my father:

—Felipe, look at that in front there!

—Where?

—There on top of the stone. Who do you think killed him?

—Killed who?

—Look, who would kill that man there?

—Which man?

—The one lying there on the stone.

—I don't see anything.

—What do you mean you don't see anything? I'm touching his feet.

—I don't see anything, María, but let's get out of here before they blame us for killing him.

The next morning, when my father got up to go to work the first thing he did was check the stone, but it was empty:

—How could María have seen a dead man there?

My mother never got out of bed again after that. The next day she woke up with chills and a fever and within a week she was gone. Later my father told the neighbors:

—You know, she must have died of fright, and not from the fever, because I took good care of her. I rubbed her down with alcohol and I gave her quinine. I think that dead man she saw on the corner of Doña Luisa's house took her away.

That was when I realized that God moves everything at His will, even the leaves on trees. My mother had a revelation and she saw the murdered man. My father didn't. Now that I'm older and I've devoted my life to the Obra Espiritual and have found the path, I believe my mother was enlightened and had a mission to complete. Although she had courage and grabbed him by the feet, she wasn't very spiritual and that's why the dead man took her.

When my mother was still alive, my father made me a squirrel doll. But he never made me anything again after that. Ever. He played deaf or else everything just went in one ear and out the other.

He skinned the squirrel. In Mixtequilla they eat squirrel meat. You cover it with salt, pepper, garlic, and vinegar or lemon. Then you put the animal on a wooden skewer to brown over the fire. Squirrel is delicious; it tastes like squirrel. My father put lime on the hide and stretched it out in the sun. When it was dry he sewed up the little paws and stuffed it, and gave it to me.

—Why is it so hard, Father?

—Because of the stuffing.

—Did you fill it with dirt?

—No, sawdust.

—What's sawdust?

—Ay, Jesusa, don't ask so many questions, just be content and play with it!

And I did play with it; I wrapped it in my rebozo and carried my doll around even though it was hard to hold on to because it was so stiff.

Since my father couldn't afford to buy me anything, I played with stones, arrows, a slingshot, and marbles that he polished himself. He looked for thick, hard, blue-colored stones that he used to round and file other little porous stones. He polished and polished them into little balls. He made wooden tops from the *pochote*, or bombax tree, which has a lot of nodules that look like little tits. He picked the biggest ones to make me *pirinolas*—you know, tops—that would dance when I spun them. While they'd spin I'd sing, well, not really sing, not like songs, but just hum along with the *pirinolas*, or I'd daydream, although I can't remember what I thought about.

I played in the dirt because I didn't know any better. I really liked the feel of it, and when you're five years old dirt still looks white to you. The Lord made His whole creation white in His own image and likeness, but it's been getting darker over the years, from use and because of evil. That's why little kids play in the dirt; it looks very pretty and clean-white to them. As they grow older, the devil enters them and their thoughts. The evil transforms everything they see, making things dirty, muddy, changing the color.

I was a tomboy. I liked playing war, hopscotch, tops, marbles, throwing stones, fighting, stoning lizards to death, smashing iguanas against rocks: boy things.

We hunted with a blowgun made out of a long, hollowed-out reed. It didn't bother me to kill little animals. Why should it? We're all meant to die sooner or later. I don't know why I was like that. I stole eggs from birds' nests before they could hatch and then I sold them, for bottle caps, and shards of broken pottery that we used as reales and medios, cuartillas, pesetas and tlacos, and centavos. Those were the coins people used back then.

Sometimes I'd build a fire and fry little iguanas. When their bodies would burst, I'd scrape them, split them open, take their guts out, salt them, and call to the boys: "Come and eat! Come and eat! Sit down, boys, and I'll serve you right away! Don't leave hungry." But they wouldn't eat that filth.

—That's not fair!

—*Éjele! Éjele!*

—Trickster! Pig!

—Liar, liar, pants on fire! . . .

Then I'd run away, with all of them chasing me. Nobody likes to be tricked.

When I was tired of playing with the boys, I'd climb trees and throw stones at them. I crawled out on the branches and looked for ways to pick fights with everyone. I'd hit them on the head, and they'd run to show my mother what I'd done. She begged me to settle down, but I wouldn't, I just couldn't from the time I was little, but that's all over now. I'm not good for much nowadays. I don't have the devil in me anymore.

My mother never scolded me or hit me. She was dark-skinned just like me and short and fat. After she died, I never played again.

My father took another woman a week after my mother died. She was just some woman. Who knows where he met her, but he kept her around for a long time. I don't remember her name, but she was a drinker. The first week I gave her two reales to buy groceries. She wanted my father to give her the money, but since he had told us she was the maid and was there to take care of Emiliano and me, I handled the money, making sure that the maid gave me the change. I slapped my father. Why would he have another woman sleep with him in my mother's place? Even as young as I was, I was filled with wickedness. Although I'd been raised in a small village where everyone lived in their own home, I thought it was wrong for someone else to sleep with my father. I don't know how I came to that conclusion on my own. I must have been born with a gift, or I knew how to take advantage of a situation. I never accepted the woman, and of course that made her mad. Since the weather was so warm we slept in hammocks. I slept with my father, and I never let him be with that woman. So she started to use the grocery money to get drunk. I don't know why.

My father did whatever I asked. When I was little he spoiled me a lot, but he wasn't affectionate. We didn't know about hugging and cuddling and things like that. We didn't. When my mother was alive, my father would say: "Don't you go scolding her or do anything to her." That's why I got to be so rude. And when she complained: "Look, Felipe, she won't let me brush her hair." He'd say: "Here, I'll brush it."

He had very gentle hands, really supple, and he was careful. I hated to have my hair pulled, it felt like sparks falling on my head, I'd only let him comb my hair. There were two of us little ones, and my mother had to do everything, braid one's hair, change the other one, heat water, wash. My father, on the other hand, spoiled me and never wanted to hear me cry.

I never saw the drunk woman sleep with my father, but she was his woman. She told me:

—I don't like it at all that you won't leave us alone. He's my husband . . .

I screamed that he was not her husband, because he was my father, and that's when she started fighting with me. When she was drunk, she yelled horrible things at me: that he didn't have to be afraid of me; since when do daughters lead their fathers around by the nose?

—You'll be sorry, she told me.

I told her that I had nothing to be sorry about, and that if she wanted my father so badly, the two of them should move away and leave me here.

Neither of us said anything to my father when he got home from work after six o'clock that night, but the next day the drunk went to the bar and spent the grocery money with other men. When I saw her coming up the path to the house, I filled my skirt with stones and threw them at her.

—Get out of here! Go away! I don't want to see you here.

That night I told my father that I'd run her off because she was always lying around drunk.

—That's fine, child, don't worry about it.

My father ended up alone with his kids again. He'd get up to make our lunch and then go to work. He was used to having that so-and-so to do the chores, but now, because we were little, he had to grind the corn in the metate himself. He tied us both to a post so we wouldn't run off. My brother Emiliano was about two years older than me. I was known for my evil ways. My father would put thick logs on the fire under a pot, and the contents would slowly boil, humming and bubbling. At twelve o'clock, when he came home, the meat or beans or whatever he had made would be ready. He also ground cornmeal for dough and made us thick tortillas, because, being a man, he couldn't make thin, flat ones.

My father worked on the railroad blasting openings in a hill with dynamite to make a pass to lay track to the Isthmus of Tehuantepec. Every day it was the same routine: he got up to cook for us. It was really rough on him; he needed a woman to take care of his children.

One day he said:

—Listen, child, I have to bring a woman in to watch you, to delouse you and to bathe you, because I have to work.

We argued a lot about that. I'd say: "You're my father, it's your responsibility to comb my hair, wash me, and feed me." Kids are very demanding that way.

When he told me that a woman would be coming to look after us, I said:

—Don't try to fool me by saying that she's the maid and then turn around and say she's something else to you. Tell me up front.

He found a woman who had a little boy. I was very precocious and I kept an eye on this one. She'd dish up the food and put my father's aside, then she'd scrape her toenails and gather up a little pile of scrapings and sprinkle it on my father's food. She wanted to drive him crazy; at least that's what I figured. I thought to myself: "What's this all about? Why put powder on his food and not on ours?" When she went to get water, I switched the plates with my father and then threw his food out. "There's a reason she's doing this and it can't be good or she'd put it all in the same pot!" I was good at figuring things out and always suspicious of what was going on. He did share his hammock with that one. When he told me that he wanted her to be his wife, what could I do? But the other one, the so-called maid, no way. I'm no fool!

The one with the toenails who had the son wasn't good to us either. She hated us. I heard her argue with my father. He'd say:

—Take care of her, comb her hair the way you would for your own daughter, you have more to gain than I do.

But she didn't even know my name. It was the same thing over and over again until I got bored and got into it with her. I was a little older and I had become very mean; no one in my family was as quarrelsome as I was. She lasted about seven or eight months, a year at the most, and after that my father left the railroad. He couldn't find work where he could take off at noon to come and feed us. He wanted a job where he would be respected, so we took off for Salina Cruz.

MY FATHER would walk down the beach to the lighthouse that was built on rocks. The rocks jutted out into the water, and when the waves broke over them, the oysters opened their shells and drank the liquid and then closed again. My father would chop the big ones off the rocks with his machete and crack them open, and we'd eat them right out of the shell while they were still alive and fresh. I've never eaten them here in Mexico City. Who knows how long they've been stored on ice? How good can they be for you if they're already dead?

The other day I bought a dozen turtle eggs because I hadn't had them in so long, not since I was little, when my father took us to hunt for them at night. The turtles come in from the ocean and bury themselves in the sand; they work hard laying dozens of eggs at a time and they get so tired. They lay a dozen eggs way down deep and cover them, and then they lay a dozen more, and they climb further out of the hole and lay another dozen on top of that and then another, covering them with sand each time and climbing even higher to lay another dozen until they've emptied their bellies. When they're ready to leave, they cover up the last layer and go back into the sea. You have to run to where the sand has been disturbed and mark the nest with a stick before the surf covers their tracks as they go back into the sea, and then you must dig really fast to get the eggs out, even if you get caught in the surf.

Otherwise the little turtles form there, alone, by themselves; they grow with the heat from the sand and the sun.

They're funny creatures. Turtles can walk as soon as they're born, and they head straight for the water, where they dive in like little fish. Snakes are like that too, baby snakes break out of their shells and slither away.

We'd hunt for turtle eggs at dusk or on nights when the moon lit the deserted beach, because turtles don't come out in the daytime. My father liked to take us along because we could tell where the turtles had crawled across the sand back into the sea, and we'd run to dig up the eggs. My father would get in the water with his clothes on and so would I, to help him, dressed just like I am and I'd get soaked. My clothes would dry on my body. We'd hunt turtles until one, two in the morning, when we'd filled the basket he carried. It was a huge basket and we wouldn't go to sleep until it was crammed with eggs, and then at dawn we ate some of them. The outside, the thick shell, is round, leathery, a tough membrane. There are big ones like that, but others are medium-sized from smaller turtles. They're always sandy. You rinse the sand off and boil them with enough salt to penetrate right through to the yolk. We boiled them and then ate them.

Other times my father stirred them; scrambled, he called it. He put tomatoes, garlic, and onions in a pot and once it was really seasoned he beat some turtle eggs into the boiling mixture. Or he fed us fish; we each got our own. He never fished with a pole. He'd get into the water and make a cave out of rocks, and when the fish swam in through the door he trapped them with a casting net. He'd pull it in and take out the big ones, which were about two feet long; sea bass, that's what was most common in that area. If there were people waiting for him on the shore, my father would sell them fresh fish; if not, he'd gut them, season them with salt, and lay them out to dry and then later sell salted fish. He sold fresh, dried, or smoked fish, or sometimes he'd smoke them and hang them.

I used to swim at five in the morning or at five in the evening, never in the heat of the day. We'd let the waves splash over us and wash the dirt off. A wave would go out and we'd wait for the next one. I don't know how people swim now, because it's been many years since I've been to the beach. They say people get in and swim out into the water. I'd rather bathe here in a puddle, where the water doesn't move, than do something silly like that. Swimming at the beach is the best, where a wave comes and you see it rise up white and foamy and it covers you completely, you brace yourself for the rush of the water against your body, dressed or naked, to feel the living water. It's beautiful when the wave approaches and suddenly it covers you and then it leaves, and you wait for the next one to smack you with its tail as if all the water had come together in a single squall. I was short and strong and I knew how to meet the waves. If I were to go back to the sea, I'd go in at about six in the evening to wait for the waves that rise up high and let them crash down all around me over and over again. When the wave rolls in, the sand looks so clean, and you stand sideways, with your legs apart and firmly planted in the sand, not facing the wave head-on and not with your back to it, but to one side, because otherwise it would drag you under.

The power of the sea is amazing. But not the way they say people swim nowadays, not like that. Don't expect me to ever do anything like that!

The port of Salina Cruz was a busy place back then. The boats passed under two iron bridges and anchored inside the bay. I don't know what life was like there, because I roamed from one day to the next, like a dog. I believe my father must have rented a plot of land and put up a small house made of sticks with a palm-thatch roof. He plastered a mud-and-hay mixture on the sticks to make walls. And that's how we lived. It was really hot there. I went barefoot because shoes got in the way when I climbed trees; I tied them together and slung them across my shoulder as I climbed from one tree to another, or left them hanging from a branch. As soon as we ate I went back out into the trees. My father would go to work, so there wasn't anyone to stop me.

My father had several jobs in Salina Cruz. He was very resourceful and could do just about anything. He cooked and washed for us, but as we got older, he said that it was impossible to leave us unattended; he could be responsible for the boy, but what would he do with me? It was hard for him. He told the woman he left us with sometimes when he went to work:

—I don't know what to do, it's such a struggle with these kids . . . I don't have anywhere to leave them . . . Who wants to be responsible for someone else's children?

—No one . . .

Then he said:

—I'm going to the dock to see if they'll hire me to work the night shift so I can be home during the day to watch out for these little ones . . .

He found work on a ship and worked all night and came home during the day. He went to work at five in the afternoon and came back at five in the morning. He fed us and put us to bed before he left and then locked us in all alone. There was no reason for us to be on the streets anyway, since it would be getting dark soon. Besides, the heat makes you sleepy. My father was a night watchman and a stevedore; his job was to load one ship and unload another during the night, but if at dawn he hadn't finished, he had to stay and work the next shift until five o'clock in the afternoon. He never got a break, just more work, work, work. He took a real beating. My father worked for a long time loading and unloading merchandise from cargo ships. I don't know if it was years or months, because I was just a kid.

That was when my oldest brother, Efrén Palancares, came to stay with us. He was dark-skinned, wasted, and a drunk. He pretty much lived in the cantinas. He seldom came home, and when he did my father usually beat him because he was drunk out of his mind. He'd stay for a week or two and then take off. Efrén lived with us when he was a child, but once he became a man he started to wander. He left home when he was about fourteen or fifteen because my father was quick to give a beating. My mother never hit us. Efrén was rebellious. When he was little he wasn't a drunk, but he was rough and reckless.

—Where's Efrén? I asked my father one morning.

—He left.

—Why?

—Bad influences . . .

My father wanted to keep him away from bad company, as I tried to do much later with Perico, but in spite of everything, he always took up with the wrong crowd. No one can change you if you're born bad. Efrén was a bigmouth. My brother Emiliano was the good-natured one; he followed my father everywhere. When my father was working as a stevedore loading ships, Emiliano stayed on the dock waiting for him. He was just a little kid and would get fried in the sun. Emiliano was right there with him when he worked on different ranches, moving from one to another. Not me. I was a wild animal. I took off for the hills. Efrén was like that too; no one ever knew where he'd been or where he was going. It didn't make any difference anyway. In one of his many comings and goings he showed up with a woman and dared my father to say something about it.

My father asked, "Why'd you bring her with you?"

God only knows what arrangement they made. The truth is that she, Ignacia, took care of me for a long time even though I fought it. She wanted to teach me how to make tortillas but I was used to running wild. From the time I was little I'd had complete freedom and I just wanted to wander around the countryside by myself.

Efrén stayed for a long time, because he had a woman, but he always came home drunk, so my father had to deal with him. Ignacia didn't complain about the abuse, what else could the poor girl do? She was probably about sixteen, and she was an orphan, so she didn't have anyone to watch out for her. She was grateful for whatever she got.

My father always took her side, and Emiliano and I really loved her, but Efrén made her life miserable: He barked at her:

—What are you doing, you lazy bitch? Get up and get me something to eat.

He wanted to be fed whenever he got around to coming home. If he didn't like what she fixed, he'd throw it at her. We always used tortillas to scoop up our food, but he'd ask for a fork and knife even though he didn't know how to use them; besides, we didn't own any. But in his drunkenness he'd yell:

—I want a knife and a fork, you fucking whore!

It would wake my father up and he'd yell:

—Why the hell did you bring her here if you're going to treat her that way?

He'd knock him out cold with a single blow, and Efrén would sleep it off wherever he landed.

One night he came home and my father wasn't there. I jumped up like a coiled spring. "Take me on, go ahead, but don't you hit her again!" I yelled.

He only slapped her once. I grabbed a thick log, and even though I could hardly lift it, I defended her, I thrashed him. I think of her whenever I hear kids singing that old song: "Ignacia is that pretty girl's name, her butt is uneven, her cheeks aren't the same," even though it makes me sad.

Ignacia used to slap me because I never learned to make tortillas right. She said that I'd learn if she slapped me enough, but I wasn't born to pat out pretty tortillas. Hers were nice; she would form little balls of dough for me to flatten, but to this day mine still turn out thick and ugly. Poor Perico would gobble them down when he was young no matter how awful they were. As punishment, my sister-in-law made me eat all the scraps of tortillas that I burned.

—You brighten the outdoors at night like a streetlight, but you darken the inside of the house, she'd shout at me.

Efrén hated the fact that we all took Ignacia's side, especially my father. She had a little girl named Felipita, whom we all loved, that baby meant the world to us. I played with her and carried her around in my rebozo, but she died when she was around eight months old. She was a bloom that lasted only a day. When she was dying, we took her to the hospital in Tehuantepec. Who knows what she died of. Little by little she turned black, and then she was completely black, as if she'd been choked. My sister-in-law never said a word. We returned to Salina Cruz without the baby; we left her body at the hospital.

We had barely gotten to the house when my father grabbed my brother:

—You kicked this woman when she was carrying your child inside her! That's why it died! You kicked her in the stomach!

He beat Efrén until he had vented his anger, and then he kicked him out of the house. He told him that he didn't want to suffer any more because of him, and ordered him to take his stuff and his wife and leave.

It gets very cloudy when the fog comes in from the sea. I was wandering the streets on one of those days when a man asked me where Felipe Palancares lived.

—I know him, he's my father. Why do you want him?

—Take me to see him.

—Let's go.

He carried me—I was little then—and put me down at the door. My father was sleeping, so I woke him up:

—Vini, a man is here for you.

The man came in. Since the doors are made of sticks you can hear everything that's said inside. He told my father that his name was Cayetano, and that he had rescued my older sister Petra. He heard a woman being beaten and crying for several nights in a house close to his, so he finally called the police, and they sent a squad to the house. Cayetano knocked at the door, demanding that it be opened. The man who beat my sister hid her inside a trunk, threatening to kill her if she said anything.

—No one else lives here, he told the policemen.

—A woman has been heard crying.

—That's not true. I haven't heard anything.

But they had a warrant to search the house even though it looked empty. Cayetano heard a scratching sound, and when he lifted the lid of the trunk he found a woman who was bruised and weeping. They arrested the man, and in her statement Petra said that he was the foreman of a crew that was building the embankment for train tracks from Tehuantepec to the port at Salina Cruz. When they finished spreading gravel he stole her, even though she wasn't friendly with him, and they hadn't talked to each other, and he wasn't her boyfriend or anything.

Cayetano told the police that he'd heard her screaming for three years.

The judge asked Petra:

—Who was this foreman?

—He was one of my mother's customers. My mother cooked for him and the other workers who laid track . . . I didn't even know him . . . The foreman didn't show up until we were really far from Tehuantepec . . . Then he came into the railroad car where I had been thrown like a sack of potatoes . . . I don't know how long I've been living in this house, but it seems like years . . . I want to go home!

They called Cayetano's mother and asked her if she would take responsibility for Petra, since her son had saved her life.

—Yes.

—I want to go home, I want to go home, Petra screamed.

Cayetano said:

—I'm willing to work to get enough money together to take her to her parents.

They lived in Tierra Blanca in Veracruz. He struggled for a year to save for both their fares. My sister was just skin and bones when Cayetano's mother took her in. They came here from Tierra Blanca and had already spent a week going from house to house in Salina Cruz looking for us.

—Your house was the last one we were going to check, because we were leaving today.

My father asked to see the woman.

—She's outside.

When my father opened the door and saw her, he said:

—Yes, that's my daughter.

—*Bueno*, señor, I've brought her back to you, but I'd like to ask your permission to marry her.

I don't know if they married or not, but that's what I heard him tell my father. They both ended up living with us, and since Petra was now a woman, my father turned all his responsibilities over to her.

—I'm putting you in charge of your little sister. Take care of her, comb her hair, bathe her, do all the things a mother does for her daughter. *Ándale*, it's your turn now.

Since I wasn't raised with my sister, I didn't love her. I didn't even call her sister. I was used to a man's touch, to my father's touch. Petra's skin was darker than mine. My face is tan, but I'm not dark; her face and her body were dark. She had more Indian blood in her than I do. Two of us had my father's coloring and the other two were dark-skinned: Efrén and Petra, Emiliano and I, half and half. Petra was a little taller than me and very strong-willed. Imagine crying every night for three years! Anyone else would have given up. As long as they get laid most women will put up with anything. That's their way of begging for charity, the sluts! But Petra didn't give in to him, she never let him have his way with her, even though she became thin and sickly. She was fierce and bad-tempered, full of anger and pride, but she kept it all inside.

Petra was fifteen. The foreman knew who she was, but he had never talked to her or anything. In those days it wasn't like it is now, when young girls are willing to put out for the first old good-for-nothing who comes along. Not back then! Never! They knew who the men were but they would never talk to them! No way! Petra never left the kitchen. She spent all day cooking, grinding corn, and making tortillas. My father bought the groceries and put them at the door because my mother, like Petra, didn't leave the house; she wasn't raised to be roaming the streets like a dog. One afternoon my mother told Petra to bring in a blanket that had been washed that morning and was hanging on a branch to dry so I could sleep on it that night. My sister never came back; a worker wrapped her up in that very blanket and took her away.

My father found out about all this after she came back. At first they didn't even notice she was missing.

My mother was very clean. All the women from Tehuantepec were like that. She washed dishes, swept the patio with a straw broom, and scrubbed with lye and a brush every single day. She almost always fed us on the patio so her kitchen would stay clean. Her daughter was stolen because of her damned cleanliness.

Petra scared me because she was so quiet, so skinny, and you could never tell what she was thinking. I didn't like her ways, that's why I hit her, but always from a distance. I didn't let her catch me and I really gave her a hard time.

I was always full of lice. My father gave me a bath every week and would pick them off me, but the next day I'd be back out playing in the dirt, and of course my head would end up full of them again. I wouldn't let my sister bathe me. I'd climb up into a tree and stay there all day without eating. "Come closer," I'd say to her, "*ándale*, come closer," and I'd throw stones at her. I wouldn't come down to eat until my father came home.

One day Petra said to my father:

—If she won't let me delouse her or bathe her, I'm going to shave her head.

I screamed:

—Just you dare try to shave my head and you'll see what happens to you!

She never did, and I had lice for a long time, until I got worms in my head.

I don't know how many years or months we'd been living together when Cayetano came in to kill Petra. She was in bed trying to get comfortable and had finally fallen asleep when Cayetano burst in with a knife in his hand, but my little brother snuck up behind him and stopped him before he could stab her. When she heard all the noise, she opened her eyes and stared at her husband with a dagger in his hand and at little Emiliano holding him back. Of course she was terrified, but she helped Emiliano get the knife away from him. That was it for her, Petra hadn't done anything to Cayetano, she almost never spoke to him, she was never mean to anyone. That was in the afternoon. He didn't kill her, but she got sick after that. She started hearing a buzzing in her ears and every now and then she'd hear a voice say: "Be careful, Petra; watch out, Petra." Her bile overflowed and she started to dry up. She got drier and drier and her face got yellow like a lemon; she turned that color. She died of fear, I guess, because one day we found her dead.

They were digging drainage ditches in Salina Cruz at that time, and once, when he was drunk, my brother Efrén fell into an open ditch and drowned in the middle of the day. I think he passed out, and with the heat and being drunk and all, he couldn't get out. When they removed him from the ditch his eyes were wide open and covered with mud. We took Ignacia in and she lived with us for a long time. They say my sister-in-law was carrying a Palancares baby when she took up with a fisherman. My father slept with her whenever he wanted and her husband never said anything about it. So there's another little Palancares child around, but if the other man took it in and accepted it as his own, then the child doesn't know it's part of my family, so he or she is lost to us.

Shortly after Ignacia left with the fisherman, my father moved back to Tehuantepec. He didn't waste any time. He got a job as a night watchman, and that's when he met my stepmother, Evarista Valencia, the person who taught me everything I know.

MY STEPMOTHER was the daughter of the warden of the women's prison. It was an old-style prison, with a large vaulted ceiling, really long, with cells down the center and more along the sides, right up to the door that led out into the street. There were more cells than prisoners. But before you got to the street there was the room we lived in, so there wasn't any way to escape. Mostly drunken women ended up there; that's what filled the prison. It was dark and humid, and during periods of hot weather, the place heated up like a boiling cauldron and everyone's hair would be dripping wet. The women who were in for only a few days or a few months were let out on the patio to get some sun, but those who were sentenced for years were kept way in the back. During the time when Madero took Mexico City, the only prisoner left in the last cell was a poor woman. No one knew how much time she still had to serve but she was in the slammer for seven murders. Of course, she had no hope of ever getting out. She called out from behind the bars and asked my stepmother's mother to let me sleep in her cell with her because she was afraid.

The prison was huge. We slept up against the bars. I would have been about eight or nine years old or maybe ten. I didn't speak to any of the prisoners. I'm funny that way, I don't like to talk to people. People probably think I'm angry, but I'm not, I was just raised that way.

My stepmother was fat, about thirty years old; she wasn't short or tall, just average height. Her hair was wavy and she wore it braided. She always had her hands on her hips like a jug, always blaming someone for something. She dressed like a Tehuana, a woman from Tehuantepec, and she wore gold earrings and necklaces that sparkled like fireflies. In Tehuantepec they put a lot of gold in their teeth so that it flashes when they laugh.

My stepmother had land, large cultivated plots. The entire Valencia family owned lots of land: orchards, groves, fields full of corn, coconut, mango, chicozapote, oranges, pineapple, and every other kind of fruit. Her fields were immense, from here to Bondojo and even further, and the trees were heavy with fruit.

My stepmother Evarista taught me never to be idle. At the prison everyone worked from four in the morning until seven or eight at night. I got up at four, crossed myself, got dressed, and prayed; we prayed, thanking God for the sunrise and asking Him to let the sun set the same way it always did, and then I had to wash out the stoves. They were rinsed out and covered with ashes, which I had to moisten so they'd stick like cement, smooth, really white. Those hearths looked so beautiful. Stones were washed to be put in the pot to bring the coffee or whatever happened to be in it to a boil; those stones, which are scrubbed well with brushes until they're clean and shiny, are called *tenamaxtles*. Once I lit the fire, while the coffee was brewing I took a broom and swept; by five in the morning the coffee was ready; we had breakfast and went to mass, and then it was back to chores. Breakfast was at eight and you had whatever God provided. Sometimes it was refried beans with a fresh sauce made in the *molcajete*, where you combine tomatoes, chiles, and salt in a mortar and crush them with a stone, and grilled meat or lake trout and *atole*, the cornmeal-gruel drink. After breakfast we washed the dishes and all the pots and pans in the kitchen until two in the afternoon, which was lunchtime for the whole prison: soup, rice, the main dish, beans, desert, fruit.

The next day at four in the morning it was the same thing all over again: "Get to work, because that's how it's going to be." Since the prison was very large and my stepmother did the cooking, I helped her in the kitchen grinding spices, browning the rice when she made rice or stew. We usually served the prisoners rice soup, meat, and beans. We cooked a side of beef every day. One day there was stew in green sauce with pumpkin seeds and mint, the next day in tomato and red chile sauce. We also gave them *glua do shuba*, which they call *cuachala* in other places; it's a mole made of toasted corn.

Señora Evarista never talked to me; she never spoke to my father either. She hit me, but I never said a word, because I was older, I understood. I thought: "*Bueno, pues* what's the point of going from house to house? I'll put up with whatever I have to to stay with my father . . . Where could I go anyway that would be any better?" And this woman took it upon herself to teach me how to do housework; she hit me a lot with a quince switch, but it was for my own good, so I'd learn. They were a really big family, there was a lot of coming and going, a lot of people to work for. I ground tons of chile, tons of roasted corn, bushelfuls; one of chiles and one of tomatoes. And I ground chocolate and twenty-five pounds of coffee every other day. The chocolate is toasted on a flat clay dish called a comal and is ground in a metate with cinnamon and sugar. You press it between your hands to squeeze out the grease and shape it into bars. Where I'm from they're made round like tortillas and scored with a fingernail, so they can be cut into four pieces, and put out to dry. Here they make them in a mold. My stepmother taught me to beat the chocolate with a whisk, and we made it the way each person in the family liked it, and there were more than twenty of them. Some with water, some with milk, some with half a section of chocolate, a whole section, or even a section and a half. We made it with water for the prisoners, not because they were prisoners but because that's the traditional way in Oaxaca. Chocolate with *atole* is called *champurrado*. Señora Fortunata always drank *champurrado*. The trick with chocolate is to make it foamy by beating it to just the right consistency. If it isn't foamy, it isn't any good. You have to really beat it with an old-time beater for it to froth, because if it's just going to be like muddy water it's not worth drinking. I don't make chocolate now, because I get too tired. But I do buy it. The Morelia's is the most tolerable. La Abuela's has too much dirt in it. I've had it and it feels like grit in my mouth. But the way they made it before, that was really something.

My stepmother cooked the food, and my stepgrandmother served it. I loved them because they taught me to do so many things. My stepmother's mother, Señora Fortunata, was an old-fashioned lady with a puffy bun. In those days, the older women left the chores to their daughters and expected them to get everything done. They just gave orders, and everything was very respectful.

Señora Fortunata would say:

—Light the stoves.

Everyone obeyed:

—Fill the kettles to boil water.

She'd go out onto the patio:

—It hasn't been swept out here! Where's the broom?

And one of us would come running:

—I'm coming, I'm coming, just a minute . . .

—You better!

Señora Fortunata kept walking around, and if by chance she found one of us sitting down, she'd say:

—Are you waiting to have your picture taken?

So I never had the freedom to play or sit around talking, and I wasn't raised to be visiting people in their homes; all I did was work since I was little. When my mother was alive, people didn't go visiting or sit around talking either. And when my parents went to the market, they tied us to stakes like roosters, Emiliano in one corner of the room and me in the other.

At night when I'd finished my chores, I slipped behind the bars to sleep with the convicted woman. My father worked as a night watchman while I slept in the prison. Then he was promoted to warden when Francisco Madero's revolution broke out. As a night watchman, he patrolled the streets carrying a lantern. He'd yell: "*Sereno alerta*,"—"Watchman on guard"—from one corner to the next. As he turned to the right, the other watchman would answer. And you heard "*Sereno alerta*" until dawn. Sometimes his post was at the prison and then he yelled: "*Centinela alerta*"—"Sentry on guard"—from the rooftops all night, so no one would escape. The new prisoners couldn't sleep with that yelling, but they'd get used to it and then everyone would sleep peacefully.

We lived in the prison because they gave my stepgrandmother a house there so she could look after the prisoners. Her husband was the mayor of Tehuantepec and he asked that his wife and daughter relieve him of responsibility for the jail. The family was very large: sons and daughters, sons-in-law and daughters-in-law; ten children, seven males and three females. They were all married then and they had brought their wives to live there. The youngest daughter was also of marrying age, she was twelve or thirteen, but we were never friends. Emiliano and I were raised there, we lived with them while my father was with my stepmother; she had to take all of us in together. Since Emiliano was a boy, he went with my father; I only saw him in the afternoon or in the evening. He left early and he came back to eat when it got dark. Emiliano was with my father all day and all night. He really loved him. If my father yelled at him for something, Emiliano would feel terrible: "*Ay, mi papacito! Ay, mi papacito!*" My stepmother treated him well; just like all the other boys in that house.

In 1911, Madero took Mexico City, the capital, and that's when the earthquake happened. At four in the morning, buildings, lampposts, and monuments fell. I was alone with the prisoner.

Every night my stepgrandmother would show up in her black shawl with her handful of keys.

—Come on, child . . .

We'd cross the prisoners' courtyard and she'd open the last cell for me to get inside:

—*Ándale*, inside!

That night the inmate said:

—No stories tonight. They're really just a pack of lies anyway.

She liked to talk out loud and she told me about her life and I started to like her, but that night she was jumpy.

—Let's go to sleep, child.

—*Si, señora.*

She rolled over and got comfortable. That's the last thing I remember until the earthquake, when the poor thing ran to the bars and begged for me to follow her. I opened my eyes and saw that the dome of the jail had cracked into four parts. She knelt down and called out desperately, with all the strength in her soul, for them to have compassion and open the door. But my stepmother and her mother had gone out into the street and didn't hear her. There was so much noise. Everyone was outside kneeling down, on the sidewalk, on the patio, along the river, in the fields, on the hillside among the *tescalera* and the huisache cactus, where they had already begun tending the corn that was beginning to sprout, doing their chores. In Mexico City, they say, the quake lasted fifteen minutes, the ground turned inside out, furiously tossing houses around. Who knows how long it lasted in Tehuantepec, but it was terrible. The prison was wrecked. No one came to get me out until it was all over.

—Look at the roof, I said to my stepmother.

They took all the drunks out during the earthquake but not her. They left her inside. She was very frightened, so they let her come closer to the other prisoners' cells. Although they didn't talk to each other, she could feel their warmth. I've never been afraid of earthquakes, because I've felt them since I was little; my whole life has trembled. Where I'm from, the ground shakes two or three times a day and you can hear it creaking; it thunders and pounds everything. It's the earth's roar, it roars like a lioness in heat. It stamps its hooves and snorts. The water rises out of the ocean. If it's your turn to die crushed in an earthquake, *pues*, then it's God's will. Who knows why there are earthquakes. They say that near the ocean waves loosen rocks and they start rolling, and the force of the rocks shakes up the earth. They also say that there's a huge restless animal inside the earth and every time it yawns it breaks things. Do you think that's true? The rocks on the hillside fall when it wants to come out, which makes a huge commotion. That's what they say, but no one really knows . . .

After the earthquake, they moved the lifer from the last cell to the first one and she spent the whole day watching people through the bars. She would say to Señora Fortunata:

—Don't be mean, give me a centavo for a candle . . .

My stepgrandmother would have someone buy a candle for her. The prisoner was saying the novena of the Jesus child of Atocha and she asked for charity every day and someone gave her a tlaco . . . There were two or three days left in the novena when a six- or seven-year-old boy showed up with a basket in his hand and called out her name for them to give her the basket. She was surprised, because there wasn't anyone left around to remember her. The boy continued to bring her breakfast every morning and three days later he started bringing her dinner. We took the basket because we thought he was a real flesh-and-blood boy, a Christian child, because that's what he looked like to us: just a kid. The prisoner would say:

—I'll be damned if I know who that little fellow is . . . But he brings me food, so I'll eat it . . .

She ate everything he brought, and when the nine days were up, instead of the boy and the basket, a young man in a gray suit, about twenty years old, looking like a lawyer, asked to see her. He had a roll of papers from City Hall and he gave Señora Fortunata a card telling her to release the prisoner to him to appear in court. Only God and the prisoner know what went on there, but at around two in the afternoon, she returned and said to my stepgrandmother:

—Give me my things, because I'm getting out!

She'd been given her freedom. My stepmother and her mother saw that the papers were real and gave her the bundle. The lawyer was waiting outside for her:

—Head straight down this road. There's a chapel at the entrance to the town. Wait for me there, he ordered.

She started walking and the trip seemed real short. It was getting dark when she saw the chapel and she sat down at the side of the road to wait. The lawyer had said: "If it gets late, ask for the Niño de Atocha . . ." She asked, but no one knew what she was talking about; everyone was in a hurry and no one paid any attention to her until someone answered:

—The only Niño de Atocha is the one in the chapel.

When she pushed the door open and saw his statue in the niche holding his little basket, she realized he had the same face as the attorney who had represented her. She fell to her knees, began to cry, and asked the child to forgive her sins. When the people outside heard her crying with such sorrow, they wanted to know where she was from.

—I got out of the prison in Tehuantepec at two this afternoon.

—Which Tehuantepec?

—Tehuantepec, in the state of Oaxaca.

—That's not possible, it's very far away, very far.

—Really, it was two this afternoon and I just arrived.

They all came closer and crossed themselves. It was one of the Niño's miracles, because the chapel of the Niño de Atocha is in Fresnillo, Zacatecas, which was about eleven hundred kilometers away, and the prisoner got there the very day she had started out. Only she and God know how she got to the chapel.

In Fresnillo, she did everything in her power to return to Tehuantepec. She struggled for many years to put enough money together for the fare, and the first thing she did when she arrived was to go to the prison. She asked for my stepmother and for Señora Fortunata and she told them what had happened; that she was freed of her death sentence, repentant, she had confessed all her sins, and the priest in Fresnillo had absolved her. It was the Niño that had performed the miracle . . . I heard about it all later, because I'd left the prison the year she came back.

My father was always on the road and traveling to different places. He never stayed anywhere long enough to settle in. My poor mother put up with it because he was her husband, but she couldn't have more than the clothes on her back and the *petate*, the straw mat where they slept, and that was it, end of story. Why would she want stuff if from one day to the next my father would say: "We're leaving at such and such time," no arguments, we're going and that's it. Her metate always rode on her back because that's where she prepared our food. It was the only thing she carried, her metate and the pot where she cooked beans or whatever God provided. But it was a different story with my stepmother. There was no way she could follow him around. When he said:

—I'm leaving for such and such place . . .

—Well, take care. I won't leave my mother to follow you to one place one day and another the next, so go on. When you get tired of running around and come home, welcome back, and if not, may God bless you.

My father took us with him. When he got bored with where he was, we went to stay with my stepmother, Evarista. He sold merchandise in different villages, Salina Cruz, San Jerónimo, or worked as a peon, a day laborer, but he never stayed put. That's the way he was. All of a sudden he'd order:

—We're taking off tomorrow.

And Emiliano and I were right behind him. It didn't matter if I had a lot of chores to do and really loved the house and all, we had to roll up the *petate* and set off to follow God's lead. But it made me really happy to be the only woman with my father.

Cartloads of fruit were brought to Tehuantepec from the fields: bananas, mangoes, guavas, mameys. I really liked fruit, I did then and I still do; bananas, chicozapotes, guavas. At night, since I was still hungry, I ate green mangoes with salt and chile even though it was spicy. Green fruit didn't make me sick. One day I ate a hundred green plums with salt. I ate ripe mangoes, seed and all, because the seed is soft and tastes delicious. Where I'm from they grow oranges, coconuts, melons, and chirimoyas, and besides the fruit my stepmother gave me, I took bunches of bananas and whole mameys, caimitos, pineapples, and *tiluyas* from the baskets. They had watermelon stacked up on the patio and piles of guavas and anonas. Every night I took fruit out of the baskets, picking the biggest ones, which would fill me up the fastest. I'd eat lying on my mat. I always had cravings. They say that an orphan is never full because it doesn't have a mother's hand to feed it. I'd eat from five in the morning until eight at night.

I was very strong-willed but I never talked back to my stepmother. I'd pull my hair and bang my head against the walls because of her beatings. That was how I handled it. I banged my head against the wall, really, really hard, in a rage. I didn't feel it, but I do remember angrily biting my arms and hands. After a while I quit. What was the point of biting myself? But I used to think, "Why don't I die from all her beatings?" And here I still am; all these years and I haven't been able to die. My stepmother beat me every day with burning logs; I was burned on the hands, the arms, by the sparks that flew when she threw them at me. *Uy*, did I suffer a lot! Back then people were really forceful when it came to punishing their kids. That was when Evarista stabbed me because I dropped the dishes and they all broke. She had a knife in her hand and without thinking she threw it and it stuck me. I still have the scar on my back here, I felt it yesterday; the tip of my finger almost fits in the hole. That day I just kept on grinding. My stepgrandmother was the one who noticed it, because I passed by her to pick up a basket. I don't know whether it was full of chiles or tomatoes, and when I bent down she saw the dried blood. I was wearing a sheer black dress, and of course you could see the white slip underneath through the black. Señora Fortunata grabbed me and I screamed.

—What's wrong with you? she asked me.

I didn't realize what had happened, but when she pulled my dress away from the wound, it started to bleed again. I was very young, so it seemed strange to her.

—What's wrong with you, child?

—Nothing.

—What do you mean, nothing? Come here and let me see.

And she lifted up my slip and saw the bloody wound.

—Who hit you?

—Nobody.

—*Ja!* What do you mean, no one? . . . I'm going to find out now.

And she took down the leather whip and wet it:

—You hit her, she said to my stepmother. You hit her, Evarista. I'm going to whip you so you know how it feels.

She grabbed the bullwhip, but I got between them.

—Don't hit her, Mama Abuela, don't hit her, leave her alone.

Evarista knelt down:

—Go ahead and hit me, Mother. What do I care?

I hugged her so the blows wouldn't strike her, but she still got her good. A wet bullwhip is so flexible it rips the skin.

What was her point? The deed was done. Even if she'd half killed her, it wouldn't have taken away my injury. Then she threw her out of the house. My stepmother was not the mayor's child, she was his stepdaughter. She was already born when my step-grandmother came to the mayor's house. She was the eldest daughter, the other nine were by the mayor. That's why after she whipped her and ripped the flesh on her arms, my grandmother yelled:

—Get out!

When my father came home Señora Fortunata told him:

—I beat my daughter and threw her out because she was cruel and I'm going to do the same to you. Instead of looking after your daughter you let Evarista abuse her. You see, she's having a rough time and you don't stick up for her. You should never have allowed her to be beaten so much!

—I didn't know about it, because Jesusa never said anything to me . . .

—Well, I'm telling you, Felipe, because this girl suffers a lot . . .

Later my father scolded:

—What did she do to you, Jesusa?

—Nothing.

—Then how did you get hurt?

—I don't know.

When would I have told him? He had no time for me. He was always gone, so he never knew if I was being hurt or not. And my stepgrandmother was always looking after the prisoners. But she was really angry and began to beat him with the whip.

—Don't hit him, don't hit my Vini, it isn't his fault.

—Then whose fault is it? Is it Evarista's fault?

—No. It's not her fault either, it isn't hers either . . . Don't hit him . . . don't hit him.

It didn't make any difference. She had already hit him and there was no taking it back. Then they got angry at each other.

—I'm getting out of here right now, my father said.

—Good, the quicker, the better.

We never knew when or how he left, but I thought that my father and Emiliano had gone to Salina Cruz to stay with my sister-in-law Ignacia, so the warden gave me to a woman I'd never met and told me:

—She's your godmother.

—Fine, Señora Fortunata.

I ALWAYS CALLED my godmother "señora" and she called me "María de Jesús." She never spoke to me during the day. She gave me orders at night: "Tomorrow you will do this, this, and this," and the next day she never opened her mouth or said a thing to me. That's how I learned to do chores. And *ay de mí!* if I did them wrong. "Just you wait." Those were her words. "Just you wait." She was a widow, and every Thursday I had to take flowers to her dead husband's and daughter's graves. I put them in vases that had little mirrors on them; the ugliest ones—the dried cornflowers—were for the father, and the prettiest ones were for the daughter, and then I'd come back. The cemetery was on the outskirts of Tehuantepec and the sun was scorching hot: "Carry the flowers upside down so they don't wilt, María de Jesús." Every Thursday and Sunday I walked there and back because there weren't even burros and everyone walked. No burros anywhere. Now everyone probably drives.

My godmother's calling was to help sick people die. I went with her to houses where someone was dying and we didn't leave until she gave them over to death. She patiently prayed for them so that God would come fetch them. If they lingered too long, if death took its sweet time coming, then she shouted her prayers—she had very good lungs—"Have mercy on us . . ."

My godmother would warn me:

—It's coming.

The truth is, I had prayed under my breath too, just to myself, so no one could hear me: "Come on, once and for all. Don't be a wiseass, don't be so cocky, come on, come on, death, don't wear us out, don't tease, come, death, come on, we've had enough."

My godmother's name was Felisa Martínez de Henestrosa and she was a godmother of ribbons. Back then people tied ribbons around their necks—ribbons that had been blessed—to ask that a sick person be healed. She gave me a ribbon for the Señor of Esquipula, who was a black saint from the area where I was born. People wore blue ribbons for the Baby Jesus, white ribbons for the Virgin, purple for all saints, green and red and yellow for the patron saints. People were pious in those days. Now the priest just comes out and says: "The blessing will cost you so much . . ."

In those years of our Lord, godmothers chose the child before it was born. When they saw a pregnant mother who looked like she'd have a good delivery, they'd ask:

—Will you pledge me your child so I can take it to be baptized?

The babies were presented at church before they were forty days old, wearing a long fancy robe that reached the floor. That first trip to mass was called the *sacamisa*. The godmother presented the infant and the mother to the Virgin in remembrance of the Virgin presenting her son to Zachariah.

Baptism parties were really nice in those days because they were orderly, dignified, not like nowadays, when people eat like pigs and get drunk, dance and God only knows what else. Have another drink. Did you get enough of everything? And did they wolf down everything that was left? It doesn't honor the child being baptized, the little mite doesn't even know what's going on! The truth is, I don't know if my godmother requested me or if the warden found her, but she did have money. She was an elegant woman.

She had a son who was studying to be a doctor in the capital, another one who ran the drugstore in Tehuantepec, the Botica Mercantil, but she was the owner. The house took up the whole block, but there's nothing left of my godmother Felisa now. Señor Teófilo knew about medicine and the third son was a lawyer. She had two daughters, one was in the cemetery, and the other one,

Celerina, lived in Salina Cruz with an artillery lieutenant from Morelia. She also owned property.

I covered the whole house doing chores. I swept, cleaned the bedrooms, washed the dishes, dusted the shelves in the drugstore, the storeroom, watered the plants, mopped the hallways. I climbed up and down the ladders in the drugstore like a monkey, wiping down the glass shelves, the medicine bottles, the mortars. I ground the ingredients for remedies and set them out to dry. I put citrus blossoms, orange and lemon, boldo leaves, mint, out in the sun for teas. That's how I learned to nurse the sick, because Teófilo, the druggist, would send me to deliver the potions. But I didn't just leave them at the door, I went inside and gave the medicine directly to the patient. I had a gentle touch and they would hold on to me:

—Stay a little longer, Chuchita . . . Stay here . . . Straighten my serapes and cover me up better. Food only tastes good when you're here. Make me something . . .

I ground their food really well so they could swallow it, and I spoon-fed them, and of course that made me get back late.

My godmother sat behind the cash register, but she didn't fill prescriptions; she just made notes with a pencil that had purple lead. She would wet it on her tongue, and after a while her lips turned violet. Her son made up the medicines and stocked them; ten drops of wormwood, ipecac powder, a touch of violet gentian . . . a little bit of nux vomica. My godmother ordered everyone around from behind the register, with her hair pulled up in a bun, the old-fashioned way, very severe. The women of Tehuantepec have a special character, they're not like the ones from Mexico City who have gruel in their veins. Señora Felisa had nerves of steel. She gave me orders and didn't check up on me. She didn't have me running around for her all the time like city women: I need this, get me that.

I had to be at the courthouse at eleven in the morning with the jug of fresh juice for all the lawyers; I made pineapple, watermelon, melon, orgeat, which is made from barley and almonds, and I carried it on a tray along with glasses. Once I added a little nux vomica to the water to build up the lawyers' appetites, but they thought it was bitter, so I didn't do that again. There were about eight lawyers. The courthouse was a block away next to the Municipal Palace, so I'd cross the plaza under the tamarind trees.

At three o'clock it was time to eat. Everyone ate at a different time. First my godmother, then the lawyer, then the druggist. If the other lawyers came, they were fed also. There was a narrow opening in the wall to the kitchen where the cook passed the dishes through. They called it a service window. They made two different kinds of soup, one with broth and a thicker one, because they ate fish every day, and two meat dishes. We never served beans, because they didn't eat a lot of beans, and we gave them clean forks, knives, spoons, and plates for each course; clean silverware each time. Then the kitchen maid washed the mountains of dishes. There was an enormous stove that was stoked with big logs. The platters were big like trays and there were huge potbellied kettles that were really deep. Everything was big in that house.

I had the keys to the pantry and it was my job to distribute everything that was needed to prepare the food. I gave out the meat for lunch, took out the soups, thick and thin, and I had to make sure that there was always a large pot of soup stock on the stove for main courses. At breakfast I served some people chocolate, and others coffee, and then I locked the pantry.

When a sprinkling of stars was still in the sky, I had to unlock the *mozos'*, or menservants', rooms so they could go to work. Once they were gone I unlocked the maids' rooms. Then it was up to the main house, to the feather dusters, brooms, mops, scrub brushes, bleach, soap, and water, and to work! Once everyone had started their job, I lit the fire and set a big kettle of water—which I could hardly lift—on the stove for my godmother's bath. I was the only one allowed into the lawyer's study to wipe down his books and dust his furniture, arrange his blotter, fill the inkwell, and empty his wastebasket.

Besides taking up a whole block, the house had several orchards and a stable. At dawn, some of the laborers went out to milk cows, others to deliver milk, others to carry water, others to chop wood, others to sweep the patio and the sidewalk, still others went out into the fields to plant or pick fruit, or pack it into crates.

There was a lot of hustle and bustle in the house. Everything had its place. By six in the morning I was already bathed. Sometimes I ran out to the corral, where they were milking cows, to give the *mozos* a message from my godmother. She trusted me with the keys. How could I say no to her? And I worked but wasn't paid a salary or given food. Well, I did eat, but on the run, like a muleteer. I stopped long enough to make myself tacos and kept on going. The cook would say to me:

—Aren't you going to come and eat? *Ándele.* That's not good for you.

—I don't have time. Fix up a plate for me and I'll be back to eat when I get a chance.

They ran me ragged when I was a child!

I never sat down, much less talked to anyone. You didn't listen in on other people's conversations the way kids do now. In those days, when a guest came, you would leave without them having to say: "You can go now!" or "Get out of here!" Your mother would just turn her head and you would go out to the patio. Nowadays, with this modern education, they teach kids things and let them hear things they shouldn't. Before, they were taught what they needed to know when it was time. Children have to learn their place; they have to respect you and you should respect them too. Nowadays, a seven- or eight-year-old will tell you everything there is to know. I didn't have any idea how babies were born. Why should I? Why would my stepmother sit around and talk to me if I was a child? She didn't even sit around and talk to grown-ups. She did her work and that was it; each person did their job and there wasn't any talking about things; not about what was or wasn't bothering you. You never knew anything about them and they didn't know anything about you. There was no need for anyone to go around saying anything. When something happened to me, I never went running to my stepmother: "Look what just happened . . ." Why would I go around saying things I had no business talking about if she didn't even speak to me? Even more so with Felisa, my godmother. Now people tell each other everything. In those days, if you had your period, you had it, and that was the end of it. If it came, fine, and if it didn't, it didn't. No one ever told me about using rags or anything. I always bathed two or three times a day my whole life anyway. I never wore one of those filthy things that stank like a dead fish. And I never stained my dress. There was no reason to. I'd bathe, change my clothes, hang them out to dry, and I'd be clean again. I never suffered with it, I never gave it any thought, and it never hurt me, ever, and I never said anything about it to anyone.

I slept in my godmother's bedroom, but out on the balcony like a dog. It was one of those balconies that have iron railings. I didn't get cold, because it's always hot there. I had a *petate* and my pillow was a brick. That was harder than when I was a *soldadera* traveling with the troops. But I was young, and you can put up with anything when you're young! It's not that my godmother was a mean person; all rich people are like that. At least they were in those days. I don't know if it's different now. I think rich people have always been the same, since the beginning of time.

I locked the maids in at nine at night. Then I waited until the *mozos* started to show up and I locked them in too, and once I had bolted the door on the last one I went to the balcony to sleep so I could be up early to open the doors for them the next day. Praxedis, who was in charge of the water carrying, was in the biggest hurry to be let out early; if he didn't get going, he couldn't get all the buckets filled by eight o'clock. One day he said to another boy, who was a water carrier and drove two donkeys back and forth very early because he had to get to the river from the San Jerónimo barrio:

—Ay, it's late, it's late! Ay, I can't finish filling all the pails! Can you wake her up when you pass by the first time so she'll let us out earlier?

—How? The balcony is so high up.

—*Pues*, with a stick, said Praxedis.

So the boy would brush my face with a rose branch and then leave it when he went by on his first trip at four in the morning. He would stand underneath the side of the balcony where my head stuck through the railing and my hair hung down, and I'd feel the flowers on my face. He cut roses every day and he must have taken off the thorns, because I felt only soft leaves and petals.

•

I could make out that it was four in the morning on the Palacio clock. I watched him as he went toward the river between his two donkeys, until I lost sight of him. I carried the flowers around with me all day.

One day I asked Praxedis:

—Who's the person who throws me a branch of roses every day?

—*Ándale*, so you're the muleteer's girlfriend now . . . I'm going to bring him to meet you.

One afternoon he brought him by: a boy about seventeen years old. He had olive-green eyes and was skinny. We didn't talk to each other at all. The *mozo* teased us.

—*Ándale*, how come I didn't know she was your girlfriend, *manito?*

—No, my friend. How could she be my girlfriend? I've never even seen her, just her hair from under the balcony. You're the one who asked me to wake her up.

They called each other *manito* because they were friends, and they'd go out together in the afternoon. I never went, it wasn't my place. I watched them leave arm in arm. I had more than enough work and I couldn't wash my clothes until everyone was asleep. I'd wash my dress at night so it would be dry by morning and I could wear it the next day. I wore out the few rags my stepmother had given me while I worked at her house.

The boy woke me up every day, until my godmother sent me to the port of Salina Cruz. I don't know if he's even alive today. I never saw him again.

I had smallpox when I was living with my godmother. I cured myself with sand and river water. You get pimples that itch a lot. I'd go to the river and scrub my whole body with sand, everywhere I could reach. I'd soap myself and scratch all over until the welts bled. I got into the cold water to wash the blood away even if it hurt; the trick was to kill the microbes. I'd sit there and watch the blood turn to water. I got well just from that: river water and salt. When I got out of the water I put salt and lemon all over, and it stung. I said: "Something has to take this away." Since I didn't have a mother, there wasn't anyone to care if I got better. God only knows where my father was! That's when I realized I had to make it on my own, as God would have me. Otherwise I wouldn't eat.

One day when I was carrying the tray of drinks, my stepmother found me:

—Your father is with the Maderistas, Jesusa!

Then she looked me over and said:

—Oye, why are you so filthy? Why don't you change your clothes?

—Because I don't have anything else to wear, and I didn't have time to wash my dress last night.

—What do you mean, you don't have anything else?

—My clothes wore out.

—How could that be? I made you so many dresses.

—But I don't have anything left except what I'm wearing. I wash it out every night so it'll dry by morning.

My stepmother got angry and said to my father:

—You all say that I don't love her, but I beat her because I love her . . . She hasn't even earned a dress where she works, she works for nothing!

She came to my godmother's house and sat me down:

—Look, Jesusa, your father says I don't love you. My mother also says I don't love you. If I didn't love you, I wouldn't care if you did whatever you felt like, but I do, so you have to listen to me. You have to do what I say. I hit you because I want you to learn something.

And I appreciated it, because if it weren't for all the beatings, I wouldn't know how to wash dishes, or wash clothes, even if I don't do it well. How would I have supported myself? Where would I have ended up? It was like that business with school. My stepmother wanted to send me to a public school, but my father was really . . . *pues*, really dumb, if you want to know the truth, ignorant, because he never learned how to read. But if my father had been reasonable, he would have said: "Let her learn how to write her name, let her learn to read, it doesn't matter who teaches her as long as she learns her letters . . ."

My father said that I couldn't go to the public school even if they taught better than the nuns, because he wasn't a Protestant. What did being a Protestant have to do with my learning to read? I've heard that song and dance since I was little; it's something they bring on themselves, the Protestants, the Catholics. I've heard it over and over. This devil's fight has been going on for centuries and won't be over any time soon. I still don't understand the argument, but because of the damn Protestants they sent me to the nun's school, where they never taught me anything. Just to pray. Damn those nuns. They made me kneel on the balcony facing the street on top of beans or corn or garbanzo beans, or on anthills, and sometimes they even made me wear a dunce cap. Of course, that made me even more rebellious. I got even by putting gum on the benches and it stuck to their habits, and I pulled their hoods, because I couldn't think of anything else to do to them. But if I saw one of them today I'd sweep the streets with them; after all, they're skinny like brooms. I couldn't care less about praying, at least not the kind we did back then. I remember a few of the words. I wanted them to teach me to read, but that wasn't what they were interested in. Now? What for? I have one foot in the grave . . . if I make it that far.

My stepmother was of a different class. She was educated. Her mother, Señora Fortunata, was as ignorant as my father; she was a Zapotec and spoke their language. But my stepmother, Evarista, knew Zapotec and Spanish because Señora Fortunata sent her to school. She had the sense to do that. But there was no hope for me; my father took off again and my godmother sent me to Salina Cruz to her daughter, the one who was married to the soldier.

—Celerina needs a nursemaid, so that's where you're going, María de Jesús.

My father didn't take Emiliano with him that time, so we both went to Salina Cruz. I set him up with a woman from Oaxaca— Benita—to teach him a job, and since he was an obedient child, he learned well. She sent him to a hog butchery. Even though

Emiliano was older than me he did what I told him, maybe because I was the only woman he'd really ever been around, or that's just how he was. He stayed wherever I told him to. Emiliano was white, my color, with a low forehead just like my father, and big olive-green eyes. The rest of us had black eyes. None of us looked like him. I never hit Emiliano. He was such a gentle brother, that Emiliano; a lump of sugar couldn't be sweeter . . . If my father said to him:

—It's midnight, Emiliano.

—Yes, Father.

Even if it were noon, he would fold his hands. "Yes, Father." I've never been like that. He'd keep his hands folded and say: "Yes, Father, it's midnight." And the sun could be beating down on him. He never contradicted him. I had a taunting laugh. I would burst out laughing: "Ha! Ha! Ha! Ha! Ha! It's noon, *qué caray*, midnight my ass!"

My father would turn around:

—I'm going to crack you one!

—Go ahead . . . if you can.

I never backed down from anyone. And anyone who backs down from me is screwed. I got into it with my father too. It didn't do Emiliano any good to be the only one who never contradicted my father.

People say: "If you tame a horse completely, he loses his spirit, and if a man is too good, he has no balls."

I STAYED IN SALINA CRUZ taking care of my godmother's grandchildren for a long time. My father, who had gone off with Francisco Madero's people, went back to his old job at the prison in Tehuantepec, but my stepmother and her mother weren't employed there anymore. Another warden had moved into the prison with his family.

I was a nanny but I didn't get paid. I was about eleven or twelve when there was an American invasion. Who knows if it was good luck or bad, but there wasn't a lack of men to marry. I could have married one of the Chinese men who arrived on the boats. Speaking of Chinamen, there was this one who was young and very handsome. He had a little place across the street and that's where I did the shopping. I don't know if he was joking or serious, but every time I went in to buy something he'd ask me to marry him. Since I didn't really understand those kinds of things, one day I answered:

—No, you're crazy, but if you want to get married, find yourself a girlfriend and I'll be your maid of honor . . .

I've always been a maid of honor or a godmother. I've never lacked *compadres* and *comadres*, men and women friends. When I think of it now, it makes me laugh, the Chinaman wanted me to be his girlfriend and I offered to be his maid of honor.

Since I'm older, I understand he wanted to get married to have kids and not feel so Chinese. A couple of weeks later my godmother's daughter and I went to the store, and he was standing behind the counter and he greeted the Señora and then said to me:

—So, Jesusa, ale you going to mally me?

—You're crazy, you're crazy. I already told you to find a girl-friend and I'd stand up for you. I said it to him innocently, in front of the Señora.

—Well, if you don't want to mally me, I alleady have a gilflend.

Damned Chinaman, he already had someone else! And then Señora Celerina said to him:

—If she promised to be your maid of honor and she doesn't want to, we'll sponsor you.

—Leally, Señola Celelinita?

And that's how they left it. He was in a real hurry. They say that the Chinese are the marrying kind, that's why there are so many people over there and the women are like rabbits and have up to four little babies. But according to him, he was more interested in me, because before he married the other one, he still pursued me. But I stuck to my "No." You can look, but don't touch.

Whether he loved her or not, he married her. And since he didn't have any family in Salina Cruz, the party was held at Cele-rina's husband's house. He didn't take his eyes off me, and mean-while the bride kept drinking pulque and *glua do shuba*. That skirt-chasing little Chinaman's name was Juan Lei. I'll never forget the enormous looks that came out of those little eyes.

My godmother's daughter, Señora Celerina, didn't treat me badly, but she didn't pay me. At least I ate first, because I tasted everything while I was making the kids' food, so by the time the bosses sat down at the table, my food was already past my stomach and in my heels. The work wasn't very hard, since I only took care of the children, but at night I washed and ironed their diapers and little outfits. I took the younger ones to the park, the older ones to school. I raised those five kids really clean. I dressed them in the morning, at noon, and in the afternoon. At four o'clock I changed them to take them to the park. I brought them back at five, bathed them again with scented soap, gave them a snack, and put them to bed. Besides bathing them, I liked to curl their hair.

At that time long hair was in style and people made a little curl on top of the head and the tip of the curl would fall down on the forehead. My charges were well-dressed, beautiful children. And that curl took a lot of work! You wet the hair with linseed water, then rolled it with a curling iron, and the ringlet came out round, chubby, and stiff. I didn't like limp, straight hair, because it doesn't look nice! So all day I fussed over those kids: a button, a collar, the curl, wipe this little face, hold-this-here, hold-that-there. The trick was to keep the kids quiet so I could entertain myself taking care of them: be quiet, real quiet, or the bogeyman will get you. "The itsy-bitsy spider went up the waterspout. Down came the rain and washed the spider out . . ." I didn't have anyone to talk to besides the little ones, because my only friend was the metate. That's where my quietness comes from. Now, as an old lady, I've started to talk some.

One day Doña Luisa, a friend of my mother's, my dead mother, showed up to see me.

—Listen, Jesusa, your father left your stepmother. He's over around Salina Cruz living on a mountain making charcoal and he goes down to the market on Sundays to sell it . . .

—What about Emiliano?

—He's with him.

—He took him away from Señora Benita?

—Yes. And he married him off . . .

—What do you mean, he married him off?

—Yeah, he forced him to marry the girl because her mother is your father's mistress.

That's an awfully close family! I didn't know if it was true, because I couldn't see that happening, but it made me happy to think that I was going to see my father again. I said goodbye to Señora Celerina and told her that I was going with Doña Luisa. I arrived at the ranch and asked for my father; he came out of the house right away but wouldn't let us in:

—What'd you come here for?

—To find you . . .

—Who gave you my address?

I didn't answer him.

—There's no reason for you to come looking for me, because you are not my daughter.

It made me furious.

—What do you mean, I'm not your daughter?

—I don't have any daughters. Get the hell out of here!

Then I said:

—Ah! I'm not your daughter . . . ? Well, then you aren't my father either.

And I turned around.

—Then we're even! Don't even think of talking to me again!

I'll be damned if that woman wasn't his mistress. I hope God has forgiven them. Since Emiliano got married not to oppose him, it turned out that besides being his son, he became his son-in-law. That's why he slammed the door in Doña Luisa's and my face.

—Get out of here! Get out of here! I won't let you in!

Then Doña Luisa said:

—Come on, let's go, this is really screwed up here, we'd better leave and forget that there ever was a Felipe Palancares.

—He's dead and buried as far as I'm concerned.

I didn't see Emiliano. He could have been off cutting firewood on the mountain. That's what happened to him for being so meek. I thought: "He disowned me. Let them stay with their hags." Every week Emiliano went down to the plaza to sell firewood, but I never saw him. He never looked for me; I never looked for him. I didn't dwell on it, but since he and I grew up together, he was the only one I ever loved. *Sí*, just him.

I started to work for a French woman, and there was a Porfirista colonel living next door.

There was a barbed-wire fence with those spikes on top, and a colonel and his assistant, Candido, lived on the other side; Candido liked to talk to me. He was a nursemaid too. When the French woman's children and the colonel's children played together, we talked and talked, even though I'm not one to gossip, but that Candido, he was an older gentleman, about my father's age, around thirty or thirty-five, he had a laugh that made me laugh also. You could hear it from far away. He'd tell the children stories and I'd make faces, silly things that you do without thinking, and we'd laugh harder than the kids; they'd just stare at us. Then he'd say: "Let's swing them." He'd make a swing and push them hard. I liked to get up into the tree and smack them in the face with the branches, but the mother didn't like that game. Her three children were real pigs. In those days I wore a *huipil*, a sleeveless blouse, and Tehuana-style petticoats. I had to be careful not to get the floor-length skirts dirty. I was cleaner than the señora, who was always filthy. Because my stepmother had been so strict and didn't like me going around like a pig, I got spoiled. This woman wouldn't let the children be changed very often, and the little ones were used to wallowing in muck. How was I supposed to touch them? It was awful. She let them dirty themselves and then she didn't want to clean them. Why was I going to clean them? Their little bottoms were caked and so, so dry.

—I'm not cleaning that.

—That's what I pay you for.

—Then don't pay me, but don't tell me to stick my hands where they don't belong. Teach them to wipe themselves, but first, why don't you learn to wipe yourself, maybe you should try using a corncob.

And that was the end of that job. The woman told me to get out, and the sooner the better. So I took off for Doña Luisa's house, but on the way I ran into Candido:

—Where're you going, my bruised little apple?

That's what he called me: "bruised little apple" or "Tehuanita."

—Home.

Home. But what home did I have? I said that so he wouldn't think I didn't have anyone.

—Where's your house?

—Down this way.

Señor Candido walked with me as far as the market and he stopped there to do the shopping and I went on to Doña Luisa's.

—What happened? she asked.

—The French woman fired me.

When I left, someone told the French woman they'd seen

me go off with the soldier. I didn't go to my stepmother's even though Tehuantepec was close by. Instead, I took off for my dead mother's friend's house. Someone told my stepmother, Evarista, that I had taken off with a soldier. Of course she was furious and went to the French woman to demand an explanation.

—Why did you let her leave if she was here to work for you?

—Because she was useless . . . look, the depraved soldier lives next door . . .

Señora Evarista leaned over the fence and accused Candido too:

—No, no, señora, I didn't take your daughter anywhere. You're very mistaken. I was going to the market and she was heading the same way, and I asked her what she was doing and she said she was on her way to Señora Luisa, who was a friend of her mother's . . . I understand she's a friend of yours . . .

I hadn't told the assistant that my mother had died. He knew my stepmother as my mother, he didn't know that Doña Luisa was my dead mother's friend. My own mother, the mother who gave birth to me . . .

I was sound asleep on a big table when my stepmother got there, and she gave me a beating just like old times.

—You shameless . . . slut! Why did you go to someone else's house instead of coming home?

Doña Luisa interrupted:

—Listen, señora, I knew the little one's mother, her birth mother. You have to understand that she's a child . . . I took her in because I couldn't leave her out on the streets . . .

—No, no. They told me that she took off with a soldier . . .

—They lied to you! She didn't show up here with any soldier!

Since she'd already talked to the soldier, she didn't keep blaming me, but she did drag me off. Doña Luisa didn't try to stop her because she didn't feel she had any right to. Besides, she didn't even know my stepmother. She had never seen her before. I'd gone to Doña Luisa's because she was the only person I thought would take me in, but she was a real gossip, and was always snooping into other people's business and watching out the door and windows to see who was and wasn't walking by.

On the way home my stepmother asked:

—Where's your father?

—Who knows . . .

How could I tell her he lived with another woman? I didn't even tell her he'd thrown me out and said that I wasn't his daughter. I kept it all to myself. When we were about to take the train to Tehuantepec, someone told Señora Evarista that another Tehuana there, the wife of a gringo, would give me a job. So she made the arrangements and left me with that gringo's wife in Salina Cruz.

—Jesusa, where are your clothes?

—I left them at the other job.

My stepmother went to get them. The French woman told her that I was really rude.

—That's the way she is, señora. She wasn't born to be mistreated. Besides, if you didn't like her, it's good she left . . .

At the new job I helped the gringo's wife in the kitchen. She taught me how to make buns. Back then you measured everything in cups, not like now when you add ingredients by estimating. You beat eggs, butter, milk, and sugar and then add the flour and beat and beat and beat until the mixture forms little bubbles, you put the batter in molds, and bake at medium heat. I don't have an oven, so I don't make buns now, but I know that recipe by heart. Anytime you want I can give it to you. Just make sure you measure in cups. I liked cooking better than taking care of filthy kids.

I spoke Spanish from the time I was a kid and I learned the Zapotec language from my stepmother. Even today I still understand Japanese, Catalan, French, English, because I worked for gringos. I guess you could say I always worked for foreigners, and here in the city they treat me like I'm a foreigner.

One day when I was serving them dinner, the American, who owned the dam, said that a soldier had been shot. "They killed him at five this afternoon, on my dam . . ."

The next day when I went to the market, there was a snake charmer at the entrance and I stood there like an idiot watching the man with the snakes inside his shirt and curled around his neck. Just then Señora Benita saw me, the woman from Oaxaca who had taken Emiliano in, and she called out to me. But I was so fascinated by the snakes that I didn't hear her yelling my name. She got mad and left her stall, where she sold meat, and came over and said:

—Didn't you hear me talking to you? I called and called and you ignored me. Your brother was killed yesterday at five o'clock in the afternoon, so if you want to see him one last time, run on down to the docks now. There are three freight cars where they're holding wakes for three dead men. The first one died of smallpox, the second was stabbed, and your brother's in the third car. He was shot to death. You'll recognize him by the bullet wounds.

I dropped the basket I was carrying and ran to the docks. I found my brother. That was when I realized he'd really been killed, when I saw him laid out. The soldiers said:

—Ay, señora, our condolences for your husband's death.

I turned around and stared at the soldier who had spoken up for everyone there:

—My husband? Stupid! How could this be my husband? Can't you see he's my brother?

They didn't know me, there was no way for them to tell. They knew he was married and thought I was his wife: but his wife never went to see his body. I guess no one ever told her. At least I didn't see anyone who claimed to be his wife. That's why they thought I was her, because I hugged him and started crying. They kept on giving me their condolences for the way he had died and I ignored them. All the crap people say just to make themselves feel better. I turned around angrily and yelled:

—Wife! I'm not his wife! I'm not Palancares's widow or Joe Smith's widow or John Doe's widow! Don't you understand me? I'm his sister.

No one said anything and the leader asked me:

—Are you Señor Palancares's daughter? Are you Felipe's daughter?

—Yes, sir, I am.

Even though I had fought with my father, when he asked me I couldn't deny it. A little later my father showed up. He stood outside the freight car. It made me really mad and I went outside too.

—I saw my brother. I'm leaving . . .

They called out to him:

—Is that your daughter-in-law or your daughter?

—My daughter.

I heard it clearly. He said:

—My daughter.

I didn't know my brother was a soldier, and I never figured out what had really happened. That's why when the señor where I worked said that a soldier had been killed at five that afternoon, it didn't mean anything to me. Later Señora Benita, who spent all night at the wake in the freight car, told me:

—You know what your father's like . . . He joined up with the Carrancistas, and since he didn't have anyone to go to the Revolution with him, he took Emiliano. He enlisted him as a soldier and said your brother would have to die along with him.

My father and Emiliano were guards for Jesús Carranza, and for some reason the general ordered them to set up camp in Salina Cruz. The soldiers got paid and my brother went to play cards, *albures* and conquian, which are monte games, and from what I understand, when Emiliano won, the other guy didn't want to pay up and be broke, so he shot him. That's how Emiliano Palancares was killed. Everyone went out looking for the killer but couldn't find him. The ground had swallowed him up. At dawn, they were still hunting for him with big lanterns but every last stone looked clean.

I think that man must have been protected by some kind of glimmering light, because he never turned up anywhere. My brother died and that was the end of it, there was no way to avenge him. The man that killed him killed him but good. There was no way to make him appear . . . At least that's what they told me. Now who knows what the real truth is.

The señora was waiting because her gringo husband came home for lunch at noon. When I got back I told her:

—Here are the groceries, señora, but I'm not going to cook, because my brother was killed and I'm going with him . . .

That's how that job ended. I left everything. I just took off. The office to register deaths was right next door to where I worked. They had brought Emiliano from the freight car.

I went inside. My father was there but I ignored him. They settled everything with him and I asked one of the soldiers:

—Do you know what time they'll bury him?

—Probably around two in the afternoon, because right now they're going to do an autopsy.

—Autopsy?

—Open him up.

My father was there at the registry waiting for the death certificate. From there they took Emiliano to the morgue, where they do autopsies. When I saw that they were going to cut him open, I wrapped my arms around him so they couldn't touch him. I argued that if they were going to bring him back to life I'd let them; if not, they weren't going to split him open. I screamed that there wasn't anything to gain by opening him up, that I didn't want them to make mincemeat out of him, not to use him for their studies. They paid no attention to me, and I had a fit and fell down. That was when they pulled me off my brother and handed me over to my father. He told me later that they didn't do the autopsy then but attended to me because my body turned black and blue and I wouldn't wake up. They didn't know how to bring me back and they got scared. My father was scared too. When I came to at about three in the afternoon, Emiliano was already cut, sewed up, and put in his coffin. There's nothing you can do, they carve them up and then they arrange the pieces back in the box.

I had those attacks for many years. I could feel my jaws lock up and it was hard to breathe when they were coming on. I'd motion for someone to blow air in my face or throw water on me or something, and if they didn't, I'd thrash around and hurt myself. They'd pick me up off the street or wherever it happened, but no one could hold me, because I was heavy and really strong. I'd fall down dead, lifeless, like a stone in a well. The fits ended in 1920.

When I came to, I was holding a piece of cotton with two bullets in my hand. What good did the bullets do me then? I'd have been better off if they'd left me with my brother. It would've made me happy. They should've buried me next to my brother. At least I wouldn't suffer what I'm suffering now.

I watched them throw my brother's coffin into the water and then cover it with dirt. I still wasn't completely myself, but I do remember that they buried him in the water; the seawater seeped into the grave. It was about five in the afternoon when we left the cemetery, and that very afternoon General Jesús Carranza's company, which we belonged to, was leaving for the capital. I say we, because from that moment on I went with my father. He said that since he'd lost his son he didn't want to lose me.

Since General Jesús Carranza had to leave during the funeral, he arranged for General Pascual Morales y Molina to lend him soldiers and those of us who stayed for the burial would be under General Morales y Molina's command. They simply swapped men. Molina was to go to Acapulco and we departed by boat that same day. I left with the clothes I was wearing. I didn't go back for my things or the money I was owed for three months' work. My father didn't want me to . . .

—Just let it go.

We left with all my brother's friends, all the people who had buried him. General Jesús Carranza was going to meet up with us in Acapulco, but that morning was the last time his soldiers saw him alive. He was killed somewhere along the way before he reached Mexico City.

IT TOOK THREE DAYS and three nights to reach Acapulco from Salina Cruz. The company slept below on a big deck that was the size of the length and width of the boat. They set up there with their stuff like they were at home—men, women, fat and skinny, and all the children that the soldiers always take along. We went to the dining room in groups. Sometimes we went up on deck to look at the ocean, and the fresh air would feel good on my face. I didn't get seasick on the boat, I got sick on land when we got off. While I was on the boat I was really happy. I liked it because there weren't any storms and the waves gently cradled the boat and it didn't sway from side to side at all. We got off and started walking, but as soon as the air from the land hit me, my head started to spin, and I fell down flat. I couldn't open my eyes, because I'd see things, and my head was all messed up and I was reeling. For two days I didn't eat or even sip water, because the ground was shaking under my feet and I'd fall if I stood up. One of the women from the coast suggested lemon water and she and another woman put ice on my head. I lay there with my eyes closed: "Drink the lemon water so you'll feel better." But just lifting my head made me fall over. That lasted for three days and then I was fine. I haven't been on a boat in the ocean since then. I'm on the verge of dying; why would I get on a boat now unless it was to sail in my coffin?

We'd leave at three or four in the morning, after they played
reveille, and walk while it was cool because when the sun heated
up you'd get sunstroke and there was no point in passing out and
being abandoned in the middle of nowhere. We'd lay up in some
area when the sun was the strongest. The fighting only went on all
day long during combat. I liked getting up early in the morning.
My father walked; he was infantry and I had to follow him. I carried the basket of dishes and wore high-heeled shoes, not the kind
they wear now that are like bayonets and poke holes in the
ground, but the ones with good heels. He had those custom-made
for me in Acapulco, a black pair, a brown pair, and stockings. My
whole life women wore stockings. Nowadays they walk around with
bare legs and their asses peeking out, but earlier even little one-
year-old kids wore socks and nobody went around bare-legged. I
had my basket on my arm: a plate, a cup, a pitcher, a pot to make
coffee or to fry whatever my father was going to eat. I didn't have
a lot of dishes. Why would I? One plate and one cup were enough.
We went with the convoy through Chilpancingo, Iguala, Chilapa,
all the way to Puente de Ixtla; we usually got to where we were going at about five or six in the afternoon or seven at night. We'd
stop there, and the next day, at dawn, *ándenles*, forward march,
and we were back on the road.

They sent us women on ahead. We wore long skirts and everyone except me wore a straw hat. I just had my rebozo. The heat
didn't bother me. If we happened to run into the enemy and they
asked us how many Carrancistas were coming up behind us and if
they had enough weapons, we'd say there were very few and they
had very little gunpowder; if there were two or three thousand
men we would tell them there were only a thousand. We told
them the opposite and they never caught on. They'd tell us:

—Go on ahead because we're going to attack.

That's why I never knew what combat was like for the infantry,
because my father always sent me on ahead two or three hours before he set out.

When we arrived, we tried to get the food ready. There were

about ten to fifteen of us women, then came the advance guard, the ones who take the first bullets. Then the rear guard got ready to attack and was deployed to surround the enemy. The officers divided the troops up. For instance, if there were a thousand, each officer was in charge of fifty men and they set them up on the firing line. All we heard was the thundering of gunfire and we saw little white clouds that went up like little balls in the air. Sometimes an explosion would leave your ears buzzing, but that was it. When the fighting was over, they played the bugle to round everyone up and find out how many men were missing. Each officer called the names off their list and they would answer: "Present." If they didn't, and were left behind, they were screwed!

We women didn't usually pay attention to the fighting; we worried about preparing food for the soldiers. We'd get to a village, and if by chance we found people still there, they didn't want to even see our faces. Everyone took off for the hills. When the Zapatistas came they robbed them, when the Carrancistas came they robbed them, so which side were the poor folks supposed to choose? They were afraid of all of them, so they didn't wait for us to get there and they didn't want to sell us anything.

We weren't cattle rustlers, we were part of the Carrancista Constitutional Government and stealing was forbidden. That's what General Pascual Morales y Molina said. The Zapatistas did steal cattle, they slaughtered them, and caused a lot of damage in the towns. The peasants hated them. They'd turn off their lights and hide. No one warned them that the soldiers were coming, but they knew whether it was Zapata's or Carranza's people. And if it was a town that supported Carranza, they greeted us decently. If not, they took off for the hills. One of the many times we passed through Guerrero, we arrived at a place called Agua del Perro at about five o'clock. There wasn't anyone there; they'd all left and it was getting dark. We found pots with beans already cooking in them in the huts, and the nixtamal or corn ready to be ground in the metate; so we ground the nixtamal and threw on tortillas. We climbed up and got chickens right from their roosts, and plucked them while they were still warm after just being killed. Then we cleaned them real good, gutted them, and cut them up into pieces. We found spices and marinated the chicken with garlic and vinegar and salt and pepper, then put it on the fire in a big pot with lard and let it brown until the skin was crispy . . . I haven't had such good chicken since. We ate on the run and I'm sure it tasted so good because we were so hungry. Nothing tastes good to me now, since I'm not hungry anymore.

During one of those comings and goings my father found another woman, a cook who went to the barracks and won him over. He was a man, so he had to be in love. He always had his women, that's for sure. I always beat them because they were abusive, because they were greedy, because they lay around drunk, because they spent my father's money . . . That was what made me the maddest, that they spent all his money, that was just too much, that's why I beat his mistresses. They weren't going to give it away for free. They may have liked my father, but not that much. The truth is that one of them, Guayabita, was jealous of me.

It wasn't my fault that the paymaster gave me the money because he realized that my father had another woman and soldiers made very little money. I knew I had to buy my father his cigarettes and food, but I didn't have to support Guayabita.

—What a coincidence that your daughter doles out all the money! She's really your lover!

—No, she's not.

My father told her that I was his daughter.

—So shut up. You get nothing.

—What do you mean, nothing?

—You heard me. Nothing!

—You're going to be sorry . . .

I had to pay the piper for that one. Guayabita insulted me in public, she told me to go fuck myself, she swore at me, saying that I was a whore. I didn't know what to say back, I'd just cry. If only the bitch were to say it to me now! She screamed horrible things about my father to me and then one afternoon all the *soldaderas*, the women who followed the troops, got together and approached me:

—If you don't stand up to that woman we're going to ride you like a horse.

I was really afraid that they'd all gang up on me and do it. I'd seen them tie soldiers by their hands and feet and then jump on top of them. I thought: "They'll crush me if they ride me like a horse." So I asked them:

—What do I do?

—You figure out how to stand up to her . . . If she tries to hit you, we'll back you up . . .

We were all walking along a path near the barracks when they saw her.

—Here she comes! Now, go!

—Oh my God, oh my God!

—*Ándale!* God'll give you strength!

I picked up a rock. I threw it as hard as I could and it hit her in the chest. She fell back and I jumped on top of her. I pinned her hands together and held them down with my arm. Then I took off my shoe and I hit her with the heel. I hit her face and her head. Since I had hold of her hands she couldn't hit me back. But if I had let her go she would have won because she was huge, tall; she was an older woman, at least twenty. Hitting her with the rock gave me the advantage because if I'd taken her on with both of us standing up she would have clocked me good. But fear made my muscles tighten up, like steel. Fear gives you a lot of strength. Either I was going to kill her or she was going to kill me. I'd made her bleed a lot when the police chief and his guards came by and got her away from me. The women stood up for me, they told the general what had happened, and the paymaster admitted that she'd harassed me. They punished my father for allowing a woman off the street to insult his daughter. As usual, my father said that he didn't know anything about it; whatever she'd done, she'd done on her own. Since I'd never told my father about the woman's insults, there was nothing anyone could do about it! Guayabita didn't start anything with me again.

My father slept by me: he always lay down next to me. On his day off, after being on leave, he'd have to be in the barracks at six in the evening for roll call, and he never missed it. I think he screwed her right before that. That time they arrested him for ten days. I went to visit him in jail. He said:

—Good afternoon, daughter.

There wasn't any reason for him to be mad at me. Besides, what could he say? He knew that I beat all his women, except my stepmother.

The officer told me not to leave the barracks because I had really injured Guayabita's face when I hit her with the heel of my shoe, and she could try to get even.

But my father's people, the *soldaderas*, told him:

—She's with us . . . If the mistress makes trouble, we can too . . . We didn't get involved in the fight; the two of them beat each other . . . We're just trying to look after the little one . . .

My father walked out on Guayabita after that.

When he got out of jail he took me swimming behind the castle of the Fort of San Diego in Acapulco. There was a place where the waves were like back home. It's the only other place that I've gone swimming. I took off my clothes but I didn't get naked like a side of beef; I wore my undershirt and my slip. We also swam in the rivers around Chilpancingo, but you have to know how to swim in rivers. I always went with my father to where the current wasn't so strong, because otherwise it'll drag you. He'd swim too, but he'd go to another area and leave me at a bend where the water would cover me up. I did get in naked there but the mangroves covered the shore like a curtain. It's really nice when you fit into the space really well and no one can see you! You soap yourself up good and scrub and rinse because the water's so deep. I scrubbed with soap and fine sand to get all the grime off and I'd be so smooth. And then I'd dry off with a sheet or whatever I had. I never went to the river again. I didn't have a father to take me.

My braid hung down below my hips and my hair was wavy, not curly, and it went way down to here. When I came back from swimming the boys in the barracks would yell:

—Queen Xochtil has arrived! Here comes Queen Xochtil!

I don't know what they saw in my hair, but my father warned them:

—Don't harass her, because if she throws something at you and it hits you, I'm not getting involved.

It made me angry that they called me Queen Xochtil. I felt like they were insulting me. I'd say to my father:

—I'm going to hit them if they keep yelling at me like that.

I wasn't pretty, beauty was never my best quality. Calling me Queen Xochtil was just teasing, it was a game. I didn't want them to flirt with me or make fun of me, because it embarrassed me. I wanted to be a man, to put my hair up and go serenading with the boys, sing along with the guitar.

While I was doing the shopping one day, there was a shooting at the market. We were stationed in Acapulco at the Fort of San Diego, and every other day we'd go downtown to get provisions. They'd set up the market in front of the Palace on Alameda. The Palace was a short little building; in those days there wasn't anything tall in Acapulco; the tallest things were the palm trees and there weren't very many of them. They did sell a lot of coconuts; round, like cannonballs. The oil vendor would yell from the steps of the Palace, because the people set up their goods there and sold each other garlic and onions, coffee and chocolate and sugar candy. The fishmonger got the steps all wet with his soaking-wet sacks full of stinking sea creatures and every one haggled . . .

—I want it without scales.

—Then it's more . . .

—What do you mean, it's more?

—*Pues*, of course . . .

The fish smelled horrible because of the heat, even if it was really fresh. It stank like a filthy old woman. Everyone was rushing around, in and out of the stalls. That's where the Mariscaleños, Mariscal's people, started shooting at Julián Blanco, who was a Carrancista. He'd been a Zapatista just like Mariscal, but when the Carrancistas took the port, everyone became a Carrancista. They forgot that they'd been Zapatistas. That's what the Revolution was like, I'm with this group now, but tomorrow I'll be with the other one, they changed uniforms like it was nothing, the trick was to be with the strongest group, the one that had the most ammunition . . . It's like that now too. People court whoever has made it to the top. But they really worship the position, the power, not the person. When their time is up, no one can be bothered with them, you have to pay someone to hang them! They'd ordered General

Blanco into combat, but Blanco was waiting for a shipload of ammunition that was being sent from the capital.

—General, sir, I have orders to leave for the plains for combat, but I don't have any ammunition . . .

—Well, go!

—The ship should be here any day now, but I have orders to leave today. General Mariscal, why don't you give me your ammunition and you can take mine? You pick it up and keep it . . .

—No, said General Mariscal, I can't do that. You'll have to leave with what you have . . .

—You'd expose me to danger, having me go into combat without ammunition?

—That's your problem . . . You have to move out . . .

—No way am I going to expose my troops like that . . . I'm telling you that the ship will be here soon . . .

—I can't give you anything . . .

They were sending him into combat unarmed, with nothing but the chinstraps on their helmets to defend themselves. It was about ten in the morning and they were in formation in front of the Palace. The women were filling their knapsacks when Julián Blanco came out of the Palace, went down the steps, and gave the order for his troops to move out:

—Let's move out, he said. We'll do the best we can.

They let him get on his horse, and then Mariscal's men, who had control of the building, started shooting from the balcony . . . they caught him off guard. And what did this poor man do? He returned fire in retreat. His men, who had been sitting on the steps waiting for him, got on their horses very alarmed, and started to ride. He took off through a fig grove, which is on the street that leads straight to the Fort of San Diego. Since Blanco was a Carrancista, part of the ruling government, we let him enter the Castle. They were installed in the Fort and continued to fight from up above, protected by the parapets. We didn't get involved because it wasn't our battle, but they fought for as long as they could hold out, all that day and all night . . . How could they keep firing if all their ammunition was gone? General Pascual Morales y Molina gave the order to raise the drawbridge so the Mariscaleños couldn't get into the Castle . . . Since we didn't know what it was about—there was mass confusion, people on the same side were shooting each other—we raised the drawbridge and were surrounded and Julián Blanco was inside, but he was hurt and they put him and his troops in a big hall that we'd vacated so there'd be room for all of them. Their horses were left loose on the patio. Since we were infantry, we didn't have any hay for them to eat, there was only corn, so they were fed corn for eight days. No one could leave the Fort to shop or anything, so we ate beans and we ground corn; we made the nixtamal and all we had was tortillas, and more tortillas. Finally our general, Pascual Morales y Molina, went to talk to General Julián Blanco . . . You don't have to believe what I'm going to tell you, but they said that the bullet wounds weren't hurting Blanco because he had made a pact with the devil, and that the wounds were healing even though they were fatal. At eight o'clock in the morning our general, Pascual Morales y Molina, went in to see him:

—*Mi general,* it would be best if you'd negotiate, because we can't fire or take your side . . . You're recovering but my people here are suffering. They can't go out to buy food. We don't have any provisions left to support the state of siege, the horses are hungry, we're surrounded. Why don't you ask to negotiate?

—I don't know what Mariscal is up to. I don't have any dispute with him. That's why I fired only while retreating . . .

Julián Blanco ordered them to raise the white flag and at eight o'clock that night—they had the flag up for so many hours asking for peace—General Mariscal entered and went straight to the room where the injured Julián Blanco was and he shot him up from head to toe. That evil Mariscal went in to kill him when the drawbridge was down and the white flag was up . . . That isn't a brave man. He killed him the way you would a little bird that was lying there bleeding to death.

After that we returned to Chilpancingo. There were some in our company who said that Blanco had gotten us into a mess, that it wasn't fair, that the fight wasn't with us, that we'd suffered because of him. But in the Revolution everyone ran a risk equally, and it was even all the way around: you're a traitor, no, you are, let's flee to the hillside, listen, this one's already gone over to the other side, no, yes, he's a Carrancista, *pues*, wasn't he a Zapatista? The people from Guerrero were all Zapatistas, but they switched and became Carrancistas, all of them between two powder flashes, all in the same pot, all of them ignoring the rallying cry; they'd go down the slopes when they were told to surround the hills, they slipped into the crags when they should have stayed put, they forgot messages, they lost ammunition, they spent too much time digging trenches, they started fights and generals killed generals and almost all of us marched without knowing where we were going . . .

Later at night they made up *corridos*. I sang them, the one about Mariscal and Julián Blanco, I sang the ones about the Thirtieth Batallion, the City of Galeana, and I knew the one about Benito Canales too . . . so many of the *corridos* that they play on the radio now, but they don't play the whole thing, not even half, just little bits and pieces. They sing only the parts they want to, not the way they should. When someone would die they always made up a *corrido* for them:

> *Mariscal and Julián Blanco*
> *got into a shoot-out.*
> *Mariscal's men were at the Palace.*
> *Julián Blanco fled to the Fort.*
> *Shoot, bang, bang. Shoot, bang, bang.*
> *Shoot, bang, bang. Shoot, bang, bang . . .*

They made up nice *corridos* then, they were just a little long!

> *When the Thirtieth fought*
> *in the City of Galeana*
> *the Battalion lost without glory*
> *to the Government's amazement . . .*

We left the general headquarters in Acapulco and moved inland to where a nest of Zapatistas was holed up. The soldiers were fighting between Agua del Perro and Tierra Colorada, so they sent us women on ahead. Four married women were with me. The Zapatistas saw us coming and came out to meet us:

—How many people are following you?

—Not many . . .

—Come on, then, so you don't get caught in the cross fire . . .

They turned us over to General Zapata. He asked us if our people had machine guns, and we told him the complete opposite for everything he asked. And then he said:

—You're going to stay with us until your detachment gets here.

We stayed in his camp, which was well hidden, for about two weeks. He had a tent set up next to his and the cook's. Zapata ordered his people to bring provisions, and he gave us bread, coffee, sugar, rice, beans, and salted beef. We ate better than we had with the Carrancistas. The soldiers spent all day taking care of their horses, scrubbing them with hay, or building dams with rocks in the streams and rivers to cut off the water supply to the Carrancistas. They'd cut down trees and branches in the woods to build barricades. The Zapatistas were never thirsty.

When General Zapata found out that our whole company was finally in Chilpancingo he said to us:

—Come with me so that I can return you to your company.

He took off his general's uniform, put on white Indian pants, an overcoat, and a hat, and we were off. He was unarmed. His officers told him that he wouldn't be attacked if they all went with him.

—We'll escort you, *mi general.*

—No, you stay here on the bank of the river. Wait for me here. If I don't return within a reasonable period of time, then you must open fire.

They kept insisting:

—It'd be better if we escorted you.

He said no, he was going alone, and if it was his turn to die, he'd die doing a good deed. He wanted to show the Carrancistas that he was fighting for the Revolution and not stealing women.

He started walking and we followed him.

He stopped at the corner of our barracks and said to me:

—Wait here for me.

He went to the door and when he heard "Who goes there?" he answered:

—Mexico.

Then he said:

—I'm looking for Señor Felipe Palancares.

He didn't ask for the other women's husbands, just for my father, so they wouldn't get the wrong idea. My father came out and the general said:

—I'd like a word with you, please.

We were standing around the corner listening. My father said:

—I'm Felipe Palancares.

—Yes, señor, I know . . . You have a daughter named Jesusa?

—Yes.

—I'm returning her to you. I bring your daughter and these women who were sent on ahead between Agua del Perro and Tierra Colorada.

My father asked:

—Who are you?

—General Zapata.

—You're Emiliano Zapata?

—That's me.

My father looked around to see if there were any soldiers escorting him.

—It seems strange to me that you'd come alone.

—I came alone to escort these women. No one has laid a hand on them. I'm returning them to you just as they were when they left. You can be in charge of the four married ones, for they told me that they were looking after your daughter. Now, make sure their husbands don't hurt them.

And then my father said:

—That's fine.

—My people are positioned all along the outskirts of town. You know who I am. If something happens to me—if you go back on your word—there'll be a shoot-out in Chilpancingo . . .

—You returned my daughter. I have no reason to harm you.

—As long as you know. If you report this to your commander and they want to attack us, they're free to do so.

My father didn't say a word. The general turned and left.

Later, when my father got all the husbands together, he told them:

—Here are your wives. The señor, General Zapata, brought them back with my daughter. He said we can report it to our commanding officer, but I'm not going to. I'm grateful to him for bringing her back. If you have a problem with the way I've handled it, you're free to talk to the commander.

The men just stared at him. They ordered their wives not to tell anyone in the barracks that they'd been at the Zapatista camp and my father said to me:

—You aren't going to say anything about being there either.

I've never said anything until now.

Since my father didn't report anything, they didn't attack us, but two days later the shooting was real heavy on the San Antonio hillside. General Zapata sent detachments one at a time to fight, but he never mobilized all his troops at once. A lot of people stayed at the camp with the equipment and the women and children. The brigades fought by ambushing; they attacked where they were least expected. That day the shooting started at two in the morning and went on all day until five o'clock in the afternoon, when General Morales y Molina ordered all the women to move out, to abandon the plaza, and had everyone leave Chilpancingo; we all went to Mochtitlán, but the shooting continued because the Zapatistas were chasing us. We couldn't return to Chilpancingo for six months. There were a lot of casualties in that battle. The ones who fled as soon as they saw that the attack was heavy lived. My father sent me on ahead with the family of a lieutenant. I saw them again here in the city many years later, when I had my stall in front of the Tres Estrellas factory.

The Zapatistas were good fighters. They should be; they climbed trees, covered themselves with branches, and went around like a walking forest. You couldn't even tell they were human! Only the noise they made advancing gave them away. They were hidden in the trees, wrapped in leaves, you couldn't see their clothes, and suddenly the shots came from out of nowhere, like a hailstorm . . . Besides, they knew their way around because they were all from the state of Guerrero, so of course the Carrancistas lost. They concealed themselves with grass, leaving just their eyes uncovered so they could see where the Carrancistas were coming from, where the Villistas were coming from, and so they could find good positions. They dug ditches and disguised them with branches so the soldiers would fall in. And they did, horses and all! Of course they finished our people off. Sure they won! They didn't have anything, but they were clever, brave, they were real brave, even if they were Indians, without even a *petate* to fall down dead on. The Zapatistas were poor people from that area, muddy peasants . . . Why would I like them? I didn't even think about it, I was young; I never thought about whether I did or didn't like someone.

When I met General Zapata he was thin, with eyes as black as charcoal, a twisted mustache, and a wide-brimmed black hat with silver trim. He was about six feet tall, that's what it seemed like to me, with big bulging eyes, real big, and he was young. He wasn't heavy. He was really nice, I swear. He wasn't a bad man, he treated us good. Anyone else would have ordered his troops to drag us women off, but not him. That's why I say he was a good-hearted man. Zapata wasn't interested in being president like all the rest of them. He just wanted us to be free, but we never will be, that's what I think, because we'll be slaves all our lives. You want me to make it clearer? Everyone who comes takes a bite out of us, leaves us maimed, toothless, crippled, and they make their homes out of the pieces of us that they bite off. And I don't go along with that, especially now that we're worse off than ever before.

I started to get mean when I was with the troops. It wasn't that I was jealous of my father, it was just that I didn't love him anymore. When I was little, I loved him a lot and he loved me a lot, but after I was older, he took up with women. They say that we women are whores, but aren't men just as whorish the way they go around with their thing hanging out, trying to see who they can stick it in?

It had been about eight months since we'd left for Chilpancingo from Bravo and we stopped to rest in Tierra Colorada. My father got mad because I was talking Zapotec with the boys from Tehuantepec. He caught up to me and scolded me. I didn't say anything. I was traveling with the vanguard and I kept on walking, and as I walked I got madder and madder, and when we reached Tierra Colorada, I was burning with rage like an ember that keeps smoldering.

—I don't care if he gets here or not! *Ora*, I won't put any food aside for him!

I sat there and made no attempt to find him food or anything. He showed up and yelled at me again, but he was so mad he grabbed a plant, one this big, he pulled it right out of the ground, root and all, and raised it up to hit me. I was furious:

—God help you if you hit me! God help you if you think you dragged me away from my home to beat me . . . Why didn't you leave me where I was? I want you to give my brother back to me alive and to send me home.

He turned around and didn't hit me, he just took off.

I caught up with him and screamed:

—I want you to send me back home right now!

I stood there like a mad dog. I didn't move. Two or three hours later the people who had been working left, but I didn't, I stayed there alone . . . When it started to get dark, I went to General Genovevo Blanco's rear guard and asked to see him. They let me through and I said to the general:

—I'm here because my father got mad and was going to hit me. I'd like you to please send me back to Acapulco and from there to Salina Cruz and then home.

—All right, but I have to inform General Pascual Morales y Molina.

At midnight, my father came looking for me with a group of men, but I didn't show myself; I didn't even move. They searched every house but the general's, and of course they didn't find me. I could hear my father yelling: "Jesusa! Jesusa!" I was about to answer him when my jaws locked, I got a squeak in my throat, so I kept quiet.

EVERYONE RETURNED to Acapulco on horseback, but I didn't know how to ride, so I walked with the rest of the troops. General Genovevo Blanco's daughter traveled on horseback. She was older, about twenty. She wasn't my friend, and I never talked to her. She was the general's daughter. When we arrived someplace, I'd stay with her. I'd sleep close to them, anywhere, next to a wall, on the floor, no one has a bed when you're in battle. I was always with General Genovevo Blanco's family because when he realized I was so young he said:

—Listen, child, stay with my girl. Go along with her.

Señorita Lucía, the general's daughter, always pulled her own weight. When they ordered: "Hit the dirt!" she threw herself down like everyone else, and would advance and shoot her rifle. She never stayed with the equipment. Never. I figure she was a macho woman. In the evening she'd sit at the table to listen and make plans, just like her father: they were strategy sessions. I never heard her call him Father, it was always "*Mi general.*" She knew all the shortcuts around Guerrero; all of them, through the hills, the valleys. At night she walked around the camp and the men knew the sound of her boots:

—There she comes!

And they'd quickly hide the bottle. But she could hear them from miles away:

—Give that one a whipping!

She'd go to the infirmary:

—Make a tourniquet, man! What are you thinking? Can't you see he's losing too much blood? Immediately or you'll be in the slammer for three days!

Everyone obeyed her. She'd check the men's aim. She trained the cavalry. She knew the caliber of bullets, and planned attack and defense maneuvers with her father. Groom the horses! Check the supplies! Put more straw in the cart! Pick up these loose rocks! Don't just stand there! She was really devout. At night, she'd kneel down and say her rosary, and she wore not just one crucifix under her shirt but three.

As I was walking along, a young man rode up and told me to get up on his horse so I wouldn't tire myself. I was insulted.

—What's it to you if I get tired or not?

I didn't pay any attention to him, and he didn't say anything else to me, but from then on he made a point of following me. When we arrived somewhere and I went to buy something to eat, they'd tell me that it had already been paid for. Ay! *Qué caray!* I'd leave the bundle there on the counter. If I hadn't paid for it, why would I take it?

It went on like that for eight months. At every store, when I went to get my money they'd say:

—It's paid for.

—Who paid?

—It's paid for. Take it and anything else you want. Go ahead.

—I don't need it.

I never took anything. Since the young man was an officer, they treated him like a god. He told them:

—If Jesusita comes to buy something, give her whatever she asks for and I'll pay you for it.

They thought it'd be easy for them to sell me stuff.

—It's paid for, child. Everything is paid for.

—Keep your filthy merchandise.

The general's daughter would ask me:

—Did you get what you need?

—I went to buy stuff but they don't want to sell anything to me . . .

—Why not?

—They tell me it's been paid for, and since I didn't pay them, I leave it there.

She said:

—Then you can eat with us, *compañera.*

When we reached Acapulco, my father was already there. They were coming back from Chilpancingo, where they'd assembled, while we traveled through Tres Palos and other places. Suddenly the young officer who was following me came up and said:

—Señorita, señorita, your father's here. Shall we go see him?

It never occurred to me that he had a motive to see my father, and I didn't think there was any special reason for him to say that, so I said:

—Let me request permission from the general's daughter.

I found Señorita Lucía:

—This man wants to know if I can have permission to go with him to see my father.

She knew him and he was an officer, so she had no problem letting me go. We found my father and the young man spoke to him:

—Here she is.

He looked mad, and he'd aged a lot. He said to me:

—So, señora? You're here with your husband!

—What husband? I said.

The young man turned red.

—No, señor, I've come to ask for her hand, but I'm not her husband yet . . .

I hadn't talked to him or anyone, he wasn't even my boyfriend! I never thought he'd ask my father's permission to marry me without my agreement.

My father didn't even look at me. The young man repeated what he'd said:

—I did come to ask for permission to marry her but she isn't anything to me yet . . . She's been traveling with General Blanco's family and they look out for her.

Uy! When my father got something in his head, nothing could get through his thick skull, not even air, much less words!

—Father! I said.

—Jesusa, you're here with your husband, you can't stay with me anymore.

—I came to ask you for her, he repeated, so you can give her to me and we can get married. I want to have a civil ceremony.

My father said:

—Not a civil ceremony, because I'm not Protestant. If you get married it has to be in the church and not a civil ceremony . . . But I don't want to hear anything more about it from you and your wife . . .

What was I supposed to do? What was he supposed to do? He took me back to General Blanco and told him that we had talked to my father, but since my father did not want to give his consent, would he stand in for my father?

The general asked me:

—Do you want to get married?

—No, I want to leave. I have the money here for you to send me back home.

—I'll make arrangements for your trip.

The young man stood there staring at him. Then General Blanco said:

—She has her own money and she wants to go home. She doesn't want to get married, can't you see that? She doesn't love you.

—Let's wait and see if she really leaves. If she does, I'll accept it, but if not, I have to marry her.

The general went to the customs office. He asked for a ticket to Salina Cruz, but there was only a cargo ship, no passenger ships. The sailors told him that if I was a grown woman they could take me, but when he answered that I was just a girl, not even fifteen years old, they told him they wouldn't take responsibility

for me because there were only men on board. So the general
said:

—*No, pues*, if the choice is between handing her over to the
crew of the ship or to one man, I'll give her to the young man.

Since I couldn't leave, I was forced to marry the officer, against
my will, all because the captain of the ship didn't want to take
charge of me. I don't know if the officer loved me or not. I understand that if he hadn't, he could have snatched me and taken me
and that would have been the end of it, since he was an officer
fighting in the Revolution. Why did he ask for my hand? What do
soldiers care if a woman consents or not? Whether you like it or
not:

—Hurry up, bitch, and let's go, come on! That's what you're
here for anyway!

But he didn't do that; he waited until he knew they wouldn't
take me on the boat. He asked General Blanco to speak to my father and that's what he did:

—Do you give your consent for them to marry in a civil ceremony as ordered by law?

My father said no.

—Then we'll take care of it some other way.

The general kept talking to the young man because he liked
him. He said if the man didn't love me, he wouldn't even think
about marrying me, especially since I didn't have anyone to look
out for me. The young man took me back to the house, respecting
the general, who arranged the wedding and stood in for my father
at the church. We got married in the church because it was what
my father wanted, not what I wanted. When we left the church I
went with my husband; like it or not. We got married in Tres Palos, in the state of Guerrero, and my father never showed up.

My husband's name was Pedro Aguilar; he was about seventeen, two years older than me. He had no reason to cross my path.
What he did was shameless, an abuse, because I hadn't agreed to
marry him or anybody. He'd ride down the middle of the street on
his horse and follow me. He had no right to go around asking who
my father was, making plans on his own. I hated that. I hope that

ingrate is burning in a very crowded Hell, because he had no reason to make my life as miserable as he did.

Pedro Aguilar took me to his house. He locked me up there and then he went out to party.

—You stay here until you stop acting so high and mighty.

He lost all his gentleness and his courting manners. His assistant brought me breakfast, lunch, and dinner. I was married two weeks before I saw my husband again, because General Blanco ordered him to go out to the hills with his detachment. For those two weeks he kept me inside the room with nothing to do, waiting for the assistant to bring me meals. Who the hell knows where Pedro was.

When the general ordered him into combat he told him:

—Don't hurry things because of Jesusa, she'll stay with my daughter.

Pedro's response was:

—I'm sorry, *mi general*, you give me orders because I'm under your command, but you don't give my wife orders; I give my wife orders and she goes where I tell her.

He came back as furious as a mad dog and he ordered the assistant to pack everything up, and that's when he put me on the wild mare, thinking she'd kill me. "Now you're going to pay for all your rejections."

I had to leave with the detachment. It was all arranged. They were on horseback and I didn't know how to ride. My husband put me up on a beast that, just like me, only he rode. When someone else would mount her, they'd cover her eyes so she wouldn't see them. Since he was mad now, he slapped the animal with his sword and she took off wildly, like a soul possessed by the devil. I let go of the reins. "Go ahead and run, throw me and get it over with!" I grabbed on to the saddle: "She's going to kill me and I'm not going to stop her." And she galloped as far as she could. She came to a ravine; she leaped over it and kept running until she wore herself out and gave up. People tried to surround her but they couldn't catch up to her until, exhausted, she was broken. Everyone thought we were both going to get killed: the mare and me. But no. We went until she couldn't go any further, and that's where it ended. The soldiers asked me if I was all right, and the mare started to neigh as soon as she saw my husband. Since I didn't touch her or hit her, the animal realized that someone else had struck her with the sword . . . Animals may be beasts, but they understand a lot of things. I got off the horse, off that blessed mare. I grabbed the reins and she didn't pull back. The assistant said to me:

—Let me walk her, poor animal, she's real tired.

And he walked her around. Once she was rested the assistant asked me:

—Are you up for riding her again?

—She's taken me this far. Let's see if she kills me once and for all.

I mounted the mare, but this time they didn't cover her eyes. After that, the animal wouldn't let anyone else get near her. I was the only one who could ride her, feed her, and water her. She wouldn't let my husband or the assistant touch her. I tightened her belts, I brushed her up and down. She couldn't stand the sight of Pedro, she'd nip at him or kick or rear up, and all I'd have to do was touch her and she'd calm down. Maybe she was avenging me. I tamed the animal that my husband was never able to dominate; she was always with me. She got nice. I had to hold her to saddle her and then I'd mount her. I gave her sugar, tortillas, whatever I had on hand. Her name was La Muñeca, the doll. She was a chestnut mare with white legs, a beautiful animal. My husband had a chestnut just like La Muñeca. I think they were brother and sister.

I never rode as a child, not even a burro. When I was in the Revolution with my father we walked. I walked a lot, I walked and walked because I liked to. But after getting married I had to ride because my husband was in the cavalry. I wasn't afraid of riding. How hard is it to sit in a saddle? And when the horse takes off, you just hold on.

When Pedro was on a campaign, since there weren't any women around, he satisfied his urges with me, but in the ports he forgot about me. Out in the hills, the soldiers made caves out of rocks for us to go into. He never let me undress, never. I slept dressed and with my shoes on, ready for anything, anytime; the horse was saddled and ready to go. He'd come in and say: "Lie down!" That was all he said: "Lie down!" If he saw any movement, he'd yell: "Get up! Get ready, we're taking off while the going's good!"

I never took my pants off, I just pulled them down when he used me. But even if I said: "I'm going to lie down like at home, I'm going to undress because I'll be covered," no way! I had to have my pants on whenever they played reveille! My husband wasn't a man to show affection, none of that. He was a serious man. Nowadays you see couples kissing and caressing each other in the doorways. It seems strange to me, because my husband never did that stuff. He had the equipment, he did it, and that was it.

Over in Chilpancingo I had an adobe house with a thatched roof. My husband left me there to do housework. He left Palemon, the assistant, and his wife in charge of me and they kept an eye on me. There was this woman who lived across the road with her four daughters. She was a widow, I don't even remember her name, but she sold *atole* and roasted maguey leaves. Since she was very poor, she had to support the four kids some way. Her oldest girl, who was fifteen or seventeen, worked as a maid at different people's houses when they had something for her to do, but when they didn't call her, she went to the fields to pick guavas for her mother to sell. One day, she asked me to come with her. Her three sisters, who were about seven, eight, and ten, were with her too.

—We're going for guavas. What are you doing all cooped up in there?

I asked Palemon to let me go.

—Go ahead.

That made the girl happy:

—*Pues, ándile,* let's go.

We left at dawn, and at one point we walked for so long that we ended up on a really high hill and a man yelled at us to come down. We got scared:

—He's going to take the guavas away from us . . .

He kept yelling at us from down below, from a ranch:

—Come down, come dooooown!

We had no choice but to climb down the hill, thinking that the man was going to scold us because we were stealing his fruit.

—What are you girls doing?

—Picking guavas.

—Did you have breakfast? Did you eat already?

—No, we haven't.

It was about eight o'clock in the morning. We'd left at five to climb the hill.

—Come have some squash with warm milk.

—If you're offering . . .

—Wait, girls, we'll eat shortly . . .

Shamelessly, we stuffed ourselves with the milk and squash. He went into the kitchen and that day we ate roast beef with gravy, hard-boiled eggs, cheese, and beans. We spent all day with him. He was all by himself! He lived alone. He was around fifty or seventy years old.

—Don't leave yet. Help me bring in the cattle.

We helped him herd them in that afternoon, and when the sun was starting to set, we carried our guavas home.

He said:

—I'll be waiting to see you tomorrow . . . Come early for warm milk and squash and maguey.

Maybe the guavas were his, who knows, but he never complained. To the contrary, he invited us and we went to eat with him the next day. We got there early. That morning he gave us grilled squash with brown sugar. He dug a hole in the ground and put the squash inside and then covered them with leaves and put dirt on top. He lit the fire and they cooked underground all night. The next day when we got there he put out the fire, uncovered the hole, took out the squash, and served them to us with milk. We went up in the hills and in the afternoon we came down and he had a pot of beans for us like I haven't tasted since. They were cooked with milk instead of water, so you can imagine what they tasted like! After that, it sort of became an obligation to go and have warm milk with squash or maguey every day. We did that for about a month, until my husband's company came back, and then I didn't join the girls again because my husband didn't let me talk to anyone. I missed going to the hills; it was so pretty there, the green countryside; the guava trees full of fruit. I'd knock them down with a stick and tons of them fell. It was the rainy season and we'd walk through the trees with their shiny leaves.

When I lived with my father I'd go to the store to buy candy—as a child I had a sweet tooth for sweet rolls, sugarcane, coffee with lots of sugar, and those kinds of things—or I'd go just to get out of the house, but I never knew how to buy groceries for a family. I was now a married woman, but I didn't go out—because my husband wouldn't let me—so the assistant did the shopping, or maybe his wife did. Anyway, every other day I had a bag at the door, with beans, rice, butter, salt, everything you need in a house. Palemon would come in, put away my groceries, check and see if I had water, and if I didn't, he'd go get it. If there was garbage, he'd take it out, but he never asked me what I needed, or if I wanted him to do anything. He never said a word to me. He just checked to see what was missing and went and got it.

My husband left for the hills with his soldiers and was gone on a mission for something like eight months. They said they were going to meet up with General Juan Espinosa y Córdoba's company. That's when Captain Manuel Arenas's widow, a woman from Chilpancingo—she probably still lives around there—persuaded me to set up a little spot there in town. Her father made wine and she brought it for us to sell. Since I didn't go to the barracks to collect my husband's pay, I liked the idea. I figured Palemon must have felt sorry for me, seeing me so alone, and since it had been so many months, he just looked the other way. Or maybe he thought my husband wasn't coming back.

The widow persuaded me to do it with her—she was older, about eighteen—and I got into the wine-selling business. I sang with the drunks while I sold, and I made a lot of money because I'd bet ten pesos that no one could guzzle a bottle of mescal as fast as I could. I drank it like water and won my centavos. Then I'd drink a glass of lemon juice and I wouldn't get drunk. I got to where I was throwing down four or five bottles in a row. And they always had to pay because it was a bet. The men from Guerrero are big drinkers! They could really put it away. With the money I won from the bets the widow bought me clothes, because mine had worn out. I had never had such pretty dresses, lacy corsets, and bell-shaped petticoats with ruffles! Some were even silk, if you can believe it, and satin blouses! Even hairpins to put my bun up with colored ribbons! I drank because it became part of the business; she drank because she was sad, her husband was killed when the first shots were fired, and they were newlyweds.

I liked to play and sing in the little joint in Chilpancingo. I'd watch how they played the guitar and I started strumming. They'd tell me to hold it here like this and press there. With more time I'd have learned. I was really happy, it's true, and I sang a lot.

If they didn't pay me ten pesos a bottle, whether it was of tequila, cognac, or vermouth, I wouldn't drink. On a bet, yes, but not because I felt like drinking. They had to pay me then and there or I wouldn't do it.

—I'll have a glass of *nada*, nothing.

Nada was a tall glass with every kind of liquor in it. They'd fill it with a shot from each bottle: wine, cognac, tequila, whiskey, vermouth—they put everything in until the glass was full. That's why it was called a glass of nothing. I'd drink it down and then suck a lemon right away as a chaser. But there were a lot of women who got drunk for the heck of it or because of a broken heart, little by little, a drink at a time. I don't drink by the glass. If someone said: "Let's have a drink," not me. For me to drink it had to be a whole bottle and they had to bet me. I'd outdrink three or four drunks and still be fresh as a daisy because before chugging the bottle I'd suck one or two lemons and a short time later I could bet again and it wouldn't go to my head. I never threw up either.

When my husband's mission came back from the hills, he didn't find me at home. The boys told him that I had a place I went to!

So when he opened the door he found me wrestling with the drunks. *Uy,* he was ready to kill me! He asked why I'd done it, and I told him that while he wasn't there I supported myself drinking: how else was I supposed to live since I didn't have an income?

—Why didn't you go to the barracks to collect my pay?

—That's very difficult. I wasn't going to collect money from any of the bosses. If you weren't here, why would I go collect what didn't belong to me? I had to make a living the way God showed me . . .

—And this is what God told you to do?

And he let me have it. He was mad at me, but he was mad at himself too, because it was partly his fault.

—From now on you'll come on all the missions with me. And don't fight me on this or I'll kill you!

Before we left he made me put on riding pants, my overcoat, my red scarf, and my big hat. No one could tell if I was a man or a woman. He burned all my beautiful clothes because he said they'd been touched by the devil, and while they burned Pedro kept crossing himself. He slapped Captain Arenas's widow for putting evil ideas in my head, but he punished Palemon the worst: thirty lashes and he held a grudge against him on top of that.

We weren't assigned to General Genovevo Blanco anymore, but to General Juan Espinosa y Córdoba. If we'd still been with General Blanco, since he was our godfather, the one that married us, he'd have known what was going on and I'd have taken refuge with his daughter, the señorita. But they'd already transferred us. That's why Pedro got so mean and told me that he wouldn't leave me again. I rode everywhere behind him on his horse. That's when he said that if it looked like we were going to lose the war, he'd kill me first, and from then on he never left me alone and I never felt free. I taught myself how to walk between the bullets because of Pedro. Shooting is real hard to do.

When we were in Chilpancingo, General Juan Espinosa y Córdoba told us he was taking us to the capital and from there we'd leave for the north. When the troops assembled to see who was leaving, I met up with my father's men. The infantry soldiers told me that they'd left him on the side of the road with a couple of supply mules. He was wounded, so they propped him up under a tree, and that's where they figure the enemy shot him. The Zapatistas killed him. That's how I found out that my father was killed in the battle of Mochtitlán, in the state of Guerrero, between Acapulco and Chilpancingo.

It didn't make me sad, because I didn't see it happen. Since I'd already gotten married and I didn't travel with my father's company, that's as far as it went. I didn't find out anything else about him until years later when I ran into a young medium in Mexico City who gave him the power to raise his own spirit from among the thorns.

H ey, you . . .

—Who, me?

—Yeah, you . . . Go stand on that side.

In Mexico they lined people up by height; if they were tall, they were cavalry, if they were short, they were infantry. That's how they divided up the companies, and each general took the people who suited him.

—Man, you got all tall ones!

—I'll take some short ones, but they'd better be tough.

Before that they simply took a bunch of people in groups without measuring them and sent them into battle, young, old, if they were missing hands, if they limped, however it worked out, the deal was for everyone to be ready to fight. They grabbed the first thing they could get their hands on, and they were sent into combat like a herd of wild horses and were often killed before they could be taught to load their rifles. The little ones, the young ones, didn't understand how it worked, so they went out in front, and were shot, end of story. They caught them like piglets being taken off to slaughter.

Pedro, my husband, was sent to the cavalry, and so was I, even though I'm as short as a sitting dog. The ones in the cavalry worked harder. The infantry didn't work as much because by the time we rejoined them they were stacking their weapons. They were told: break ranks and we're out of here! Everyone took off! And the cavalry was more work because the horses had to be walked and fed and watered and brushed and the caked dirt taken off their hooves or they'd get sick, they had to be taken care of . . .

After he divided them up by height, General Juan Espinosa y Córdoba trained them. Some only knew how to use a machete. They had to be taught how to load a gun before they could go into combat. When would they have ever used a weapon, much less known how to clean it, gauge distances, aim and try to hit the target they were shooting at and not just shoot for the sake of shooting? General Espinosa y Córdoba would get exasperated:

—Do you think we have ammunition to waste?

Each morning he'd lead the training himself. They had to learn to march, present arms, break the guns down, and aim the way they teach recruits nowadays. Most of them didn't even know the different bugle calls: to mount, dismount, or hit the ground.

—What kind of a militia is this?

Juan Espinosa y Córdoba was a dark-skinned Indian. The old guy was ugly, very tall and fat. He looked like he'd been carved with the blunt end of an ax. He did have a pretty blond wife that he brought with him from Chilpancingo, quite a young girl. Espinosa y Córdoba had a pointed mouth and we also called him El Trompudo, or Big Snout. He was a yeller:

—Get into squads of five or ten soldiers. Let's see if you can at least grasp how to do that!

Every morning during training he gave orders.

—Put the dumbest into squads of five so that they can understand better, and watch them carefully, because they don't even know what to shoot . . .

Everyone came to training, even my husband, who'd been fighting for who knows how long and was a captain and always got sent up to the front. He complained to the general:

—But I'm a captain . . .

—Everyone has to attend the training sessions . . . You too, even if you're a captain . . . Even if you were a general you'd have to! You have to learn how to give orders the right way. If you, as a captain, don't know, how're we going to teach the militia? Here everyone gets trained! I don't want to hear any more shit about it!

He was right. Listen, in the Revolution there was a regiment that had a lot more casualties before they even met up with the enemy than after. They almost finished off the entire outfit before they even got to the fighting. Friends killed each other more than they killed the enemy. One time, we didn't have uniforms, so you couldn't tell who was who, and we wiped out a whole division that was coming to reinforce us . . . Fresh troops were coming and we shot the hell out of them . . . Everything was done ass backwards . . .

—What about the uniforms, General?

—There are only enough for those ranked corporal or higher . . .

After all that, over and over, the brigadier general, Juan Espinosa y Córdoba, formed the Northwest Fifth Division, his own unit of fifteen hundred men. A lot of people were killed out of stupidity. I think it was a misunderstood war because people simply killed each other, fathers against sons, brother against brother; Carrancistas, Villistas, Zapatistas, we were all the same ragged people, starving to death. But that's something that, as they say, you keep to yourself.

The day after the unit was formed we left for the north.

I saw a passenger train in Tehuantepec once, but those aren't like military trains. The military train is for freight and the cars are enclosed, they're all black without windows to look out of. Ours was a small, wood-burning train that moved slowly; it would run for half an hour and stop for half an hour, when it wasn't stopped at a station for several days. It went slow because there were a lot of cars, carrying horses and all the things troops need; the Indians were on the roofs and the horses were inside. Otherwise, how would a train be big enough to haul such a herd of humanity and beasts? We ate up on top of the train, we had a stove and it never went out, because we closed the lids so air wouldn't get in from underneath and sparks wouldn't fly out the top. Otherwise, it would have been a blazing fire.

Life was really hard back then. We covered our things the best we could with oilcloth ponchos so they wouldn't get wet in the rain. I always got soaked anyway. I wore a big Texan hat and made myself as comfortable as I could. We had to ride crouched on top because the horses had to be sheltered and fed all the time. When we got somewhere, if they gave orders to disembark, they'd let the animals out to be watered; the animals came first. Not a single one died on us on the train, although it didn't do us any good to be thirsty and cramped up on the roof, because the Villistas still kicked the shit out of us. The Villistas spent all their time derailing trains. That was their tactic, but we got used to it. From the time we left the capital heading north, they loosened the tracks and the engine buried itself because of the weight we were carrying. When that happened, the cars broke open and a lot of horses died and many people too. Each time the train derailed, it took who knows how many days to get it back on track or to bring in engines and cars from other places. We had to take all the horses out and bury the dead people.

In Santa Rosalia we had a derailment that even crammed people's backbones together like an accordion. That was the worst one because the engine rolled over and so did six or seven cars; the front ones had the most damage. We had to set up camp until they sent us the parts we needed. That's why it took us so many months to reach the north. Nothing happened to the passenger cars. They were well made; they've probably rotted by now, but they were made of solid pine.

I remember once when we woke up in Chihuahua at four in the morning. The soldiers were yelling:

—Look, look at all the Apaches, look at all the Indians without huaraches.

It wasn't true. People said that there weren't any Christians in Chihuahua, just Apache Indians. We were scared but we wanted to see them, we didn't really understand what it was all about. The people there looked just like the people here, it's a bunch of lies, tall tales, and it causes a lot of confusion and stirs things up. I never saw an Apache.

We traveled at a snail's pace between one explosion and the next. We'd camp at one place and then another and we never got

to any station on time. We never met up with the other group of
Carrancistas. Villa was a bandit, he didn't fight like a man. Instead,
he'd dynamite the tracks when the trains were passing through. It
would blow, and the cars, the horses, and the Indians would fly
everywhere. Is that a courageous man? He blew up passenger
trains, too, and stole their money, and the young women. He'd tie
the girls to the saddle or drag them around in the cactus. That's
not decent. I hate Villa more than anyone.

I never saw him up close, never, and it's a good thing, because
I'd have spit in his face. Now I make myself happy spitting at the
radio. I heard that they were going to engrave his name in gold
letters in the Congressional Building. Whoever planned that must
either be bandits like him or idiots! I couldn't believe it either,
when they said on the radio that he had a wife and kids. What a
bunch of lies! What family? I won't believe that even if they drag
me around by my tongue . . . He never had a wife. He grabbed the
youngest girl around, took her, brought her back when he was
bored with her and tossed her away and took another one. Now
they come out with a "wife," and they say sons and daughters. Bullshit! They want to make him look like something he never was. He
was a bandit without a soul! Of all the *guerrilleros* I detest Villa the
most. He had no mother. That Villa was an ape who made fun of
the world and you can still hear him laughing about it.

Since my husband didn't talk to me, no one else did either. All
the officers were his friends, but none of them spoke to me. When
we stopped at a station where they took the horses off, three or
four officers would go into the empty cars with their wives; they
each grabbed a spot, but Pedro didn't like the others to see us doing it and he never called me for that.

When I was under my husband's thumb I never bathed. Who
would I want to look nice for? I couldn't look at anyone or change
my clothes or comb my hair. I didn't even have a comb; the two I
had broke, even the lice comb I had from before I was married. If
I was filthy and full of lice as a child, my head was even more lice-
infested when I was with my husband. He hit me, split my head
open, and I lost my long wavy hair because of all the sores and
blood. There was filth encrusted on my head and it stayed there,

because I couldn't bathe or change. So I suffered like St. Mary in the desert. How could I make myself love him? I had a grudge against him, I hated him. I could scrape the dirt off my dress, it was so thick. I wore the same one all the time even though he bought me clothes. But I couldn't put them on. He bought them for me wherever we stopped, to impress the other soldiers and their wives.

—See how well I take care of her!

That's what he was like. What can you do about a man like that? He wasn't stupid, just selfish, because he said that no one would bother with me if I was that foul-smelling. He'd entertain himself real nice elsewhere, not with me. That's why I asked the whole celestial court to kill him. If there was a campaign and he went out with an advance party, I'd yell: "San Julano, San Perengano, free me from this Christian plague! Let them kill him or capture him, but just don't make me see him again!" And I'd kneel down and cross myself and fold my hands. I asked them to kill him even if it would condemn my soul to Hell forever. I preferred to wander outcast like a leper. Even when I was alone I wasn't allowed to have my head uncovered, because he'd come and order: "Cover yourself." I slept with my rebozo over my face, all covered up like a mummy. I was a martyr. But not now, I'm no martyr anymore. I suffer like everyone else but it's nothing compared to when I had a husband.

Pedro beat me from the time he took me out of the dive in Chilpancingo. He yelled: "You'll be sorry." "Now you'll pay!" And he never let up at all.

He never forgot it, because he was like that, real jealous, real temperamental. I didn't say anything to him, what was there to say if I never even looked up at him? I almost didn't know what his face looked like. I was afraid of him, always crouched over in front of the fire, covered with my rebozo. So how could I stand up to him? I couldn't. He didn't care if I was dead or alive. Now that I take care of myself, I think he did it to try to get rid of me, but I was real dumb then and I went wherever he said without complaining. Pedro beat me for everything, like most of the men in the company, who spoke to their women through the snap of their whip: "Walk, you cunt, move it!" The point was to make their lives miserable. Pedro would grab me and hit me on the head with the butt of his gun and my blood would boil, but I never said anything; I didn't even flinch, so he wouldn't see that it hurt me.

One day when we were camped at a station in Chihuahua—I don't remember which one—where we stayed several days or weeks—I don't know how long—he came to me and said: "Listen, *Vale.*" I never heard him use my name; who knows what that *Vale* was all about.

—Listen, *Vale,* grab your soap and let's go so you can wash my handkerchiefs.

I knew he was going to beat me even though everyone said that he was a such good man. That's what he pretended on the outside, but inside it was a different story. He seemed to be one thing, when he was something very different.

I said:

—*Bueno.*

We walked from the station until he found a little clearing where the burros roll around to scratch themselves. The place was really clean and he said:

—Stand here.

He hit me until he'd had enough. I remember I counted up to fifty blows from his machete. He hit me on the back. But I didn't bend over. I just sat on the ground with my legs crossed and covered my head with my arms and hands. I was used to it, since my stepmother treated me that way when I was a kid. I don't know why I'm still here. I don't remember if it was this hand that I held up but I have a scar, my left one; the machete went into my back. Look, he cut me open. You can see the scar here because that cut went all the way to the bone. It bled but I didn't feel it; after so many blows I didn't feel anything; I hadn't gotten over one blow when there was another one on the same spot. I never did anything to take care of the wounds, I didn't put anything on them, not even water. The wounds healed on their own.

When I came to, I was in the railroad car where we lived and my back was all cut up. The girls asked me:

—What's wrong? Are you sick?

—Yes.

—What is it?

—Nothing.

—Then why'd you say you're sick?

—I am, but what business is it of yours?

What did I have to gain by spilling my guts? Nothing. It's not as if telling them my life story would take the pain away. I don't explain anything to anyone. And since I didn't say anything, it went on that way for a long time. And Pedro would look for any excuse to beat me. He'd order me to get the soap to wash handkerchiefs.

And I'd know: "He's going to beat me." He never hit me in front of anyone and that's why he was never caught red-handed.

—Jesusa, you have such a good husband!

They never saw him angry.

—What'd you say?

—How lucky you are to have such a good husband. God bless him!

I never corrected them. Those are personal things you keep to yourself, inside, like memories. Memories don't belong to anyone else. They're just yours; like the years you live through that make you who you are. You can't pass your bag of bones off to anyone else to carry around. "Here, you carry them." You can't, right? That day I grabbed the gun. I was wearing a long blouse with two pockets and I put bullets and a gun in them. "Soap, yeah right, no way, let him kill me once and for all, or I'll kill him!" I was determined. I followed him. We got to a field far from the station and he said to me:

—This seems like as good a place as any to me. I'm going to kill you here or we'll see what you're made of . . .

I stood looking at him. I didn't cower and I answered:

—Really? Then we'll kill each other. I'm not going to die alone. You take your gun out, I have mine.

I don't know where I got so much courage, I think I was just desperate, and I took out the gun. Then he got scared, I could see real clear that he was afraid. I thought: "Well, he's real brave, let him take his gun out too and we'll shoot each other right here and now. One of us may end up alive." But then he said:

—Who's been putting ideas in your head?

—Who? You should know who. The same person who tells you to hit me, that same woman has warned me.

It was a lie. No one had said anything to me, but since he asked I answered. I'd never raised my voice to him before:

—Who told you to talk back to me?

—The same person who told you to make my life miserable . . .

Then he said to me:

—Drop the gun.

—No, you brought me here to kill me. We'll kill each other here. Take out your gun.

He didn't . . .

—I'm not going to do anything to you. Drop the gun.

—No. You can take me out of here dead, but take your gun out, too.

—No.

—Then why'd you bring me here? For a walk? For a walk in the woods? You brought me to kill me, right? *Pues*, kill me.

Then he started to talk to me real nice:

—Don't be silly . . . I . . . people tell me you do things . . .

—Why don't you spy on me if you think you know what I'm doing?

—I can't be everywhere at the same time.

—Then why do you believe what they tell you? Here's how it is . . . You're going to prove it to me right now . . . Let's go, *ándele*. You walk in front . . .

—You go ahead.

—No. Things have changed now. You don't tell me what to do anymore. I order you, and this time you go first. Let's go, and if you don't like it, I'll shoot you here.

I got braver since he didn't take his gun out. I thought: "He doesn't have a weapon . . ." So I started to talk louder.

He walked in front. I said:

—Walk over there to the paymaster's car, *ándele*.

Someone had told my husband that I was the paymaster's lover. I wasn't, but some woman told him that, they're all like that: when they aren't shaking their asses in someone's face, they're flapping their lips, to see who they can destroy with their gossip:

—Call the woman to come out. They can arrest me, but you're going to prove it to me right here or we both die.

When my husband saw he'd lost control, he called her:

—Listen, come out here; you've seen her with the paymaster. I want you to repeat what you told me now in front of her.

And the woman denied it:

—Ay no, *manito*, I didn't tell you anything.

I yelled at her:

—Yes, you did, and he beat me because of it. He hasn't killed me because it hasn't been God's will, but he took me to the woods with every intention of doing just that. Now you both have to prove it to me . . .

—No, *manito*, she said, I haven't told you anything. Don't be like that. How can you believe it? Who told you that, it wasn't me . . .

—It was you, I yelled, and I fired a shot at her feet.

At that very instant her husband came out and grabbed her and started to beat her right there.

—You've tried to make that woman's life miserable and now you're going to pay for it by listening to her . . . You explain what you said. Why did you tell Pedro that she was with the paymaster? Were you their mattress? If you weren't with them, you have no business talking . . .

And while he yelled he hit her.

Hearing the shot so close to the car, the paymaster came out, and so did the major and the lieutenant colonel. They sent for General Espinosa y Córdoba. He took my husband's sword from him and struck him with it fifty times.

—So you know how it feels.

And he gave the other husband fifty whacks for allowing his wife to behave that way. He gave her twenty-five to stop her from gossiping. I'd never met the paymaster until I saw him that day, and he didn't even know who I was. He came out of his car because he heard the fight. Big Snout yelled at both of them:

—I'm beating you for believing all the stories you hear, and you for pimping, because you let your wife go around causing trouble.

The troublemaker had curly hair. Her name was Severina. Her so-called husband brought her from a whorehouse in Morelia. My husband went there too and had a thing going with another woman for a little while, because he couldn't bring her back. But Severina would have liked Pedro to leave me for the other woman, and be with Jacinta—that's what her name was—because the two so-and-sos were real good friends, both were from Morelia.

According to what I found out later, my husband had this problem of letting women fall in love with him, and once he'd had his fun he'd say:

—You really love me? Too bad, I'm not available, I'm married.

Pedro got nicer after I threatened to shoot him. But then I got mean. From the time I was little I was mean, I was born that way, terrible, but Pedro never gave me a chance to be nasty. The blessed Revolution gave me self-confidence. When Pedro pushed me over the edge, I thought: "I'm going to defend myself or he can just kill me and be done with it." If I hadn't been mean, I would have let Pedro abuse me until he killed me. But there came a moment when God must have said to me: "Defend yourself." Because God says: "The Lord helps those who help themselves." I heard Him tell me: "Defend yourself, you've taken enough. Now you start giving it back." And I took out the gun. After that I said I wouldn't be abused and I've kept my word. I've done such a good job I'm still here to tell you about it. But did I ever suffer when I let myself be mistreated. I think there must be a special place in Hell for the women who have let men abuse them. They're probably sitting around with their asses on burning logs!

Pedro kept cheating, of course, he was a man; he was a man and he was on the prowl. He still had other women, but he was different with me because I became a real fighter, a real bitch. And through the years I developed the instinct to give it before I got it. If someone throws a punch at me, it's because I've already landed a couple first. Pedro and I would get into fistfights every now and then and it was an even fight. That stuff about squatting down and taking the blows was over. I knew how to defend myself from the day I hid the gun in my blouse. And I thank the Lord I did.

MY HUSBAND had the luck of a street dog with women. They followed him all over the place, and when he didn't pay attention to them they used a go-between to upset me.

When he was in the 77th Regiment he took up with someone else. I knew she was his mistress, but I didn't say anything; it was her husband who demanded to know what right Pedro had to be involved with his wife. Pedro, who was drunk at the time and thought he was brave, punched the man. He got the upper hand and the other one couldn't touch him. When he was beating him to a pulp the police arrived and took Pedro away. Because he was a soldier and was drunk and being disorderly in public, they threw him in jail for fifteen days. And this shameless bitch, Angelita—can you believe that name?—went to see him in his cell. She'd just gone in when I got there with a basket of food. She was lying against the bars and he was leaning from the other side, the two of them real happy there.

—What a nice picture these two pieces of shit make! Too bad the cock is penned up in another cage!

—She just came to bring me a message from the colonel, Pedro said.

And he tried to make up a good story.

—I know all about this whore; the colonel doesn't have such bad taste. We'll meet up with each other on the streets real soon . . .

I turned around and left with my basket. I didn't leave the

food: "He's paying her for something, let her bring him food and I'll bet she gives him something sweet along with it." I left furious. Why the hell did Pedro ask me to bring him food if he already had someone to do that? I went down one street and Angelita went down another. I saw her turn the corner and I cut across the street to head her off. She was so brave, she started to run. That made me madder and I chased her even though she had a head start. I thought: "Let's see what this bitch has to say for herself!" She ran and ran and went into the first open door she found. I stopped in front and stood there, tapping my foot. The owner came out and asked me:

—What are you looking for?

—For the woman who just went in!

—What woman?

She turned around quickly and saw her hiding behind a big flower pot.

—Get out! I won't have any fighting in my house!

But when she saw how mad I was, the owner didn't want to get involved, so she locked herself in the kitchen.

I stood on the corner to wait for Angelita, but when she didn't come out I jumped the stone fence and we got into it on the ground right there in the yard. I took a big hairpin out of my bun and I stuck her in the face with it.

She was covered with blood, because I'm really strong. I always have a weapon. Angelita didn't know that I usually carried a knife. Once she realized she was losing, she got away from me and started to run down the street, and locked herself in her house. Her husband yelled:

—*Ora sí*, they treat you like you treat them. Get out of here!

That poor girl ended up full of holes. Later, one of the soldiers' wives saw her at the barracks and told me:

—Ay, her face looks like a colander!

—Branded with a hairpin. And she'll be like that forever and ever, amen.

Angelita was a young girl, she had fair skin, she wasn't bad-looking, to tell you the truth. Whenever I had a fight with Pedro I'd say:

—When you make me look like an ass, find a nice thing, one that doesn't look Indian like me . . . someone worthwhile . . .

This made him laugh, but the rage made my bones hurt.

Pedro found out that I beat his mistress, but he never said anything to me about it. Just the opposite, when he got out of jail two weeks later, he bought me earrings with nice stones. I realized then that it wasn't his fault; he was just being a man, the women chased him. I saw how they followed him, shaking their asses back and forth, so legally, I say they were at fault. What were the married ones looking for from him in the first place?

Pedro got to town at six in the evening and I arrived the next day. That same night Angelita went looking for him; he had barely gotten off his horse and she was all over him and he nailed her. That's why I say that as a man he had no choice but to perform. What was Pedro supposed to do if she was offering it to him? Tell her: "Get out of here, I don't want any"?

What was the solution? He had a special kind of luck, like a street dog, I'd say. And they followed him like horny bitches.

I don't know what was wrong with those women. They must have had needs their husbands couldn't meet, so they went with Pedro to get what they wanted. It was always the same story: "It's love!" Love, my ass! That's bullshit. Those women were like cats in heat who don't realize they'll be saddled with kittens and they prowl around with their tail up in the air.

One night when I was lying in the barracks I overheard a corporal who was a good friend of Pedro's talking to his wife. They were real close to me and thought I'd fallen asleep:

—If you really watch what goes on, said the corporal, you can see it's not the boss's fault. They come looking for him, so he gives it to them.

The next morning when we were rolling up the *petates* I didn't say anything to the corporal's wife. Why stir up trouble? She'd just say I was eavesdropping. Let them say what they want . . . I no longer paid any attention to them.

I wouldn't say Pedro was handsome, but he must have had some kind of magnetism that attracted women and made them follow him, because I don't know what else it could've been. It's a different kind of luck. His hair was curly, real wavy with a curl right here in front. He had a flat nose and a pockmarked face. There's no doubt his two gold teeth looked nice, but he wasn't handsome, I don't think.

—*Ándale*, Pedrito, don't be mean, share it with us . . .

He'd just laugh. He was a man right to the end.

—Come drink with us . . . Come on, Pedrito . . .

The bitches snagged him in no time because he was so vain . . .

They even poisoned him once. The poison was actually meant for me, but my blood is black and bitter and my veins are crossed, so it didn't do anything to me. But the first glass he drank poisoned him because his blood was sweet. It seemed to make him rabid: he started running through the streets and the air twisted his head around to the back. That woman put a spell on him, she drove him crazy, she twisted his neck. Palemon, his assistant, and I had to tie him to the bed, and he stayed that way several days, saying all kinds of things he shouldn't have, until we took him to the witch doctor to cleanse him with herbs. Halfway through the treatment, the man turned to me and said:

—We won, señora.

My husband still looked the same to me, lying there like a dead man, but the witch doctor was sweating; he was kneeling in front of Pedro, brushing him with herbs, and he kept praying and praying until he ran out of prayers. Then he wrapped him up and laid him down. He made a package out of the crap he took out of him. He left and didn't come back until six in the evening the next day with another bundle of herbs from the woods to cleanse him again. When he finished, he said, showing me a bottle with yellow water:

—Look what I have here. Can you see what's inside?

—It's a little figure . . .

—It's him.

It was Pedro, an exact likeness of my husband made of wax stuck in the bottle. He asked me:

—What do you want me to do with him?

—I don't know.

—Señora, if I throw it out he dies, if I burn it he dies, if I bury it he dies too, so you decide . . .

—No, I don't know, I don't know. Do whatever the Lord bids you to do.

—I'll put him in an anthill, because they can't get him out of there.

He took the bottle with the little figure of my husband and the herbs from the woods and after the third treatment Pedro was conscious. The witch doctor told him:

—Now that you're back to your senses, I'll tell you that your illness came from a drink that you got God only knows where. I want to warn you, your blood is very sweet, you don't have any defenses against curses. I'm willing to help you out, but if this happens again, you'll go back to where you came from, or you'll be an idiot the rest of your life, living with everyone's pity.

After his accident, my husband started to take me out in public, and one day when we were shopping I heard him say to Palemon:

—Here comes that bitch . . .

I turned around and saw her. Pedro said it again:

—Here's that bitch. I order you to put her on the train to Ciudad Juárez, no matter what it takes. Better yet, throw her into the pigpen.

—I came to see you, she said, real happy, ignoring me as if I was just a picture painted on the wall.

—You have no reason to come here, my husband answered, and he repeated the order to his assistant.

—Put her on the train. If she's here when I get back, I'll shoot her . . . and don't be surprised if I shoot you too.

—But why? she said innocently. I came here to be with you. I don't care about the danger.

—You have no reason to come looking for me. You already know I'm married, and that one standing over there is my wife. She may be small, but if you don't get out of here, she's going to beat the shit out of you.

I merely listened, because it wasn't time for me to do anything.

—*Ándale*, let's go, he said to me. Don't stand there like you've been skinned alive.

He left her there with the assistant, and I heard Palemon tell the woman:

—If you don't want to get shot, you better get on the next train and leave . . .

He made a big show of helping her up very carefully, but you could hear blows from the butt of a gun, and that was the last time I saw her. She was a large woman, big hips, not pretty at all, from a whorehouse in Morelia. But different people like different things. Pedro met her and had fun with her for a while, but she stuck to him like a thick-lipped bedbug. This Jacinta must have really fallen hard for Pedro, lower than she'd fallen in the whorehouse. That's what I think. Poor thing, but it's not like he was the only man around. There were lots of them, and that's something she knew from her own experience. You'd think he was the last man on earth. Besides, he was taken, so how could it work? You have to find a man who's alone, who doesn't already have a woman screaming at him, so you can do the screaming. It makes no sense to love a man who's already taken.

I wasn't jealous of my husband. Why would I be jealous if I couldn't care less about his life? It just made me mad that people gossiped, so I had to speak up, because I'm not made of stone. In the end, even though I was fed up, I beat him and his mistresses. I didn't want to be his fool. What were they looking for if Pedro already had someone to give it to him? What were those bitches after?

And what about the men who get in where they don't belong? To put it crudely, all women have the same thing between their legs. I don't agree with all that running around from one shameless whore to another. Pedro had enough for all of them. If they'd roll around with him, they were rewarded; he bought them dresses, shoes, he fed them, and they didn't want for anything. My husband didn't expect to get it for nothing, even if it was offered. He had at least a dozen, God knows how many more. I caught one. I caught Angelita and I gave it to her so she understood. But she was just one, and Pedro had a shitload of tramps.

Pedro didn't marry me because he liked me but because he thought: "This one's not going to get away." He had more than enough women, what did he need me for? When I met him, he was being serviced by women in every house, they washed his clothes, ironed his shirts, he had breakfast with one and got clean things there; the clothes he had worn with me he left at the house where he went for dinner. He slept at another house, and another and then another. He had a comal and a metate everywhere. I'd see him every now and then when he spent the night with me. He never went around worshiping me: "Sweetheart, I love you. Sweetheart, I'm dying to be with you." None of that crap that goes on nowadays! He never kissed me either. I'm not used to kissing. Judas kissed Jesus and look what happened to him. Let them do what they want to do so badly, but don't go making it fancy!

Pedro was very macho, he was real energetic and full of the devil. All I can say is I didn't make it easy for him, because he couldn't break me. Other women would be drawn into his arms, but I never offered myself to him. That's why I don't know what love is. I never had it, I never felt anything, and neither did he. He just wanted to humiliate me. I was happy when he didn't come to me. I'd see his boots when he came in the mornings and I'd ask him:

—Can I get you breakfast?

If he was in a good mood he'd say yes, and if he was mad he'd say:

—I'm not asking you for anything.

—Then don't ask me.

I'd grab the pan or the casserole or whatever and throw the food out, dish and all, into the middle of the street. That's how I got even, I'd throw the food out. But then I didn't get any either, because what I had cooked stayed right where I'd thrown it. I wasn't one of those who'd say: "The food's ready, I'm going to eat." Why should I care if he eats or not? I wouldn't even taste it, and I'd never say I was starving to death. I was strong, and I'm still strong, it's my nature. My body's used to doing without the basics of life. I could take it. Rage, that's what kept me going. I've had a bad temper my whole life. I'm strong-willed. If I didn't eat I'd say to myself: "I'm not really hungry anyway." And my hunger would go away from sheer effort. Two stray dogs who wandered the streets would enjoy what I'd cooked.

In spite of all his weaknesses Pedro made sure I had everything I needed. Since he didn't want me visiting anyone, he never said: "Go ask so-and-so if you can borrow chiles and tomatoes." No way. My husband wasn't one of those. He made sure I had chiles and tomatoes, garlic, onions, flour, coffee, sugar, rice, brown sugar, everything I needed. He bought it in bulk. I took a horse with all the supplies I needed, along with my mare La Muñeca, when we were on a mission. When we went out to fight a battle, Palemon or Zeferino, the other assistant, would bring me water and I'd make tortillas and cook rice or beans, or whatever was available then. Pedro ordered the two assistants to pound in posts—two big ones and four little ones so the tent would be close to the ground and we wouldn't get wet. Everyone had to pitch their own tent. Single men slept two or three to a tent. The ones with wives were with just their wife and kids. There were a lot of children about five, six, seven years old who stayed behind with their mothers and the equipment. Not many women went into battle; Pedro took me even though he didn't have orders from General Espinosa y Córdoba; that's why he made me dress like a man, so they'd look the other way and not report me. He covered my head with a scarf and a hat. Most of the women went into battle for the same reason I did, because their husbands made them; others went because they were trying to be men. But most of them remained behind. I can tell you about things that went on in lots of different places. If I'd stayed at the station I wouldn't have seen or heard anything. The truth is, it's really something special because it isn't just a story; I saw it for myself. I got used to it and I liked to go into battle, but it didn't last for long.

I always carried a pistol in my belt, as well as a rifle because a cavalryman carries his rifle on the back of his horse. My job was to load Pedro's Mauser, mine and his; while he'd fire one I'd load the empty one so he could switch back and forth. We'd be riding, and La Muñeca would keep pace with the other horse, right next to it. That damn animal knew exactly what she was doing. She knew how to fight! I'd load the Mauser with those big bullets that we had in our cartridge belts; they came in packs of five. I was never scared. I don't know if I killed anyone. If they were close, I might have. If not, I didn't have any reason to shoot at them. Fear doesn't exist for me. Fear of what? Just fear of God. He's the one who turns us to dust. But fear of the world, *pues*, what for? If your time is up, then it's your turn. It's all the same to me, that's how things go.

During the battles all you see are little figures fighting. They don't look very big. You can see them move from there to over here, some coming, others going, and you ready your gun to hit them. If you don't have good aim, the bullets go whistling past their ears or over their heads. But if you have good aim, then the little monkeys fall down and stay down. Pedro was a good shot. He carried an extra cartridge belt as a backup on the horn of his saddle. I never even heard the bullets, I just saw smoke. I never saw a dead person's face! No one would get down off their horse to look at the dead people. They were left there, dead or alive. We had to keep chasing the people who were up ahead. Usually the families didn't even know that their loved ones had been killed. The buzzards were their cemetery; after all, they were just piles of clothes lying there on the ground.

We fought at night too. We shot the bullets wherever there was a glimmer, following the powder flashes, the same as they did, in the direction of the glow of the enemy camp. But the hardest thing was not knowing which way the enemy was coming from or where they were.

—There he comes through the rocky mountain pass.

But it wasn't true. Then again:

—They sighted them on the hill.

Nothing. The sentries had you jumping with their false alarms. Sometimes we couldn't even see our own faces, much less spy the enemy camp, because of the blanket of fog. We had to put up with the foul weather, and a lot of times we groped our way around and we'd go to sleep not even knowing where we were. Once, an unexpected downpour forced us to return to the station, where the equipment had been left. We were covered with mud, dragging our rotting equipment behind us. We had a lot of losses too. We abandoned the trenches until General Espinosa y Córdoba angrily ordered us, filthy as we were, to go back to our positions. But when he saw that the rain wasn't letting up, he gave a counter-order and we took cover again. The next day at the station you could see all the clothing that the women had hung on the cable so it would dry out. And since all of us in the barracks made friends with what didn't belong to us, I knew ahead of time that even though our shirts and pants were in shreds we'd never see them again . . .

Up north the snow would be close to a meter deep, piled up from the constant snowing. The train engines would die. They wouldn't move any farther. From the door of the train I could see that beautiful snow between Ciudad Juárez and Villa González. It would come down from the sierra through San Antonio Arenales and it was amazing. I'd wander around to get into all that white. I loved watching the little white feathers fall. I'd cover myself with my shawl and go off into the whiteness. I was fifteen and it all seemed like a game. Now you couldn't drag me outside if it started snowing, but back then the cold didn't bother me. Since I'd never seen snow, it delighted me. I'd bury my legs in the white and spend all morning rolling around in it. I'd feel warm until the cold soaked through me, I think, because I was out in it for so many hours, and I'd climb on top of the boxcar and put my feet almost into the fire so they wouldn't feel numb. After doing that three or four times I became crippled. My feet cramped up and ended up gnarled. At night the pain would be so unbearable that I couldn't sleep, because when I'd try to stretch out I wouldn't be able to move my legs. And at that point, even though he was usually terrible to me, my husband would say to Palemon:

—Go get me a little tar from the axles . . . Bring me a piece of burlap.

And Pedro would cover me with the tar and the burlap from the train. Every night he rubbed my legs and wrapped them up carefully. I couldn't straighten out. My hands were like claws, too. With the asphalt and the massages the pain lessened until I could walk again.

IN THOSE DAYS the San Antonio Arenales sierra was beautiful but brutal, with its steep precipices, ravines, and loose rocks. At night, we could hear the gravel falling and I was always afraid that the mountain was coming down on top of us. We camped at the foot of a hill in a huge empty plain, without a single tree. I don't know if the town was close by or far away, but the peasants came on burros to sell us provisions. We paid them with colored bills like the peso notes they use now. The government made that money in the capital. For money the Villistas had thin white tissue paper that looked like spiderwebs. I don't know who made the sheets for Villa, but they weren't worth the paper they were printed on and they had to force people to take their money. Everyone carried their own paper; the little orange slips were twenty centavos, the ten centavos were blue, and the fives were red. They were all fake. That was the change you got for a peso. There was a lot of gold and silver around, but it was buried, because during the Revolution everyone hid their money. Nobody knows where it's hidden now, especially in the towns where the peasants buried their seeds too. They dug big holes and hid their beans, corn, rice, so they wouldn't have to sell it, because the paper money wasn't worth much for very long. The government soldiers earned a peso and five centavos a day, but my husband never gave me his salary the way my father did. When I came to the capital I learned about gold ounces, coins this big worth forty pesos, thick, solid gold. Yes, they were pretty. The silver pesos were big too, and they made a nice sound. But in San Antonio Arenales we paid for everything with red paper.

"We're staying here for a while!" General Juan Espinosa y Córdoba advised his officers. "I haven't received orders yet. So go ahead and get settled in as best you can."

The officers would approach him every four or five days when they'd see him come out of the tent where he lived with his blonde.

—What news is there? they'd ask.

—None. It sure is cold! Have you gathered enough firewood?

—*Pues no, mi general,* just enough for you . . .

—Don't be lazy, don't be lazy . . . Go ahead and get firewood for yourselves too!

—How long are we staying?

—There hasn't been any news.

And he'd go back into his tent, rubbing his hands together and pulling the collar of his jacket up, as though it didn't bother him in the least.

In the rocky mountains of the San Antonio sierra, the soldiers began collecting wood for a fire, and Pedro went along with them looking for branches to make us a house. On one of those trips, at a bend in the river, they found a little coyote. When that little animal saw people, she was so trusting, she walked over to them and they picked her up.

—What a beautiful puppy! my husband said.

I raised her with *atole* made of flour, which I'd feed to her with a rag, and the animal got very attached to me. She'd sleep on my legs and wouldn't let anyone get near me. I loved that little coyote so much. She was real furry, which was good in the cold. At night, my husband would sit by the fire to read. He'd read two chapters of the novel *Nostradamus,* or from *Catherine of Medici, A Thousand and One Arabian Nights, The Great Prevoste,* and *Luisa de Montmorency.* He also read to me from *The Cardinal's Daughter.* That one's real interesting, about the daughter of a cardinal and a queen. He was the queen's confessor and after hearing her at confession he fell in love with her, but he couldn't do anything about it because the king was around. When the king went off to war, the queen got pregnant with the confessor's child. But the girl was raised by a nursemaid in a villa where the cardinal hid her. I memorized that whole novel. My husband read quite well, he explained everything so it made sense. Then he'd ask:

—Tell me, what did you understand?

—*Pues*, this and that . . . but the queen went too far . . .

I didn't know then that even queens do things they shouldn't.

—I can't talk to you about anything! No, that's not how it went, you didn't pay attention.

And he'd read it to me again, only slower.

—Did you understand or not? Let's see, tell me what you understood.

And I'd tell him.

—No, I told you that the cardinal is devious. He should've had it out with the king, man to man.

And he'd continue reading and I figured it out pretty good, even if I said whatever came into my head. The thing is, he never taught me how to talk, and then all of a sudden he decided to ask me questions. He'd start reading, and he probably got bored with talking to himself all the time like a crazy person, talking out loud, with me there real quiet, just watching him, waiting for him to ask for his coffee. But I do have to give him credit, he did read real nice, and I did understand what he read, because there are things that are engraved in my mind, and I'll never forget them. Besides, Pedro would read the same chapters over and over, sometimes six times. As you can imagine, something had to stick with me, it was the same story every day! When we stayed in a town, at a farm, in the sierra, wherever we ended up, Pedro read, but if he was out on a mission, he was busy watching to see where the bullets were coming from and he'd forget about the book. He had his own ideas and habits; he probably wanted to talk. I didn't understand it, but he was different, a strange bird, a real loner. He'd spend the day hanging around with the other soldiers, but in the towns he'd go back to his old ways. He always took several books, his assistant Ze-

ferino packed them in a box, and out in the hills of San Antonio
Arenales, Pedro would read every night. Who knows who taught
him to read! Who knows! I don't. If I asked him, which I never
would've done, I'm sure he'd have said:

—I don't remember.

He was like that. Who knows why. When he read, his eyes
would brighten. The daylight would be fading, it would be getting
dark, and he'd keep reading until he was dazed, late into the
night. Then he'd close the book real careful and lie down to sleep,
without asking me to warm up his dinner.

One morning the colonel came looking for my husband to play
the assembly bugle, because there was news, and since Pedro was
out in the woods at that moment, I went ahead and blew the horn.
The coyote followed me, and when the colonel tried to grab my
arm, she jumped on him and bit him. He took out his gun and
shot her. I got so mad.

—Why'd you kill her? That animal was protecting me . . .

—Yeah, he said to me, but it was a ferocious animal. Look, it
bit me.

—She was protecting me. It wasn't her fault. You grabbed me.
How was she supposed to know why you grabbed me?

I felt even worse when I saw the smoking gun.

—You have no soul! You all knew. You knew that no one could
come near me. The animal got mad because you came up and
touched me. I want her alive again . . . Why'd you shoot her?

—Why'd it bite me?

—You know why . . . You could've spoken to me, but instead,
you grabbed me and she was protecting me. It was your fault, not
hers.

—I'll give you a hundred pesos for your animal.

—I don't want the money, I want my coyote. Come on, bring
her back . . .

—Don't be ignorant. How do you expect me to revive the animal? I'm not God.

—Give her life back to her, bring her back.

He ignored me and walked away. When all the soldiers assembled and were given the order to move out toward Rancho del Guajolote, my husband asked me what happened.

—The colonel killed my coyote.

After that I dreamed about her. I missed her a lot. I told Pedro:

—I'm not taking care of any more animals. What for, so someone can kill them? No way . . .

—That coyote was meaner than a dog, *Vale*, she was real brave; but he offered to pay you for her . . .

—But I don't want the money, I want my animal.

Later on I raised a couple of piglets that someone gave Pedro. I carried them around in the pockets of my overcoat, one on each side. Then there was a sow and a dog that someone gave him. One was just as mean as the other, but I still missed the coyote and I refused to get attached to them. I raised all four of them with *atole* and a rag. The sow was real mean too; no one could get close to me, because she'd bite at them.

I was the only one in the unit who had a dog. He was very white, so I called him Jazmín. When it was our turn to get on the train, he'd wrap his front paws around me. Palemon and I put the sow in a crate on the roof of the train and we made a covering with sticks so she wouldn't get sunburned. Jazmín slept with me. He was short and fat and looked like a pigeon. I gave him milk with flour tortillas in the morning, at noon he had soup with a bone, and he didn't eat anything at night. He was a lot of company.

They killed my coyote. Then Jazmín died and when I thought the sow was going to die too, I told my husband:

—Give her away to someone. See what you can do with her. I don't want her anymore. See if you can sell her too, because I'm not taking care of any more animals . . .

He sold her to a merchant from Piedras Negras. I didn't have a pet again after that, and a short time later they killed Pedro too. Why would I want more animals?

We traveled all over, around the area called Rancho del Guajolote, which was close to where General Saturnino Cedillo was from. We were there for a long time. Everyone was left on their own and my husband went into slaughtering. General Espinosa y Córdoba settled in there with his blonde and paid no attention to us. As long as there weren't orders from the government, he was free to do whatever he felt like.

Pedro killed hogs and fried pork rinds. The kids from the town would stand around the pot and he'd feed them:

—*Ándile, ándile,* don't be shy, have some rinds, take whatever there is . . .

I'd buy two packs of tortillas to feed everyone who wanted to have a taco with him. As soon as he fried the rinds he'd give them away, tortilla and all.

—Listen, he'd say to me, make sure there are enough tortillas. Have a lot made so the kids can come and have something to eat.

Pedro was good to everyone; whenever he killed a hog he asked people to help him. Some brought firewood and made the fire and another would start heating a pot of water. When they left, he gave each one a piece of meat . . . He was always like that. When I'd take him food at the barracks I had to take enough for everyone, because he'd invite whoever was there to eat:

—*Ándele,* come and eat, have some lard with that.

He was very generous. That's just the way he was.

There wasn't any water where we were camped, so a boy named Refugio Galván, who was about twelve years old, would carry water from a hill that was pretty far away and sell it to the troops and the townspeople. That's how he supported his family, because his mother and his brothers and sisters were real poor. I usually gave them whatever was left in the bottom of the pot, and the mother would make tacos with thick tortillas. She kept the pork rind in a pan and fed her children for the rest of the week, or however long it would last.

The family had some seeds and Pedro would give them meat in exchange for the seed, but when he realized how dirt poor they were, he just gave them the meat.

He liked to talk to young Refugio Galván, and sometimes he even went to the head of the stream with him to bring back water. Who knows what all Pedro told him. He talked about cannons, real cannons, about machine guns, about bullets, and told the boy that no one was ever going to win . . .

—Why aren't you going to win?

—We're not.

—But why not?

—Because this has been going on for a long time and it'll go on for a lot longer. It's a never-ending story.

The boy asked a lot of questions. Even though he was shaky, probably from hunger, he was a very curious child; he understood everything and wanted to know about everything. He was skinny, but he'd go back and forth and back and forth again and again with his buckets of water, even though he'd be bent over under the weight. He'd run to catch up with Pedro:

—Captain, Captain, here I am . . . !

One afternoon Refugio Galván's mother came to the house to ask my husband to bless the boy as his godfather, but I didn't understand what she was trying to explain to me; I thought they were going to confirm him.

—No, she said, he's deathly sick.

It turned out that her son was already dying. Pedro had gone to Ciudad del Maíz, and so the woman asked me to help her.

A long time ago it was the custom for the baptismal godparents to bless a godchild who was very sick, and if it was God's will, he'd get better, and if not, he died. Since this boy's godparents weren't around, they begged me to do it. I asked for a bowl of water, a candle, some grains of salt, and a piece of cotton. I blessed him with the water, I put the salt on his tongue, and I asked him if he was leaving.

Then the little fellow made a sign that he was going.

I asked him:

—Don't you want to wait for the captain?

He shook his head. There wasn't time to wait.

—*Bueno, pues* I give you your son, I said to the mother.

When I put him in her arms the little one died. I left him there and went out.

While I was at home I kept thinking: "The poor little thing is dead . . . What's Pedro going to say about me blessing the boy without his permission?"

An officer who went with me to see little Refugio said:

—Señora, we're going to let the boss know so he can bring everything we need for the wake.

—Do whatever you want. I don't know anything about how that works.

The corporal sent word to Pedro to buy the stuff for the St. Joseph outfit, the fireworks, the liquor, the brown sugar, all the things for the wake. On a piece of paper he wrote: "You're the godfather. Señora Jesusa blessed the child before he left this earth."

When my husband got back he gave me the material to make the St. Joseph outfit for the little angel and he went to see him. From there, he went to the store to buy sugar, coffee, brown sugar, sweet bread, corn to grind, and more fireworks because he realized that what he had brought wouldn't be enough for all the people who were at the Galváns'. I sewed the gown, a green dress with a yellow cape with stars on it, and laid it in the round basket with the crown and the sandals. Then all the little children came and made two rows from the door of my house to Refugito's house, the boys on one side and the girls on the other. When I arrived, they welcomed me with music and firecrackers. I dressed him, my husband put the little sandals on his feet, and then I tied the cape around him and reddened his cheeks with colored paper. When he was ready, Pedro put the crown on his head and took off the silk scarf he was wearing around his own neck and covered the boy's face to keep the worms from eating his flesh, because they won't eat the dead if they're wrapped in silk. The worms respect the fabric because it comes from them.

At the wake, they spent the whole time talking about Refugio, reciting his name like a litany; God has reasons for what He does, divine mercy, everything is already written, he's been liberated from the devil in time, he'll rest eternally, he was so young, he was so good, such a hard worker, such a responsible little boy. They prayed for the souls in Purgatory; Lord remember the soul of

Your humble servant Refugio Galván, that You have just gathered to Your breast—and a bunch of other things.

—What happened to Refugito?

—He climbed a post and fell and ended up with pneumonia from the fall.

—Why'd he climb the pole?

—To save the pork rinds.

I pricked up my ears, because his mother was talking about how Refugio had gotten sick.

—I gave him the pot with the pork rinds and the little ones surrounded him: "Ay, *dame*, give me some, don't be mean!" I guess they thought there was too much for one person. Refugio ran away with the pot and climbed the pole and I found him lying on the ground, without the food, because it'd all been stolen . . . He was sick for two weeks. He didn't break any bones, but he had a high fever . . .

—And what did you do?

—I waited. What else could I do . . . ? Waited for God to decide . . .

While I listened I started to think that if they had told me, Refugio wouldn't have died, because I would have boiled some kind of infusion to dissolve the blood clot and he'd have gotten better. Avocado leaves with bamboo and corn tassels are real good for bumps and dissolve the coagulation of blood that gets stuck. It's like taking arnica. It hurts when the clots break up, but then you feel better. Who could revive him now that he was already under the ground? He was twelve years old when he died. She was a foolish woman, dumb as a rock. I sat next to her. I looked at her blank face, the face of a woman who accepted everything without a fight, and it made me madder. I said:

—Ay, señora, it's your fault he died because you didn't even fight to save him. The tumor clotted inside, and then with such a high fever, there's no way he'd make it.

—It was God's will . . .

I'd have liked to send her to God, but there she was with her arms crossed, squashed against her chair.

The fireworks went off all night long and the music played. The men finished the two jugs of liquor.

—Can I serve you another?

—Sure, for Refugito.

—Cheers.

Then someone else came in and asked the mother:

—How did he die?

I'd have said: "Go to hell," but she just wiped her eyelashes and told the story again.

The next day we took him to the cemetery, playing music along the way. Four men carried the coffin, but they switched off because they'd been up all night drinking and were hung over. When they buried him, they shot off more fire rockets to use up the ones that were left. The funeral wasn't sad. We're just on loan when we come to Earth; it's not true that we come to live on it. We're passing through, and many children fulfill their duty by just being born, but they don't have permission to stay, so they go back right away. They last only a few hours or days or months. Here on Earth we say: "He died from this or he died from that." But the date is already written down and at the moment that God says: "This is it," He lifts them off the Earth. People from the villages seem to understand that and accept it. They return the dead the proper way. They don't grab on to them crying and say: "God, why did You take him from me . . . ?" "Sweet Jesus . . . it's so unfair!" because most people say: "God was so mean to take my child away." But it wasn't unfair. They're sent to be on Earth until a certain age. You have to take care of them and heal them, you have to fulfill your obligation, yes, but if you fight to save your children and it doesn't comfort them, God doesn't want to leave them with you and then you have to resign yourself to His decision and give them up.

That's why they bury the dead with fireworks and music and are festive. If they cry, it takes their glory away and God doesn't receive them with pleasure, because they have to be returned the way they were sent to Earth. If the physical parents on Earth don't want to let go of them and hold on to them screaming and protesting to God, it hurts the one who has just died; it can even cost them eternal life.

Pedro started drinking when we got back from the cemetery and stayed drunk for a week. He didn't attend to his troops, he didn't take care of himself. I don't know if it was because he was so hurt or not, but he was lost. He drank for a week. He started with the whiskey and didn't stay at the house, but roamed the streets of the town like a drunken bum, talking to himself, muttering who knows what, no one could understand him. All he cared about was drinking. He even forgot what the witch doctor told him. After a week, he pulled himself together. He didn't have any money left and was in debt. He got a couple of hogs on credit, butchered them, and sold the meat. Then he started to get back on his feet, but he was almost unrecognizable for days.

One moon-filled night when Pedro wasn't home because he'd gone to get the hogs, I saw the *nagual*. It was the silhouette of a person walking toward my door. The weather is very warm near Cuidad del Maíz, which is between Río Verde and San Luis Potosí, and the houses are made of sticks, so that the air can come in through the cracks. Pedro had put a fence around our house and he mixed mesquite and huisache branches between the poles, with the thorns pointing toward the outside, and the same with the door. I saw a shadow walk toward my room through that mesh. Pedro had built a little patio with a roof next to the room—a palm-frond roof—so when he slaughtered hogs the meat wouldn't dry out or spoil. That night there was such a beautiful moon that I could clearly see the *nagual* stealing through the cracks. So I screamed at the top of my lungs:

—What do you want? What do you want? If you take a step inside I'll blast you . . .

He crouched down and ran away on all fours like a dog to a big shade tree, where the peddlers from Ciudad Valles came to sell their goods. I lost sight of him there, but his tail was dragging on the ground. When my husband got home I told him about it.

The *nagual* is a human who disguises himself as an animal to steal from people. He's a man with the fur of a dog and he walks on all fours, but he stands up so he can reach what he throws in his sack. When he's discovered he runs away howling and everyone crosses themselves in horror. He comes out on moonlit nights so he can see better. He's really just a thief who transforms into an animal—a dog, coyote, or wolf. People of weak faith are really scared of them, but not me, because I've seen them in real life. I did see the *nagual*. I was home all alone, so the next morning I told the boy who helped me out to put the pot of lard on top of the table.

I'd get up to stir it so it would turn white. You have to stir lard or it stays black and looks bad. After the last stirring, Pedro and I would leave it outside to settle.

We had stuff stolen from us several times; one night a pork leg, and later two shoulder blades. That day I had salted a lot of pieces of meat too, strips about a meter to two meters long, flank and shredded meat. Other times, when I got up the next morning, the meat was all messed up. That *nagual* had taken the best pieces, and he even brought a big pot to scoop up the fresh lard. I finally said:

—This time I'm staying awake to see who shows up . . .

I didn't go to bed. I turned off the light and left a candle burning—no matter where I am I light a candle or a pot of wax with a wick in it—and I sat in the doorway holding my gun. I clearly saw the *nagual* go through the fence and come up to the door, and just as he was about to open it, I said real quiet (after all I had my gun):

—What's up?

I shined the light on him. And you know what? It was Pedro's friend who always came to the house to eat and I'd give him pork rinds and pork. My husband helped him enlist in the army, brought him to San Luis Potosí, to Ciudad del Maíz. He'd put a hog skin on his back, the animal's eyes glistened real ugly, and when I jumped on him and beat him with a stick, you wouldn't believe how he took off through that huisache fence, scratching himself on the thorns! I said: "Some friends Pedro has!"

The next day when Pedro came back with that same friend, I told him:

—I met the guy who passes himself off as a *nagual* and steals from us.

I said it to the very same *nagual*. His eyes weren't shining anymore, his name was Ciriaco, and from then on I realized the *nagual* wasn't an animal. Sometimes in small towns they say a girl was stolen by the *nagual*, but now I'm sure her boyfriend snuck away with her, because she'd never be allowed to be with him otherwise. So he shows up dressed like an animal and steals her away. They both just play dumb. It's all made up so they can do what they want, and she's just as shameless as he is.

We didn't stay in Rancho del Guajolote much longer because my husband asked for a few days' leave to go farther north, to Hacienda del Salado in the state of Coahuila, to see his grandmother. The two of us left on horseback. Pedro was born there and he couldn't stop talking he was so excited. We were just arriving at about three in the afternoon when a goat walked up. After sniffing him all over she started to bleat:

—This is my mother, he said to me.

I turned around and all I saw was the goat and I said:

—Where?

—Right here. She's my mother . . .

—You expect me to believe your mother's an animal? You sure don't have a lot of respect for her.

—Believe it or not, this animal is my mother. I never knew my mother. This animal raised me . . . I think of her as my mother.

The goat came over and stood on her hind legs and licked him and nuzzled him with her goatee. Pedro grabbed her by the back of the neck and rubbed her.

Then his grandmother came out and said:

—You're here, son . . .

When he was young his grandmother would go to town to run an errand, and Pedro would start to cry. The goat would run over to where he was lying and squat down; she'd spread her legs and let him suckle. So that's how the big-tit goat raised Pedro. And he caressed her lovingly and the goat bleated and bleated, and sniffed and sniffed him. Who knows if his mother died, he never told me. I don't know anything about his father either. He never talked to me about that. Why would he? I didn't want to know, I wasn't interested in his life. I do know that the day after we left the goat died.

I'd been talking to the grandmother for less than fifteen minutes when Pedro came back from town, where he had gone for a ride. The townspeople didn't even let him get as far as the plaza! Word got around real quick that he was back and they started to surround him, because before we got married, when he was already involved in the Revolution, he had rustled horses from the rich people of the hacienda where he was raised and he brought them to add to the horses the armed forces already had. That's why they made him a captain. There was no way the ranchers would have forgotten that! There was always someone willing to spread the word that Pedro Aguilar was around. His friends warned him:

—They're coming to capture you . . .

—How can that be? I thought things had changed with the Revolution . . .

—The Revolution hasn't changed anything. We're still dying of hunger . . .

He ran back and said:

—*Ándale*, let's get out of here . . .

He yelled to his grandmother:

—If I stay here, they'll kill me!

And he spurred his horse.

We couldn't even say goodbye to the poor grandmother, who just stood there with her arms fallen to her sides. That day Pedro was unarmed because we didn't bring the Mauser. He had a gun and so did I, but they weren't enough. He knew all the trails around there, so we took off toward a narrow path, and that's why they didn't catch us. But we heard the gunshots in the woods. The two of us were alone and we reported to the commanders when we got back. I was glad to see our people. We didn't even stay for a day at his grandmother's. He had a chance to ask for her blessing, and he wasn't going back there again.

Villa's close by!

—Yeah . . . They passed through Conchos, and trashed it . . .

—It's a pigsty . . . They burned the cornfields . . . They rode their horses inside the church and looted . . . They cut the heads off the saints . . . They took everything! They say the streets are stained with blood . . .

—What about Villa?

—That pighead was there the whole time, laughing! He had them ring all the church bells so we'd know it was him!

The troops just crossed themselves, as if that would do any good. While Pedro and I went to Hacienda del Salado, they ordered General Juan Espinosa y Córdoba's people to break camp because the Villistas had blown up a passenger train between Conchos and Chihuahua and killed all the guards. They made mincemeat of everyone. They were all civilians escorted by a few military men, and when someone yelled: "Down with the Carrancistas!" the Villistas wiped them out. Women, men, children, all naked with their eyes open so that the vultures could pick them out easier. There were three train cars piled with the dead. That's how they arrived at Villa Ahumada, or Villa González, as they call it now, and Espinosa y Córdoba ordered them to throw the bodies on top of each other into three big holes, men and women with the little children, all tangled up together. That's what the famous Division of the North was like. Hopefully they're roasting in Hell right now. The dead were naked because their clothes had been stolen; everyone on the train had been wearing nice clothes. When we got there we couldn't tell which were civilians and which were soldiers; they were all just like God had sent them to this world, and we threw them into the hole fast because they were already starting to smell bad. The snow was all red with blood. At about two in the morning, after breaking camp, they played reveille and we set out to chase Villa and his bandits. Espinosa y Córdoba was furious and he sent us toward Ojinaga. I left with Pedro; only the equipment was left behind.

The company was crossing the sierra at a full gallop when all of a sudden we heard a clamoring, a chorus of screams: "Here come the Carranclanes, sons of Goat Beard. Beat them over the head, hard . . . !" Some people froze, but Espinosa y Córdoba gave the order to move ahead.

The combat started at three in the morning, in the dark, and we had a lot of casualties. We shot toward wherever we saw gun bursts, but those bandits were protected by parapets; they were behind the rocks. General Espinosa y Córdoba ordered an about-face, but since we didn't hear the counterorder we kept going, shooting at those sons of you-know-whats. Dawn broke, and we fought all day. I rode next to Pedro carrying the Mauser for him. The troops had dispersed and we kept going, taking out those thieves like it was nothing. I was handing him the loaded Mauser, and when he didn't take it, I turned around to see what was wrong and Pedro wasn't on his horse. At about four in the afternoon my husband was shot in the chest and that's when I realized that he and I were out there all alone. I saw him lying on the ground. When I got off my horse to pick him up he was already dead, with his arms folded across his chest. He didn't bleed much. A little later the two assistants caught up with us, and they helped me tie him on his horse. The enemy fired and hit Pedro, as if they wanted to kill him again, but he was already good and dead.

The major arrived in a cloud of dust followed by soldiers. I yelled that we were alone and my husband had been killed.

—What should we do? he asked me.

—What do you want us to do, Major? We should retreat firing.

He looked stunned and he asked me again as if he didn't understand:

—What do we do? What do we do? Ay, Virgin of Guadalupe! What do we do?

—What do you want to do, Major? Retreat firing . . .

—You take charge, because I can't handle it . . .

And he stood there opening and closing his jaws like an alligator. I told Palemon:

—Let's move out, fire as we retreat toward the Rio Grande, and don't leave any of the boys behind.

Zeferino and Palemon helped me round everyone up and we got to the river at five that afternoon. We had to cross, but we didn't want to be easy targets on the bridge, so we left the dead under a rock that jutted out and we crossed, swimming on horseback. A gringo captain captured us when we got to the other side. Through an interpreter he told me to hand over our weapons because we were prisoners. I answered that I wasn't giving him anything.

—You have to hand over your troops, your weapons, and your supplies because your general surrendered and turned over his weapons at noon.

—You mean the general crossed the river at noon?

—Yes.

I just stood there looking stunned. Son of a bitch!

—You mean he turned over his weapons?

—Yes. Since he did, so must you, but if we come to an agreement and you return to Mexico, we'll give everything back to you, exactly what we received.

They made a list as I handed over twenty-five weapons and the twenty-seven double cartridge belts; two of my husband's, two of mine, and two from each of the soldiers who had escaped with me.

We found General Juan Espinosa y Córdoba sleeping, lying

there in his tent, real calm. They didn't finish us off, but they did put an end to us. He was totally at ease because, after all, he'd saved his own hide.

—General, the captain's dead and I need you to give me some soldiers to go get his body . . .

—No. We're prisoners here. I can't give you any soldiers, because we're all prisoners . . .

—You may know what you're doing, but give me some soldiers to go and bring him back. He can't stay on the other side of the river . . .

Finally the gringos let me take a small squad. Four Mexican soldiers and one of their guards to protect us. I got there when it was dark and the coyotes were already eating Pedro. He didn't have hands, or ears, pieces of his nose were missing and part of his neck. We picked him up and took him to Marfa, Texas, in the United States to bury him, near Presidio, and that's where he stayed.

It made me really mad that our general had gone over to the United States. I told him that since we still had weapons and ammunition he had no reason to take his ass up north. He should have ordered us to pursue the enemy until we couldn't anymore.

—Jesusa, there wasn't any other choice. There were so many Villistas and they pushed me back here.

—At least you could have given a counterorder so all of us could have come together, and not just leave us behind. My husband was killed between Ojinaga and Cuchillo Parado. He'd be here if you weren't such a coward. . . Now I understand what they mean when they say your motto is "If there are a lot of them let's turn and run, if there are few we'll use caution, and if there isn't anyone coming then let's move forward, sons of Coahuila, we were born to die . . . !" That's some way to fight a war, General.

He bowed his head and said:

—There's no choice now.

—There's none for you, General, and we're prisoners because of what you chose to do, but I belong on that side of the river, not here. I'm not trying to show you up, but come on!

We were in Marfa for a month, until General Joaquín Amaro

asked the gringos to return us to Mexico. I said goodbye to Pedro
and we crossed the bridge and from there we went to Villa
González, where the equipment had been left. General Juan Espinosa y Córdoba reassembled his troops and went back to Mexico
too. I was last and I joined my husband's company. Since the gringos had listed me separately when I crossed the border, I didn't
get sent back to Espinosa y Córdoba; instead the gringos returned
the weapons and supplies that were on the list along with the
troops that Pedro had consigned to me. That's why once we
reached Villa González I said to our general:

—I'm handing over the troops that were left to me, the ones I
crossed over with.

There were twenty-five soldiers as well as corporals, sergeants,
lieutenants, the major, who was still shell-shocked, and me. It was
the major's duty to hand over the troops. But since he hadn't
wanted to take charge of the retreat because he was weak, or
scared or who knows what, when we got to Mexico, General Espinosa y Córdoba saw that I was in charge and he said:

—You stay in command of the deceased Captain Aguilar's
troops . . . The soldiers explained that you led them when your
husband was killed and the major stepped aside . . .

I could see Palemon making gestures to me to say no. So I said
to the general:

—No, señor, I'm not a soldier and they can't name me commander.

—Then you don't accept the command?

—No.

—Why not?

—Because I don't, señor.

Up in the north they grabbed women and abused them.
Neither Zapata nor General Morales y Molina were as bad as Juan
Espinosa y Córdoba, that shameless bandit. He thought himself a
real ladies' man. Besides, he had bad intentions, because the general was spiteful. He wanted me to stay with the soldiers to harass
me because of the things I'd said to him:

—You've decided?

—Listen, I'm not here because I'm a soldier. I was following my husband even though I didn't want to.

—Then I won't give you your marching pay. I won't pay you for the last ten days or the past three months . . .

—Then don't pay me . . . I need the money but it's up to you. It should be my inheritance from my husband . . . You can take the money and shove it wherever it fits; after all, it's only toilet paper anyway.

This really burned him because his nickname was toilet paper; he wasn't worth anything.

My husband's assistants were good soldiers. They were older married men, who brought their wives and their children along with the equipment. While my husband was alive it was their duty to look after me: they bought me groceries, and brought water or whatever else I needed, and the government paid them. They were really good to me, but when Pedro died they couldn't follow me around anymore or look after me as before.

Zeferino and Palemon, the assistants, almost never talked to me, never said anything to me. Pedro would order them: "Clean the horses," "Water them," "Take care of the errands," and they'd brush his clothes, clean his saddle, and I saw to everything else he needed. But when he died they came to me:

—Don't stay here. Get your pay and go home . . . We have to wait for another captain or colonel to ask us to work for them, so we can't protect you from everyone. Now you're on your own.

All the widows got together and helped me get money for the ticket. We came to Durango to speak to General Amaro, who had arranged for us to be returned to Mexico from the United States. Since he was the chief of operations in Durango, you couldn't just walk in and talk to him. People had to make an appointment a day ahead and he'd see them the next day, if he'd see them at all. I was with eighteen other women when they stopped me on the patio of the barracks. "No admittance beyond this point." The sentry and the quartermaster crossed their bayonets to block our way. I said:

—Why not? I'm here to see General Amaro . . .

—If you don't have an appointment, you have to wait till to-morrow.

—No. I want to see him now, and I will see him now.

The general could hear me from upstairs and recognized my voice at that point because I was speaking very loud. He looked out the window:

—What's up, Aguilar?

—Nothing, *mi general*, I said. They won't let me in to talk to you. The captain died in the battle of Ojinaga and Cuchillo Parado and we ended up across the border.

—Come in, come in. Don't be yelling at me from down there.

So they admitted me, and all the people with appointments were left waiting. The general opened the door and let me come in along with the whole delegation of dusty women. I told him that General Juan Espinosa y Córdoba didn't pay me because he wanted me to stay in command of my husband's men and wouldn't discharge me. I didn't join up and was only in it because I was following my husband; because I was forced to and not because I wanted to. I didn't have any rank; I was just the captain's woman.

—The general is under my command, Aguilar, and it's not up to him to stop the deceased's pay . . .

He got very angry and sent a telegraph telling them to send the three months' pay they owed Pedro and ten days' marching pay to Durango. And the general with no balls had to send the money right away, since he had to follow orders . . . General Amaro said to me:

—Little one, you're going back home.

He himself loaded me and the eighteen other women on the trains, right there in Durango. Each would be able to go where she needed to go. He also gave me a pass so that I'd be paid a widow's pension when I got to Tehuantepec.

I wasn't even eighteen years old when Pedro was shot through the heart. He always said that when it looked like things were over, he was going to kill me. He wanted to send me on ahead, but it didn't happen that way. I'm still here raising hell.

I had to change trains in Mexico City to go to Tehuantepec. I

handed my four suitcases through the window to a porter standing on the platform at the station. All the clothes I owned, my husband's and mine, the shirts I had sewed for him—because in those
days the wife made the man's clothes—my pay, which like a fool
I'd put in one of the suitcases, the money I'd tied up in a handkerchief, the leather boots, four suitcases full of stuff, I lost all of
it. I never saw that porter again.

Each of the other women took off for home, but since I'd been
robbed at the Buenavista station, I stayed there alone, abandoned,
in Mexico City, scratching myself with my nails. I looked like a
turkey that's lost her chicks, stretching out her neck and looking
all around, crying, "Gobble . . . gobble . . . gobble . . ."

OF THE EIGHTEEN WOMEN, only me and the one going to Chilpancingo were left. We walked along the Tacuba highway from the old Buenavista station. She went her way, and there I was in Alameda Park, not knowing where to go. The cold chilled my hands to the bone. I was left without a centavo, no clothes, nothing, stripped of everything. Did I notice what the city looked like? Why would I care? I'd just realized it was a city of thieves.

People began to steal during the Revolution. Before that, Porfirio Díaz wouldn't allow that to go on. If someone stole, they were killed; if they murdered, they were killed; if they raped a girl, they were killed; if they deserted, they were killed. Díaz wasn't one to say: "Give me so many thousand pesos and get on with your business!" No. There was respect and a lot of fear. People thought: "If I commit a crime they'll kill me, so I better not."

I crouched down against the wall. That's where the police found me when it got dark, and asked me where I was going. I told them number 15 Parcialidad Street. There was a sentry with a lantern on every corner. Nowadays the streets are empty, and there's no protection, but there was back then. They walked me block by block, passing me from one to the next, and the next, and the next, until I got to number 15 Parcialidad Street. All that's left of those streets now are whispers.

Up north, when all the women got together to give me money for a ticket, I made friends with Adelina Román, General Abacu's wife, and she told me to look up her sister Raquel, who was married to General Juan Ponce. But instead of going to the door and asking for her, I sat on the curb and waited there until ten o'clock that night. It started to drizzle, and the porter came out to close up, and since I was in the middle of the doorway she asked me:

—Girl, aren't you coming in?

—No, I'm waiting for Raquelito . . .

—Raquelito's inside.

I didn't know how things worked since I was from the countryside. Mexico City is quite different; everyone tries to take advantage of you . . . The porter brought me into the tenement house and called out: "Señora Raquelito! Señora Raquelito! There's someone here to see you." She came out and I told her that her sister Adelina had sent me and said that they'd put me up.

I spent many days on the curb on Parcialidad Street while they were eating because I was an uninvited guest. When they ate, I'd go out to the curb because I was embarrassed to sit there and stare. When they were finished, I went back in and drank some water. They didn't see that I was hungry. It wasn't their problem to worry about me. I've had it really rough at times. Sometimes I ate only a tortilla.

It wasn't Raquelito's responsibility to feed me. I was just there. That's not mistreatment. Why would it be if everything is preordained by God's omnipotent hand? It was unavoidable. I didn't work for them, so I didn't have a place there. They were doing a lot for me by letting me sleep in a corner of the hallway. I slept on the floor without a *petate* or anything. If there isn't any more wax than what's burning, you have to make do. I didn't have a centavo, and Raquelito wasn't rich either. She was a general's wife, but in those days generals didn't have much money. The generals nowadays are thieves; they're rich because they steal the country's treasures! Besides, the general had died, so Raquel had only the pension from the government and it hardly covered the expense of going to collect it. She lived with some relatives on Parcialidad and the money from that pension provided for everyone. The first thing she asked me was:

—Did the government give you a pension?

—Yes, but they're sending it to my home in Tehuantepec.

—Are you going home?

—How can I?

How was I going to go home if I didn't have even a centavo in my pocket? I had only what was on my back because all my documents had been stolen. What proof did I have? Then Raquelito told me not to be in a hurry; she'd arrange for them to send my money here to the capital.

During that time, Goat Beard, President Carranza, Venustiano, was running the government. Raquel took me to the National Palace, the government house; it was filled with women, a world of women, so many you couldn't even see where to get in. All the doors were jam-packed with petticoats, widows trying to arrange to receive pensions. We went into the Presidential Hall one at a time, taking turns, into a big ballroom, where Goat Beard was sitting on a throne. I recognized him. I'd seen him up close in the taking of Celaya, where they cut off Obregón's arm. He didn't remember me, because generals see so many troops. When I went in he said to me:

—If you were old, the government would give you a pension, but since you're young, I can't give the order for them to continue paying you. You could remarry and there's no reason for the dead man to support your new husband.

I grabbed the papers that Raquel had gotten for me, and I ripped them up and threw them in his face.

—Ay, such rudeness!

—You're even ruder, worse than rude, you're a thief, because you steal from the dead. And you'll do to all the rest of the women you don't like just what you've done to me.

The secretary was the only other person in the room. He didn't say a word. I was fighting for my rights, and he couldn't have gotten involved even if he wanted to, because I was arguing with the President.

It made me real mad. I could feel the anger rising inside me and I started to sweat. What did he care if I was young or old? He had to pay me because it wasn't his money to keep; it was what the deceased had left me to support myself. But Carranza kept my money, the bastard. The revolutionaries who had gone on to Heaven were supporting him, their pay continued going to him; my husband's, my brother's, my father's, and the pay of all the rest who died because of him, because of the mess he made that sent so many people to the next world for no rhyme or reason. I hope all the generals are turned into salt and water and end up in Hell.

Since I didn't have anyone to look out for me, Goat Beard held my regular pay and my marching pay. He's the thief who screwed me. When I hear them talk about him on the radio I scream at it: "Damn thief!" His brother Jesús Carranza was a good man, but Venustiano was the worst there could ever be, evil disguised as good. Each government boasts about whoever suits them at the time. Now they call him Man of the Four Swamps, and I think it's because he had mud instead of a soul.

They forced Carranza on us like a straitjacket. He seized most of the gold Porfirio Díaz had left in the National Palace, filling boxes and boxes with gold and silver bars. Obregón's men blew up the train that ran from the villa in Santa Clara, took the money, and chased him into a trap at his ranch near Tlaxcala . . . But they don't tell you that on the radio. They talk about what suits their purpose, not what really went on, and they never mention that Goat Beard was always running from something, always fleeing . . .

Those revolutionaries make me feel like I've been kicked in the balls . . . I mean, if I had balls. They're just bandits, highway robbers who're protected by the law. When a soldier dies or deserts, they don't take his name off the list they send to headquarters in the capital. When they call the roll they pay someone a peseta to answer "Present!" for him. They sign the payroll and it's sent stating: "The troops are all present or accounted for." Sometimes they don't even have two half platoons. The colonel or the general who's in charge of that company keeps the missing soldiers' pay. They all do it, all of them, and it's the same with the horses. The allowance for a horse is more than for a soldier and the cavalry generals keep it for themselves. The soldiers walk from one place to another because there aren't any horses, they exist only on paper: "Three died and they have to be replaced . . ." That's why they all fight to be cavalry generals; in a year or two they're rich.

Why did Porfirio Díaz lose? Because he thought he had a lot of soldiers: he got the payrolls showing that his troops were all on hand, and he sent their pay, but most of them had already gone over to the enemy side. They all do it, because one is just as much a bandit as the next. Those revolutionary bastards!

Since I didn't have anyone to look out for me, I'd go out to find work, but I'd just walk up and down the streets, and then come back. I thought I was looking for work, but since I didn't talk to anyone or ask anything, because I wasn't used to talking to people—and to this day I'm still stubborn as a mule—I never got anywhere. I just talked to myself, real quiet to myself, and ideas would swirl around in my head like little balls and make me dizzy. I'd think about the past, all the huisaches I'd crossed, what was going to become of me, about how life had me hanging by a thread, and I kept racking my brain but I just didn't know what to do next. I've never thought as much as I did then; so much that my head hurt. Or maybe it was from hunger. I'd go straight up and down Santa Ana, up to where La Esmeralda, the jewelry store, is on the corner of Tacuba, and from there I'd come back again to Santa Ana Street. I wouldn't cross the street because I was afraid of getting lost, so that's what I did, over and over, one step at a time, thinking about sad things.

I walked for a long time, about ten months. I didn't eat anything. I don't know how God still has me on this earth. And later, when I was older, I'd think: "Blessed be God because I've suffered so much. I'm sure I was born for it. I've swallowed some real bitter pills, so many that I don't know how I'm still alive." It would be getting late. I'd come back to Parcialidad Street and I'd sit at the door until dark. Once everyone had gone to bed I'd go in to where Raquelito had given me permission to sleep. I'd lay some newspapers on the floor and cover up with my shawl. I did that for months, I don't know how long, because I never learned how to read a calendar. I did learn how to tell time with a watch. But I accepted it: the world is the way it is and tomorrow will be another day.

The next day or month or the next year, I don't know which, nor do I care, after going up and down the streets, God sent me a guardian angel. That girl must have seen me before, that heavenly soul that God sent to help me, because one time she asked me:

—Where're you going?

—I don't know . . .

—What do you mean? I see that you go straight down this street and you come back the same way every day . . .

I simply stood there. She kept insisting so much that I said:

—I'm looking for work.

—Don't be dumb, she said. Every door where you see this sign . . . Listen, do you know how to read?

—No, I don't . . .

—Every place you see these signs saying "Maid wanted," you can find work . . .

And she showed me where they'd put up "Maid wanted" signs on the doors and balconies. That young woman took me through the streets of Mexico City, and at every window and at every doorway where she saw a sign, she'd stop:

—Look, there's work here . . . Let's go on ahead and find another one.

And we started walking again. We got to another window and she'd repeat the same thing so I'd understand. We crossed street after street after street; she took me by the Hospital and we came back through Ciudadela. She explained a lot of things to me, everything she knew . . . And then she said:

—It's late. Let's go and eat.

—You go ahead. I'll wait here . . .

—No, let's both eat.

—I don't have money to buy food.

—Listen, I'm not asking you if you're buying the food. Let's go and eat.

She took me to the Juan Carbonero market that's near 2 de Abril Street, and she fed me. My stomach hurt, because after being hungry for so long your body doesn't want to take in food. I ate just a little. And then she said:

—Let's go to your house now.

—I live behind the Teipan . . .

The Teipan is a school for orphans close to the Santiago prison in front of Tlatelolco Park. She took me through there and I showed her Parcialidad Street:

—I have a friend who lives here!

She went into the tenement with me and started walking toward the same house where I was staying.

—Raquelito, Raquelito, she said. I have a friend here with me.

—Who's your friend?

That young woman who took me all over the streets of the city was Isabel Chamorro. She talked with Raquelito and told her that she had arranged work for me. That's when I got a good look at her, because I hadn't before. I was ashamed for her to see the hunger in my eyes. She wasn't young or old, tall or short, normal, not fat or skinny, she was a lovable little thing with short wavy hair, a nice personality, she was really good to me. I think she was poor, because I never saw her house. The next day she came early to take me to work.

The blond Spanish woman that I worked for first was the owner of a wine store across the street from the San Marcos market. She lived in a tenement house that was divided into two parts: the house on this side and the wine cellar on the other. The house was on a corner. The wine store and the warehouse faced the street, and all the rooms were in a row around the corner. The kitchen was very big.

I don't know what they filled the bottles with—it was supposed to be some kind of wine—but I never saw grapes or any other fruit. The husband managed the store, and we were over on the other side of the building. He was with the barrels and the señora was in the house.

At that time of year, there were these slugs called *tlaconetes* in all the houses, long and slimy things, and Señora Pepita showed me how they shriveled up if you put salt on them. They terrified me, and since I didn't have anything to cover myself with when I slept, I put newspapers down in the kitchen and poured salt around everything so they wouldn't climb on me. I had to do all the chores for Señora Pepita—wash, iron, clean floors. Back then the floors were wood and had to be washed every week with a brush and lye and they were painted with yellow congo every Saturday. I liked it when they were freshly painted because they looked real nice, like the yolk of an egg. First I scrubbed them so that the wood was real clean, without any dirt that would absorb the color. Then I'd paint them with a brush, two coats. The yellow congo is dissolved in lemon water so it'll stick. It made me feel pretty, as if I was all yellow inside, even though the lye made my hands peel because it had so much soda ash in it.

Every now and then when the señora went to Tepito she bought me old used dresses so I could change my clothes, just the rags they sell at the market. I had to wear them because I didn't have anything else to put on. They cost anywhere from six or seven up to fifteen centavos, depending on what she was willing to pay, and everything there was used.

Those Spaniards agreed to pay me three pesos a month. I didn't understand about the money in Mexico City, and it's a good thing, because they never even paid me a centavo. This blond woman wasn't a screamer; she didn't have any reason to yell since she was alone in the house. But she brought her stinginess from her homeland. At that time bread rolls were three for five, not like now when they cost ten. She'd buy five rolls and give me one in the morning with a cup of black tea and another one at night with tea too. I've hated black tea ever since. I like lemon tea. At noon she'd send me to buy three centavos of dough, a kilo was six centavos, and she made it into balls for me to make tortillas. She'd count them to make sure none were missing. Later she'd count the tortillas, she'd leave me three and take the rest. Sometimes she gave me beans and sometimes just the broth. She always used the leftovers, so I never tasted her cooking. She made paella and put everything from the week in it. I've never seen anything sadder-looking.

I guess I lasted there about half a year or more until I got rheumatism. I'd take off my shoes, the ones I'd gotten up north, so they wouldn't wear out; I only wore them when I went out or to run an errand, but they were already very old. Since I washed down the doorway and the patio every day the dampness made me sick. And Pepita, the Spanish woman, ordered me to leave because she couldn't have me in her house if I was sick. I got real mad, and when she asked me real two-faced what I planned to do, I said:

—I'm going to set up a stall and sell *pepitas*, which are seeds.

She just stared at me and yelled:

—Get out of here before I belt you!

It took a lot of effort to get back to Parcialidad Street because my legs had cramped up on me. When Raquelito saw me she asked:

—What happened? Why are you dragging your feet?

—I was thrown out because I can't work.

—What's wrong?

—I got crippled working at the wine store . . .

When Raquelito and her relatives saw how bad I was and that I was almost naked because the rags I was wearing couldn't be mended anymore, she went and told Isabel Chamorro, the girl who had taken me to work for the Spanish woman. Raquelito figured out how much I should have gotten from the time I started working until I left, and they demanded that the Spanish woman pay me for the time I had lasted.

—If you don't pay Jesusa the three pesos a month, we're going to take this a step further, we're going to sue you.

So Señora Pepita took eighteen pesos out of her change purse. I have no idea how many months that would've been, I really don't. Raquelito added it up and they brought me the money and that's what I lived on. Raquelito and Isabel Chamorro tried to explain about the months to me, how many days in each month,

when it was one month and when it was the next, because I was
clueless, really clueless . . .

I stayed with Raquelito while the eighteen pesos lasted, but at
mealtime I'd leave the house and eat on my own. Since some of
the people in the neighborhood spoke to me, I was getting used
to it there, and I wasn't so ashamed. One day Raquelito told me
that she was losing the house because she hadn't paid the rent.
She left with her family and there was no way I could follow
her . . .

I met the wife of a navy lieutenant near Parcialidad Street and she
took me in. Señora Coyame didn't have kids, she lived alone with
her husband, like Pepita, the Spanish woman. I slept on the floor
behind a stove. After all, I was a freeloader and had to sleep in the
doorway with the dog. They say that the dead and freeloaders start
to smell bad after twenty-four hours. I had no money, so how
could I eat? Why would they give me food? I wasn't their responsibility. They were doing a lot by giving me a corner to sleep in, in
the middle of their own poverty. No, there's no such thing as kindness, nobody's considerate, don't you believe it. Why should they
give me a taco? I didn't eat. Look, I drank water. I keep going because it's God's will. He's helped me. Even though I'm bad, God
hasn't let me down. Right now I haven't eaten since morning and
I'm still not hungry. I was born that way, so what do you want me
to do? There are debts that are owed and have to be paid. To
make a long story short, I'm used to it now.

The sailor's wife was so jealous that she sent me to spy on her
husband so he wouldn't go off with another woman. I had to follow the man, from a block away, from the Teipan to Luis Moya, to
the sailors' barracks, then to the San Miguel church, where he
worked. She wanted me to tell her who he talked to and where he
stopped and I tracked him like a dog. The poor man would go
straight to his house without turning around to look at anyone
and there I was a block behind, like the secret police following
him. Until I got bored: What is there to spy on? What did it matter
to me?

The only thing Señora Coyame lived for was her jealousy and every day it got worse. She was afraid someone would take her husband away from her, but who'd want such an ugly, dark-skinned old man. Who even pays attention to a dark man? One day I thought: "This woman isn't paying me anything. Let her live with her imagination. I've had enough." She had a younger sister who wasn't married who lived in the same tenement and when she saw that I spent all my time on the patio she said:

—Don't give up. Let's go look for work at the box factory.

—Okay, but then your sister won't let me sleep in her house . . .

—It doesn't matter. You can stay here with us in the porter's place.

I was fed up and had already thought I'd be luckier somewhere else, so I moved in with the sister and it worked out much better.

Behind the Santiago prison there was a man who hired girls with experience making boxes.

—Have you done this type of work before? the man asked me.

—Yes.

Leocadia, the porter's daughter, and the other girls told me to say yes. They had warned me ahead of time and I had to tell the man yes, but I said it very softly. I started work as an apprentice making shoe boxes. I didn't even know what cardboard was, or what color the paper was, if it had a front and back; and the paper does have a front and back, and you have to be able to tell the difference. That was the problem, because it all looked the same to me. The man was awful nice. He showed me how to tell the difference; he marked a carton for me to use as a pattern to trace and cut the boxes. After two months they put me on a machine that cut boxes. That's when the owner realized that I didn't know what I was doing, but I must have grown on him by then, because he never mentioned it. I never heard a mean word from that man. Just the opposite. He paid me fifty centavos a day. Compared with the three pesos a month I'd earned as a maid, fifty centavos a day was like a million to me.

Don Panchito went bankrupt. But he didn't throw me out on the street. He tried to teach me his trade, but I was real dumb and he disgusted me.

Don Panchito said:

—Learn how to weave wigs. You can support yourself that way . . .

—The hair horrifies me. It's from dead people. They take it off their head in the cemetery . . .

—No, woman, no . . . ! Learn . . . You don't want to understand . . .

Now that I'm older, I understand, but then I was real slow. A lot of women wore fake braids and they'd comb them out real long. I have short braids now; if I wanted to wear them long I'd buy them. But why would I want to wear fake hair as long as I have at least three strands on my head? Raquelito wore hairpieces because she lost her hair, there was hardly any there, and so she bought two handfuls. And I could see that she lengthened her hair with those long curls. Girls walked around with long braids but they weren't theirs. The whole point is to show off what's yours and not someone else's. But she'd say:

—I just don't feel right without braids . . .

—But how can you wear that hair? God only knows who it belonged to . . .

—It's been disinfected . . .

—It doesn't matter to me if it's disinfected, it's someone else's!

On Sundays I went to the movies with Leocadia. Sometimes other girls from the factory would go along with us, and for ten centavos we watched movies until eleven at night. All old movies. I like the American ones the best, the Lon Chaney ones, and even now I understand them better, because they're complete stories. The ones from Mexico are all serials, once you start getting into it, it's "THE END," you're left hanging; they just get you warmed up and boom, it's all over. That's no good. I like a story that starts at the beginning and goes to the end. Back then it took three days to see all the episodes. Now all the movies are short ones, about an hour and a half, and they cost three pesos! I'd never pay that! The movies were about love stories or adventures, always an entire story, right up to the very end. I'm not a big fan of that crap they make here in Mexico, because they aren't real movies, and the ones about the Revolution are the worst. I don't know how they can brag about the shit they come up with.

There were about ten of us who were with Don Panchito, and we left when his business went under. Since there wasn't all that union bullshit, you could get work almost anywhere, so we went to a box factory around Tepito. We made boxes for face powder. You had to cut small circles for the top and the bottom and then the strips for the sides. I didn't like it, because it was little tiny work and real slow and I liked the big, fast stuff. Besides, they paid us the same as Don Panchito: fifty centavos. But we had to make thousands of little boxes, like matchboxes but round. The girls asked me if I thought it was fair and I said:

—No, because the work is boring and we don't see the end product. This takes a lot more patience. They should pay us more for it.

The girls agreed that it was a pain in the neck, and we each took off to go our own ways. I went to work in a factory in San Antonio Abad where they offered me seventy-five centavos a day to make shoe boxes.

The San Antonio Abad factory was big. It was run by a Spaniard. There were seventy women and fifty men working there. He'd let us in in the morning and we went to our places and didn't have anything to do with each other until the next day when we came back to work. The first shift started at five in the morning and we got out at one in the afternoon, when the one-to-nine shift started. There were instructors who taught the factory workers and trained them until they could do the job alone, and foremen who watched us. They taught assembling, cutting, and lining, and there were others for tracing and cardboard covering, where you had to stretch it and cover it with paper.

Since I was the newest one there, the instructors told me that if I didn't buy drinks and drink with them, they'd ride me like a horse. I was afraid of those women. One of the boys warned me:

—Watch yourself because they're all going to catch you. There are a lot of them, and they'll climb on you and break your back. Don't be a fool. Tell them you'll buy them drinks.

The boy's name was Nicanor Servín. He was a box liner and I lined cardboard. I'd take my cardboard out into the sun on a cart after wetting it, spread it out on the ground, and when it was dry I'd pick it up and carry it on my head to hand in at the warehouse. They'd give it to me at the warehouse and I had to return it covered. Nicanor Servín was in a row with all the liners, and I'd spread the cardboard out in the front row. We didn't talk to each other there, but we talked on the way out to the street. He was a real nice boy, he didn't try to take advantage of me. He'd do you a favor without expecting you to pay him back, you can guess how. Nicanor saw how all the women were harassing me because I'd only started two days earlier and they treated me like an idiot who had just come down from the hills, like a country bumpkin. When he realized that I didn't have anyone to look out for me he said:

—You have to buy these women drinks . . . I'll lend you what you need.

I told them to leave me alone, that I'd buy the drinks. I asked for a bottle of pulque and I started pouring until they all fell on the floor drunk. They stayed right there in the factory, and was the owner mad when he found them:

—What happened here?

—You can see for yourself, señor, Nicanor Servín said.

—Who got them drunk? The new girl?

—The women wanted to jump her, so she bought them drinks. You have to decide whether to stand up for the girl or punish all of us.

The man found the instructor under a table drunk. I'd ordered two bottles, not one, and then I made them drink it all. There was no way they could've ever handled it, and they all got totally smashed. The owner punished them and they didn't mess with me anymore after that. But then I took up drinking, and when I'd leave work I'd say to them:

—Let's go have a few drinks. *Ándeles.* You're going to buy me a lot of pulque because I'm going to teach you how to drink.

I learned to drink in Chilpancingo, except then I didn't have money. When I started to get paid fifty centavos a day I still had a tough time living on it because I had to buy clothes and food. But with seventy-five centavos a day I could drink even if I didn't eat well. You could get a serving of beans and a serving of tortillas—six tortillas for three centavos, and they were big, handmade tortillas, not like that crap they sell now. So I'd buy myself tortillas and put rice and beans on top and I'd be well fed. In the morning I'd drink a mug of *atole* for a centavo and three tamales for a centavo also, big tamales, like the ones that cost twenty or thirty-five centavos now and barely have any meat in them. I rented a room that had a door facing the street and one into the patio, with a stove and a terrace. The room was number 77 San Antonio Abad, at the corner of Jesús María. They tore it down and built warehouses there. I still slept on the floor, but I had a place of my own. The *petate* cost me ten centavos and I covered myself with a new blanket that cost one-fifty. I could make myself coffee and cook beans; I took food to work. The same thing over and over! I was making progress. One time I even took beefsteaks, because you could get five big steaks for ten pesos.

I stayed at the box factory for about two years. From there some co-workers and I went to another factory over on Magdalena Mixhuca Street. At that time there was a lot of money in Mexico, and they paid in gold coins. They paid three or four of us with one coin and we'd go buy the groceries for the week at the company store, which belonged to the widow who owned the factory. We never had any money, because we gave it all back to the same business. So that shrewd widow knew how to keep her gold, we just held it for a little while. Everyone had to spend their part there to make change for the coin. You weren't free to buy anywhere else; the money went out and it came back in! And from then on, it was factories and factories and workshops and bars and taverns where they sold pulque and more taverns and cantinas and dance halls and more factories and workshops and laundries and annoying señoras and hard tortillas and more drinking; pulque, tequila, and spiked coffee in the morning for hangovers. And girlfriends and boyfriends who were worthless, and dogs that left me to follow their bitches, and men who were worse than dogs, and thieving policemen and abusive bums. I was always alone, and the boy that I took in when he was little left me and I was even more alone, say goodbye and never come back, and it isn't that way, María, turn around, and me, imprisoned in my pots and pans, but I'm not much of a fighter anymore or as mean on the streets now, because I got old and now my blood doesn't boil and I've lost my strength and my hair fell out and I just have pegs for teeth, I'd scratch myself, but I don't have any fingernails left after so many got ingrown and came out in the laundry sink. And here I am now, just waiting for it to strike five in the morning because I can't sleep and it all comes back to me, everything I've been through since I was little and I walked around barefoot, fighting in the Revolution like playing blindman's buff, being beaten, more unwrapped each time in this fucked-up life.

EVERY NIGHT after work I'd get drunk, dancing and drinking with the people from La Montañagrina. I'd leave that bar and go to El Bosque. They were right across from each other on Pino Suárez, the street that was named after the man killed along with Madero. La Montañagrina was a block long, with tables, chairs, a bar, and a wooden floor for dancing. In the winter, they put a big coffeepot over a gasoline lamp and boiled cinnamon for punch that was spiked with a lot of liquor. We'd chug it down, real hot, and get drunk and all warm inside. The punch was ten centavos at the bar and fifteen at the table because the waitresses made a five-centavo tip. You could see the men and women who came in and out in a huge mirror over the bar. The door would open and close every once in a while.

I worked as a box maker. The owner of the factory, Don Chicho, who was also a Spaniard, sent me to run his errands. One time he had me go to his mother's who lived on a street that ran into the statue of a man wearing a cape that covers his whole body. I think it's Morelos or someone like that.

On the way home it was shorter for me to cut through streets to get back faster. I heard someone say "pchpchpchchchchchch . . . pstttt . . . psssstttttt . . ." and since that's not my name and I'm not a dog, I didn't pay any attention. When the jerk got tired of going "pchpchchchch and pstttt" he caught up to me and bam, he grabbed my hair!

—I'm talking to you. You're ignoring me!

I hauled off and slapped him. That's when he reached in his pocket and pulled out a whistle and called the police. He showed them his reserve officer papers and the police had to follow his orders. They took me to the Sixth Precinct, on the corner of Vizcaínas and Niño Perdido, where I gave my statement and the chief clerk asked me:

—Why'd you hit a reserve officer?

—Why'd he insult me? This man doesn't know me and I don't know him, and the fact that he's in the reserves makes his behavior even worse. Why? He has no right to grab my hair.

—I thought you were coming from the Public Health Department.

—What do you mean, from the Public Health Department?

—Yeah, where those women come out.

—Why do I care if women come in or go out of there. It's just a street and it was quicker to go that way.

—Right, what a joke, you acting so uptight, being the kind of loose woman you are . . .

And I tried to jump on him to punch him in the face, but the chief held me back. He asked the reservist:

—Where'd you see her come out of?

He didn't answer, like he hadn't even been asked, and he said to me:

—You were coming down that street and I've seen you go by a lot of times. Don't act innocent, because I'll have you checked out . . .

The chief clerk stepped between us:

—Listen, there's no reason to pull someone's hair. Can't you tell the difference between the real thing and a fake? It's one thing for you to be an agent and another for you to act like an animal . . . No matter how much you wanted her to be one of them, she isn't what you think she is.

Between the yes she is and the no she isn't, it struck noon. I asked the judge to let me call my boss so he could explain who I was and what I was doing. When he picked up the phone I told him that I'd hit a man and been locked up:

—I'm on my way over.

As soon as Don Chicho got there I told him not to pay any fines, that I'd hit the agent because he'd done something wrong, not me. The judge was a good man. Up to that point I hadn't been detained in a cell; I'd been in the clerk's office.

They let me go at about three in the afternoon. As we were walking along, my boss turned to me and said:

—You really are trouble. I thought you just talked nasty. I didn't realize you actually got into fistfights.

—He pulled my hair first. Was I supposed to let him manhandle me? I don't even know the guy . . .

I just slapped him, but it left a mark. I could really beat the hell out of people. I don't hit anymore. I'm not a fighter, because I realized it isn't good, even if you win you end up losing; but back then my hands would even get itchy for a fight.

The owner waited two weeks before he fired me.

There used to be a park in Lagunilla next to the market that they tore down and turned into tenements. The loaders sat on the benches to eat. When the benches were free I'd sit there, and if not, I'd sit on the grass. Since I didn't have a job, I just walked around Lagunilla. A woman showed up one day to see if any of us were available. She'd already hired two girls and she took me too.

Adelina de la Parra owned a business on Netzahualcoyotl Street and I was her maid. Her house was like a store, like a restaurant, who knows what it was, but people went there to dance. I cleaned and made up the bedrooms. This was a big family: there were eight bedrooms, and there were a bunch of girls because it was a drinking and dancing place. They sold tacos, sandwiches, and drinks and they regularly had to deal with drunks and mean men. I was there just to sweep and dust, but when I finished the señora would say to me:

—Go ahead, dance, wait tables, so you aren't just standing around staring . . .

That's when I started to like dancing better than cleaning.

I'd go home at ten at night or wherever I wanted until the next

day. I usually took off for La Montañagrina. I earned my centavos
at Netzahualcoyotl but I had to pay to drink just like everyone else
who came in there. People fought all the time. Once it got really
good. I was talking to someone and a man who had fallen in love
with me came in. He was really crazy about me but I ignored him.
He was a tanner and he always smelled like tannin. His name was
Carlos something or other. "When I get here you wait on me and
leave whoever you're with." I'm sure that day I wasn't in a good
mood and I didn't pay any attention to him. I noticed that Tannin
Carlos had buzzed in like a tannery fly.

—Didn't you see me come in?

—So what? I'm waiting on these gentlemen.

He turned around and left and I couldn't have cared less. I
thought it was funny that he got so mad, so I told the piano player:

—Play "Sighs and Tears" for me.

He started to play and I grabbed one of the young guys I was
drinking with.

We were waltzing when the other one came back. He was really
burned because I'd scorned him. He was just a customer who paid
the same as everyone else. You get what you pay for. He thought
he had the right to tell me what to do. Why would I leave the people I was with?

—I'm here to work, not to pamper jerks like you.

Carlos wanted to pick a fight with my partner and I said:

—Your fight isn't with him. You have no right to attack him.

—I'm not one of your stable of studs. Anyone who messes with
me is asking to get stabbed.

—And who do you think you are? The owner of the house, the
one that pays my rent? Or maybe you think you feed everyone
here?

—From now on you take care of me or I'll take care of you
with a good beating!

—The house pays me and I do what they want; I'm waiting on
this guy and his friends. You got here too late, *manito* . . .

Uuuuyy! So he took out a knife this long, a tanning knife, and
he wanted to get into it with the others.

—I'm going to slaughter them.

—I said, don't mess with them, your fight's with me. You're a real man, *ándale*, come on . . . I have a knife too. Don't get into this, guys, I'll work it out with him! You have no right to come yell at me.

I pushed him out into the street. When they saw the knife, all the women who were working ran out with the clients. And we really got it on.

—I love you and I want you to understand me . . .

—Is it my fault you love me? I love everyone the same way. If you can live with that, fine. If not, say goodbye and don't come back!

He had a wife. I know because a couple of times he brought me his little one, who was about two years old. Can you believe the nerve? I'm sure he wanted me to raise him. That was his problem. Married men don't appeal to me; they're always complaining about how hard things are, always whining that they don't get fed on time. They say things like I really love you and she just trapped me . . . Besides, I'm a screamer, so they better not yell at me.

—There isn't anything for us to work out. Go on your way and leave me in peace. Take your kid back to the fool that bore him.

After I slapped him across the face, I bit his hand. He let go of the knife and I grabbed it and I said:

—Stop right there. Go ahead, you're a big man.

—I'm going to make you pay for this.

—If you can, go ahead and try.

He tried to drag me, so I kicked him and he rolled on the ground, and that's where I jumped on him and started hitting and biting him. I pulled his pants down and hung on to his bunch of grapes. He was screaming bloody murder! I let him go after giving his balls a good twist. He could barely move, he just wanted me to let go. He ran off covering himself with the front of his jacket.

—Get out of here!

Back then no one could handle me, even if they were stronger. I'd won because I was a cunning fighter. I felt anger burn throughout my whole body and without realizing it I'd calculate: "I'll land a punch here . . . and kick there." Youth! That's why I'm alone, because I don't like anyone to tell me what to do . . . And if you don't believe that, check with Pedro . . .

The girls would ask me:

—Who are you waiting for?

—Who is there to wait for? After all, I only have one life. If it's my turn, then it's my turn. Later is too late. I won't stand for someone coming and raising hell out of jealousy, no way. Get lost! I wait on everyone and treat them all the same as long as they pay. Let me hear the coins dropping on the counter! And I'm not falling in love with them no matter how handsome they think they are. I can't even stand most of these pains in the asses. Take me dancing, take me drinking and I can hold my own, invite me to take a spin around the city; give me enough to eat, because I like to eat and drink, but don't tell me to pay you back with what God gave me. No way.

—You think you're real tough, but your King of Hearts will come one day, the waitresses said.

—We'll see! You take it but I don't. Why should I let them use me? Even the god Huitzilopochtli wouldn't have a chance of making it with me.

I never liked any of them, ever; as friends, yes, honest friends, that's fine, but none for money. If we're going to drink, let's go, but nothing more than that, please. I had a lot of men friends and I don't regret it, because they were straight with me. I broke anyone who tried to be devious. All that crap about I want you just for myself, no way! And if you don't want my friendship, then see you later . . .

—Ay, you're unbelievable, fiercer than a female fighting cock!

The women really took it from the men. All those bastard truckers had to do was yell at them and they'd give in. They were such dopes that they let them do a lot of things that just weren't right.

—Lie down there, get going, *ándale*, come on.

It was like they thought they'd purchased slaves and the girls had to put up with it, however many times they felt like sticking it in them, and then the fools walked around idolizing the men. I know, because I let myself be used too. But that was before. I lost my foolishness when I got to the city. I said to myself: "The more you let yourself be used, the more they ruin you. And the ones who keep letting it happen deserve what they get and more. Let them swell up like donkeys that have eaten too much grass . . ."

From the time I was real young, my male friends knew what I was like, because when my father was alive they dressed me up like a man and I'd hang around the troops. My father would tell them:

—You take care of her for me . . .

—Yes, sir, we'll take care of her.

I'd hide my long hair under my hat and go out with them; singing to the guitar, serenading all the hot women, strolling through the streets of Acapulco, drinking straight out of the bottle, and no one ever laid a hand on me. It was like that when I worked in Netzahualcoyotl. I hung around with the lowlifes but we were all friends.

—Aren't you coming, Jesusa?

—I'll catch up with you.

—I'm coming too, said a quiet waitress named Rosita.

—No way!

—Ay, why not?

—The fewer donkeys there are, the more corn each one gets.

—Don't be mean!

—Damn it, girl! This is a man's thing! We don't want any whining women.

One guy was a chauffeur, another was a banker, another a policeman. Valentín Flores was a fruit vendor, he could really yell loud. He was from Michoacán and he sold his fruit from one of those wooden flatcars. When he didn't have oranges he had avocados, and if not, then cheese made from cactus fruit, or goat's milk. He also made really good lemon sorbet. If he didn't have time, then he made snow cones, which are easier. You just fill the bottles with different-colored syrups and you're ready. He'd make four or five trips through the market, and when we'd hear him shouting in the street we'd say:

"Here comes the crazy man! Here comes the crazy man!"

We took things from that poor peddler. We stole his merchandise because he was almost always drunk. He was a sweet man and we got to be friends because I stood up for him one day when all the women from the factory jumped him.

—Don't be like that, we already ate all his merchandise, let's help him get back on his feet.

He left for La Merced happy, with what we were able to scrape together for him. Something is better than nothing. He was an older man, about forty or fifty, and one day when he was really drunk, I hid his supplies. He was drunk as a skunk and he knelt down in front of me and said:

—Ay, *mamacita*, give me back my cheeses! I have to sell them.

—I'm not giving you anything, because you'll lose it.

That's when a group of people from the bar saw us and they nicknamed him Don Juan Tenorio and me Doña Inés. Valentín tied up his Dr. Bell pain medicine in a handkerchief along with the centavos he earned. But he'd buy everyone drinks and then he had to go around begging to make it back and keep selling his goods.

Valentín Flores was the nicest man I ever knew. He was poor, too willing for this mule of a life. "Keep calm and we'll awaken, *caramba*," he'd say. "I've fallen down the hill and I can't climb back up, that's how it is for us, and there's nothing we can do about it." Even though he was a soldier when Porfirio Díaz was president and he had a reputation as a hell-raiser, I still say that Valentín Flores was a kind man. They called him names like gimpy, because the Federales broke his hands when they forced him to enlist. Even maimed like that he was terrible, and when the boys asked him why he fought so much even though he was crippled, he'd tell them it was because you shouldn't ever let anyone take advantage of you. And he didn't take abuse, he really didn't. But when the police caught him drunk and took him in, he'd tell pitiful stories: "I'm a mutilated man, how could I hit anyone?" He'd move his twisted little hands like this, shaking them. So they'd let him go:

"I can't hurt anyone," he'd leave the police station saying real sad, "I can't fight," and tears would even roll down his face. It was all hypocritical because the first person who crossed his path learned what his right hook to the jaw felt like.

We had a close friendship because we were both troublemakers. Once I got sick, and he was the only one who came to make me hot camomile tea. He wrung out towels and put cold compresses on me. And because I was in so much pain, I thought: "Who cares if he's a man, it doesn't matter to me, as long as he takes care of me, it doesn't matter if he sees me the way God sent me to this earth." And if Valentín was willing to help me, then it was his problem if he had bad thoughts, but I never noticed anything while he helped me.

There was another guy, Raimundo, that we called Charalito, little eel, because he was skinny. The gang at the canteen called another one Warehouse Ladder because he was tall and straight. Raimundo Patino, Charalito, was a porter but he also sold bread at the San Lucas market and in the afternoons he went to the circus tents to sell ice, pastries, and soft drinks. He'd go to Netzahualcoyotl at about seven in the evening to dance. We were real good friends. He'd say:

—When they close here, come over to such and such place with me. We'll dance there and then go somewhere else until we're dog-tired and can't move anymore.

He was a loyal friend. And from then on I'd go with him to sell his stuff and I watched over him like a mother hen. Everyone said I was his wife, but his wife was real pretty, young, and she already had three beautiful kids with him; you could tell they were conceived in love. He'd bring the five-year-old and we'd take walks. He hung around with me but we were just friends, and screw anyone who thought the wrong thing.

All of us women who worked at Netzahualcoyotl went to the beauty shop once a week to have our hair styled in a Marcel wave. They charged us a peso and fifty centavos and it lasted all week. It was a pretty hairdo and there hasn't been one as nice since. Back then they chose the best hairstyle for the shape of your face; they

didn't just curl it any old way without knowing what they were doing. The hairdresser would look at your face and at the pho-
tographs of different hairstyles that were tacked on the wall. Then
she'd say:

—Look at this one. She has your profile. Do you like this style?

And they did your hair the right way; real tall, wavy, they used
a curling iron to make ringlets that fell down to here; curly
ringlets, round, three of them that made your face look pretty.
Even if the woman was ugly, I mean really ugly, it improved her
face. They always put five waves in my hair. I've never worn a part.
I've pulled my hair straight back my whole life. Where I'm from
only the tortilla makers parted their hair in a line straight down
the middle of their head. Why would I do that if I wasn't one of
them? I've always combed my hair back. I only wear two thin
braids now that I'm an old woman, and believe me it breaks my
heart to look at myself.

One night when I was drinking with the boys at El Bosque, an
artillery captain came in.

—Are you a waitress?

—No, señor, the waitresses are those girls over there.

—Since I saw you drinking with the boys I thought you worked
here . . .

—No, señor, I don't.

—Listen, would you like to be a waitress over in San Juan
Teotihuacán?

—I don't know, being a waitress doesn't appeal to me, because
I don't like to hassle with drunks.

—It's not a bar. You'd serve food. We serve drinks, pulque and
beer, to go along with the food. You could work on Sundays. I can
arrange the job if you won't back out on me.

—Who me?

Since it was only on Sundays, Señora Adelina de la Parra let me
go. Besides, I was free to go to the bars to drink and dance, or do
whatever I felt like after ten o'clock; the evening was mine. I've always liked nighttime. I think it's blessed.

On Sunday mornings I left for San Juan Teotihuacán and
came back that same evening. It was an hour there and another

hour back on the train; the stay was short but it was worth it. They paid my fare, besides the three-peso salary, and I made good tips. The customers were all foreigners and old at that; I never made less than twenty or twenty-five pesos plus wages. I did that for about a year. The pyramids looked like hills, as if they'd been pushed up by the Earth, and everyone who saw them fell under their spell. I climbed them once but not to the very top. We didn't have time to check them out, but they were beautiful, furry. I don't know what they're like now, but I'm sure not great, because everything in Mexico falls apart.

The restaurant was in an underground cave, sunken, you know, a big cave. Up top was a patio and you went down through there. They could sit twelve people to a table, and there were twenty-four tables. The kitchen was at the entrance, and the North American woman, the captain's wife, heaped mayonnaise and olives on the sandwiches they served. If they had a banquet during the week the owner would send someone to let me know:

—There's a dinner honoring General So-and-so. Come early.

And I'd head over.

I was still dancing and drinking at Netzahualcoyotl. But we didn't dance like they do nowadays, where they swing their whole body from one side to the other, or jump or open their legs. Back then it was real dancing, you didn't let everything hang out and shake it so much. We danced in a box; the floors had squares on them and no one was supposed to go out of their square. I danced *danzones* carefully, paying attention. I just moved my hips, not like today when they bend way down and shake, like they're having a seizure. And tangos, and waltzes and *corridos* where we went up and down the whole hall keeping the beat. They don't dance the good ones nowadays, they just do ridiculous stuff.

I liked dancing with Antonio Pérez, the driver, the most. When we got tired he'd drive me home in his car. He must have been about nineteen, or around that. We were like brother and sister, something like that, it was respectful, we loved each other a lot, and we were real careful how we treated each other. His older brother was in the military, a lieutenant colonel, and sometimes he'd say:

—Tell me, what's really going on between you and Jesusa?

—Nothing, she's a friend.

—Isn't she your mistress?

—No.

—It looks to me like both of your eyes are turning green. Why don't you bring her to the house?

—What for? So you can all say things that aren't true? No. We respect each other.

—That's not love.

—Yes, I love her, and that's why I visit her.

—Jeez, who understands you?

—Jesusa does, brother. Jesusa does.

I'D SPLIT MY GUT making fun of other people. Back then I was always looking for trouble and I'd do all kinds of things to cause a fight.

When a spiritist brother came to instruct us I figured he was crazy. He sat all the girls on chairs and they were actually stuck to them. He went into high communication with the Omnipotent Light, the Father, the Son, the Messenger Elías, and put them all to sleep. He was a young man, only about eighteen years old, thin, unassuming. I couldn't see his eyes.

One day the young man told the waitresses that he had spiritist powers.

The girls were evenly spaced around the room. He passed his hand over each one without touching them and then told them to stand up. They were able to move, chair and all, but they couldn't get off their seats. I was spying from the doorway, I watched his gestures, his movements, his expressions. I was real skeptical.

One time he said to me:

—I'm going to stick you to the chair too . . .

He struggled with me but couldn't do it. I could see him sweating from the effort. Then I said:

—See, you can't. They aren't really stuck either . . . They're just acting like idiots.

—No, we're not, we really can't get up. You pull us off. See if you can.

—Not me. I'm not going to pull you off. Let him do it, he stuck you there.

The boy said to me again:

—I'm going to glue you to the chair too . . .

—Go ahead, if you can.

He tried again and couldn't, even when he summoned all his powers. Then he got real humble:

—Lend me your will . . .

—It's yours.

He prayed, got rid of the bad currents, the rebellious spirits, and who knows what all he did to me, but he couldn't control me with his mind.

—You don't know how to give yourself up to it.

I swore at him, like a wild animal, a skittish mare. He was really young and besides, I didn't believe him. He could manipulate the others but not me. I imagine he had only one protector, Madero, and I have three really high-level ones, but I hadn't accepted them yet and I lacked faith. My protector is higher than Madero. Madero was a spiritist himself, when he was alive. The beings in space guided him and that's why he knew everything that was going to happen during the Revolution, except for the part about Huerta. This boy was Madero's mouthpiece, and the dead president manifested himself through him.

So I wouldn't miss anything, I watched that brother's gestures and listened to what he said when he prayed, what he asked for, because everything I hear stays in my mind, everything, and that stuck with me. But I didn't believe in it, so I made fun of it.

—Listen, girl, don't be a fool. Ask me for whatever kind of proof you want.

—I don't need proof of anything, because everything you're saying is a lie . . .

—I'll prove it to you whether you want me to or not. I have to control you, to overpower you.

—You can't . . .

—Ask one of your dead loved ones to give you a sign.

—I don't have any.

—Don't be foolish. Who do you want to speak to from the Otherworld?

—I don't want to speak to anyone, because I don't have anyone to talk to . . . I don't have any family . . .

—You have to. Everyone has family either above or below ground.

He insisted so much that I thought: "I'll tell him to call Pedro just for the heck of it . . ."

—I don't have anyone, but if you'll leave me alone you can call Pedro.

—Pedro who?

—You just tell Pedro I'm asking for him. He'll know.

He called him through a medium that he'd chosen from the group right there in the room, without them even knowing it. Doña Adelina had closed the business, all the doors that faced the street, so the spiritual beings would manifest themselves through the vessel, that humble waitress, right there in the big hall with all the tables and the piano. He was a very high being and when he put the medium to sleep between the Otherworld and Earth, she received the spirit. A voice spoke:

—The being that you've called says he doesn't know you . . .

Pedro was wilder than I was; either that or he wanted them to beg him to come.

—Right, I said. See what liars you are. How could he not know me? I'm not surprised that he'd insult me when I'm doing him a favor by remembering him!

The boy said:

—Call someone else. This one failed you.

—No, I'm not calling anyone. I'm not going to be the butt of your joke.

—Call another one of your dead . . . You have to believe!

—I believe in God, and only from hearsay, because I've never seen Him myself. Well, once, when I meditated real deep, I saw Him on a slope dressed in purple . . .

—Call someone else, please.

I felt like my jaws were moving.

—*Bueno, bueno, pues*, if you insist on bringing me a soul, get whoever you want.

The medium went to look among the dead souls in space and came back:

—I can't find anyone.

—Then look for them on Earth.

The medium started to agonize. She said she'd found him but couldn't reach him.

—There're too many thorns . . . I can't get to him.

The brother removed the bad aura, the currents that surround a body in space, and he said:

—You can get through now, they won't prick you.

The medium kept walking.

—I found him, he's under a tree, but I can't lift him because there's too much cactus.

She was given spiritual strength to get through the plants.

—Bring him! Bring him!

That's when she picked up the spirit and described him. She said he had cartridge belts across his chest, a big hat, squeaky brown shoes; he was average, not tall or short, not dark-skinned or white, the color of a pine seed.

They made me leave the room and closed the door. The brother ordered me to stay in the doorway.

I leaned on the door listening from the outside, and when I heard him say: "Good evening," I recognized my father's voice. It wasn't the woman who was in the trance, it was my father, like when he was alive, commanding, and it said:

—Good evening.

The boy answered:

—Good evening, brother. What can I do for you?

—Nothing. I was called, so here I am.

—We've called you. Do you know anyone here?

—I don't know any of the people present. But you just sent someone out. She's my daughter.

I was listening to all this. His flesh had already turned to dust . . . He died in 1913. The vultures, the coyotes, God only knows what other animals ate him, because my father wasn't buried, he was left under a tree in Mochtitlán. From what the soldiers told me later, that's where his company was defeated. He was leading two supply mules when he was injured. The fighting was over, so he leaned up against a tree to rest, and that's where it happened. The Zapatistas surprised him and killed him. His spirit was what was grazing in the field, surrounded by underbrush and thorns. The Supreme Being didn't have him on his list yet so he hadn't been raised up.

—Before I talk to my daughter, I want to speak to the owner of the house to ask her a couple of favors.

They call Doña Adelina. The señora also wore her hair in a Marcel wave.

—Señora, since you run this establishment I ask you to watch out for my daughter, because I don't like what she does here. Please give her a different job . . . Keep her away from drinking.

He told her that I was very young and didn't really understand people, and wasn't a good judge of character, that I was alone and unprotected on Earth, and it really upset him that he couldn't take care of me.

Señora Adelina told him not to worry; she'd look out for me.

And then the boy said to me:

—Come here, he's calling you.

I didn't want to get close, because I thought: "He's going to slap me."

—Don't be afraid, child, come closer, my father said. I want to give you some advice because I couldn't when I was alive. Do me a favor. Stop making us suffer, tone down your behavior, we're always in chains up here because of the things you do. Stop swearing and don't fight with people on the street anymore, because when you do, my wife, your mother, and I get locked up. Don't be so foolish. Control yourself.

My father didn't speak anymore. Souls don't have the right to materialize, to say earthly things. They just say two or three words so that you can understand and that's all. I started to believe after that testimony.

WHEN I WAS LYING DOWN in the room, at around three one afternoon, I saw something that looked like smoke go by and I stared at it. Who's smoking? I went to find out and I didn't see anyone. I kept watching the smoke, and then I remembered that the girl the young spiritist had put into a trance lived in the room next door! I stood up, grabbed a chair and put it in the middle of the room, and called her.

—Listen, child, come here . . .

—What do you want?

—Sit in that chair.

She sat in the middle of the room.

—What're you going to do?

—Nothing. Look at me . . .

With the force that had possessed me, through that stream of smoke I ordered her to look at me.

I didn't even know how to do it, but it must not have been me talking, because she stared at me and started closing her eyes on her own. Since I wasn't a believer, I thought: "This one is making a fool of me, but I'm going to stick her." I lit a candle. I grabbed a pin, the kind they used to use to hold a hat so it wouldn't fly off down the street on you. I put the pin in the flame and when it was red-hot I stabbed it into her arm. She didn't move. She didn't feel it. Then I stabbed her other arm. Nothing. Since she was asleep,

I thought: "It's not her. She's dead." And that's what it was. Her flesh was dead and only her brain and her soul were alive. I said:

—Are you going to answer every question I ask you?

—Yes.

I thought of dumb things, just nonsense, and I told her straight out:

—I want you to take over my body and go to the Portal de Mercedes and show yourself to Antonio Pérez, the driver, and bring him to me . . .

Antonio always brought me chocolates. He wasn't my boyfriend, but he liked to give me sweets or waxed gardenias with my name on them. I sent for him just to tease him. I kept repeating it over and over to the girl, like the sound of a rattle shaking:

—Go find Antonio. Go find Antonio for me . . . Go get Antonio, go get Antonio, go get Antonio, go get Antonio . . .

I don't remember the medium's name. I just called her child. She was dark-complexioned, fat. Right after she fell asleep she'd get convulsions and then she'd start talking and talking, even though it took a lot of effort.

Antonio was a driver in the Colmena area. Now the cars leave from there to go to 16 de Septiembre Street, near the Cathedral. There was a big store there called La Colmena, the hive, and the old jalopies parked along the sidewalk out in front. They waited there for someone to hire them or they picked people up at their residences. Not like now; now they just yell: "Taxi . . . taxi!"

She went looking for Antonio in spirit form and said:

—He's not here.

Then she moved a little in her chair.

—They say he left to take a fare to Luna and Sol streets.

—Keep looking until you find him.

—But . . .

—Ay, *hija, pues* go look for him there!

I was having fun. But that poor soul had to go flying after Antonio because it's the soul that goes out. From where she was, the soul answered through the mouthpiece of the medium.

—I found him! He's around Luna and Sol streets!

—Now that you've found him, materialize and show yourself to him . . .

She gestured to him and Antonio saw me in her.

—He's following in the car but he can't catch up to me! the girl said.

—*Pues*, come on! You come back and let him come here too.

—He's at the corner! What do I do now?

—Leave him there.

—He's honking.

And I heard a honk. I opened the balcony and I looked out and Antonio asked me:

—Were you outside?

—No, why?

—I saw you walking down the sidewalk . . .

—Well, you must be crazy, because I'm here . . .

—But I've been following you since Luna and Sol streets, where I left a fare.

The poor girl was asleep in the middle of the room, she could have died on me. A little later Antonio said:

—I'll be by at ten . . .

—All right . . .

After he left I continued with the medium until eight o'clock at night. I didn't realize so many hours had gone by. From three in the afternoon until eight at night is really too long for a brain. All of a sudden at eight o'clock she turned around. She stared at me, then she looked at the floor and said:

—Yes, yes, yes, yes, yes, yes, yes, yes, yes, yes, yes, yes . . .

When she started repeating herself, I felt like something really, really cold was entering me, like something cold was being thrown on my head, and it made me shake all over. I started to shiver and at that instant I thought: "This woman is going crazy on me!" She turned to the right and kept opening and closing her mouth saying: "Yes, yes, yes, yes," and looking at the floor . . . "Now how do I wake this girl up? What do I do? Oh my God, how do I revive her?" This went on for a long time, then she turned to me and said:

—Sister, there's a brother here who wants to talk to you . . .

I acted brave. Real fast, like I was someone special, I asked:

—Yeah? And what does he want? Who is he? Do you know him? Describe him to me!

—He's an old man with glasses, a little priest. He's sitting on a bench in a garden. He has a book in his hand, and there's a pile of books next to him.

This meant that he was in the spiritual gardens giving lessons to the other beings. That's how I understood it. I told the medium:

—Does he want to talk to me? Let him come . . . Come on, let him come through. I know who he is.

I remembered the picture of a man that Concha, the laundress in Netzahualcoyotl, had given me. Concha must have belonged to the Obra Espiritual, because she brought it to me and said:

—Listen, if you ever find yourself in a jam and you need something, ask this Father for what you want and he'll grant it to you.

I took the little picture as if it were no big deal, I hung it up and I never called him or anything, even though his face was engraved in my mind. He looked like a priest from a church.

And what happened? Ay, I felt like a rat trying to get out of a trap! I thought I was going to talk to just anyone but as soon as he entered I felt something ugly, chilling, that penetrated all the way down to my feet. I went numb. And when he took over her body the medium stood up, raised her hand, and said:

—In the high and powerful name of the Eternal and Divine Master I give you my spiritual greeting. I have come to ask who has given you permission to work with this vessel and possess a body that doesn't belong to you.

My jaws locked. I didn't know what to say.

—Why don't you answer me if you know who I am? What will you do if this flesh through which I am manifesting myself falls to fertilize the earth?

—What does that mean, "fertilize the earth"? I don't understand what you're saying . . .

—You must understand me, and I will repeat it: What will you do if this human vessel falls to fertilize the earth? I'm going to watch you. You've known me for many moons from my picture . . .

—Yes, they showed me your picture, but I lost it . . .

—I am a soul in space. I see and watch over the brotherhood of humanity.

—I don't understand what it's all about . . .

That was all I could say to him: "I don't understand . . . I don't understand a thing . . ."

—You have to understand. I have come with the permission of our Eternal Father to give you a mission. You must study every day from three in the afternoon until eight at night, but study and not entertain yourself as you have done all afternoon.

Then the Spiritual Being departed, but before he left he said: "May the peace of the Lord be with my brothers." I didn't know that I was supposed to answer: "May the peace of the Divine Lord go with you and may a ray of light illuminate you on the spiritual path," so I kept quiet. Shortly thereafter, the medium woke up from her drowsiness and neither one of us said anything. She just got up from the chair and went to her room dragging her legs.

Every day I put her in a trance. We did our chores in the morning; we hurried and at three in the afternoon when the rest of them were lying down like elephants, we were already working away at our spiritual study.

There were times when I put the girl in a trance that I really sweated it. Beings from the darkness passed through that vessel and hit and slapped me, and I didn't know how to stop them, because if you grab an entranced person with your hands it kills them. Dark beings came forward and I'd shake: "Ay, what do I do now?" But the old man, my protector, helped me a lot. He took over my brain and made me talk. That's how he taught me to distinguish between the beings from light and those from obscurity. Some spirits that had died in fights were very rebellious and came aiming their guns at me and slashing the air with their knives. It was a struggle to convince them that they were only souls, that their guns and knives were useless, and that they should stop acting like clowns. The medium was the one who paid the piper; she'd twist and writhe like she was fighting herself. You should've seen how sad it was when they realized they were souls! They'd cry. *Bueno*, it was painful to hear them. I had to pray to them to wake them up from their drowsiness and make them look at their own dead bodies!

—Light that illuminates the high throne of my father, Lord, illuminate these beings that go forward in the shadows and cannot see that light; divine light, merciful light, light of infinite kindness, lend us your help, Lord, to take away the evil.

I was learning as they were illuminated. The blindfold of darkness was removed so that they could see and then they'd let out a long sigh:

—What do you see, brother?

—A tiny light . . . like a candle on a cake . . .

—Now it's your turn, brother, to fight to make that light bigger. What do you see to your right?

—I see a man swarming with worms.

—Look closely to see who it is!

When I gave them the light they'd blink like they were dazzled. They realized that the object lying on the ground was their own body. Sometimes they were recently dead and it horrified them. Other times they'd see their skeleton already eaten away. Then they'd awaken from their lethargy and be resurrected to a life of grace. But there are tons of souls that stay in the darkness, and they're a very noisy crowd.

At first, since I didn't know what I was doing, I really screwed up and I made the medium real tired asking useless things like: "Are two and two four?" and I turned spirits against each other, stirring up quite a row. There were a lot of spirits that never spoke to each other again, because of me, even though they were father and son or husband and wife, but when my protector possessed me I began to be responsible and I stopped causing a lot of the trouble that was going on in higher space.

Later I found out that the name of the old man, my protector, was Franz Anton Mesmer.

The girls at Netzahualcoyotl began to pay more attention to me because a friend who was a banker invited me out every Saturday.

—*Ándale*, let's go for a ride.

The banker paid all of them to go with us:

—I'll give each of you ten pesos to come along.

We'd go for a drive in the car, and then after dinner he'd take each one home until he and I were alone. He called me "Mama" and he'd say: "I'm the dad and you're the mom." They got so used to the banker that they'd ask me:

—Isn't the gringo coming back?

They liked it because he never took me alone. He'd show up and say to Señora Adelina:

—I'll pay for all of them! They're not going to work now. Close the shop and let's all go dancing!

And he danced with all of them and they all tried to get him to take them out:

—My poor daughters! he'd say. Right, old lady? I need to take them out for a drive. Let's all go! Call for a car, two cars, whatever we need.

We also went to the theater and he'd ask me:

—How many girls are we going to take today, Mom?

—As many as you want . . .

—You choose . . . Girls, do you want to come with your papa and mama?

—*Bueno, pues vamos*. After all, you've been paid, Doña Adelina . . .

He took us all over Mexico from here to there, eating sorbet and pastry. The line of cars, one after the other, went to Molino de Flores, to Santa Anita near Ixtapalapa, to Xochimilco, to have a picnic. He liked to go places surrounded by us, a big man with so many women. He took us to the chinampas, the floating gardens of Xochimilco, where he hired some Indians who thought he was their god because he paid them very well. The Indians would see him coming and would run to cut ears of corn. He took us there just to eat tender buttered corn. They'd drench it in butter all the way to the very tip, and he brought a saltshaker in his pocket for us. But it had to be roasted over the fire with the leaves and all, and each person got their own ear of corn. That man was crazy about corn! Well, he was a little crazy about me too . . .

They made him roast duck in Santa Anita. We'd stop at a big house there—it's since been torn down—and there they'd ask the gringo:

—What would you like to eat?

—Whatever your specialty is . . .

—We have duck in *pipián*, which is a white chile sauce . . .

—Yes, yes, that's what I'll have . . . Mom, you go and watch so you can learn how to make it.

I asked the cooks: "Let me have the recipe," and they explained that you wash the ducks real good and rub them real hard with onion stalks until the juice penetrates, then they're rinsed again to get rid of the smell of the lagoon, and they're covered with salt, pepper, and vinegar and then browned until they're golden.

The *pipián* sauce is made separately with chile seeds, pumpkin seeds, peanuts, and sesame seeds. Once everything is ground real well you dissolve it in the broth and heat it until it boils and thickens. Then you add the pieces of duck to the pan. *Pipián* duck was made only with breasts; when he had roasted duck they'd put the whole thing in front of him on a platter, and all you heard was the sound of little bones breaking.

He was a nice man, blond, fat, tall, not old, but no spring chicken either, he was probably about forty-five or fifty. He was very attentive. He greeted everyone with a lot of fanfare. He'd kiss my hand. He knew how to treat women and was never insulting, he never argued with anyone. Do you think if he'd had bad intentions he'd have taken seven or eight girls out at the same time? Not like nowadays when they invite girls to go somewhere with a plan in mind and try to get in their pants the first chance they get. That's not good manners.

What I liked about the rides was being out in the fresh air until dawn, to see the countryside, the corn sprouting in the fields; it reminded me of the green and blue of my homeland. I always liked to get up early even though my feet got muddy, because at dawn the ground gets wet from the fog and so do you; you get soaked with water from the hills. I wiped the sleep from my eyes with tender leaves from the trees. That was how I woke up. I knew all the brambly terrain of my homeland and returned to the house only when I was starving. One of these days I'm going back all by myself to feel the rain again, the rain from the mountain, it's not like the rain here in the city that doesn't even soak the ground, it just makes it dirty.

There were two gringos who talked to me about love: the banker and a captain I met in the United States, in Marfa, a few days after they captured us. The interpreter told me:

—The gringo captain is in love with you . . . Marry him.

—Why should I get married? I didn't come here to marry anyone. I crossed the border because I was with my soldiers, not to look for a husband. I'm a prisoner, and I have to return to my own country . . . I'd have to be stupid to get married, I'm not crazy.

The banker loved me so much that he even proposed marriage. I told him:

—No, I won't marry you. Think of what that would look like, me so dark and you so fair . . .

He was from another class and birds of a feather flock together. He could've married a Mexican, but no matter how pretty she was, I assure you that one day he would look down on her.

—Jesusita, don't you want to marry me?

—There are a lot of girls here. One of them will marry you . . . But not me . . .

I thought: "Like I'd ever get married again! No way! I'd rather stay the way I am, poor as dirt!"

So I refused him, but it's better to reject someone than to have them reject you. It wasn't that I was afraid that the white people in the United States would treat me bad, but as they say, for the second time I rejected my destiny. I also said no to the tall, thin twenty-five-year-old captain who guarded all the prisoners in Marfa. I don't even know what that one's name was. I turned him down. I just said no. But it seemed the interpreter must have given him hope, because the captain kept repeating all the reasons I should agree to his proposal. It must not have been my turn. But I did have several opportunities, because besides the gringos there was the Chinaman; Juan Lei was the first to pursue me. So I guess my future could have been with foreigners.

I was very young, and when you're young you don't understand anything. You figure that the moon is cheese, that all mountains are covered with oregano. You're real dumb. Since I suffered so much with Pedro I said to myself: "You're better off alone." If the bull can lick himself just fine all alone, why can't the cow? How could I tell if it would go well for me if I was married to a foreigner? A man can be mean whether he's foreign or Mexican. They all hit the same way. They all beat you. It's like the lion and the lioness. When the lion is trying to win the lioness over, he licks her, he flatters her, he follows her around. As soon as he has her in his clutches, he snaps at her. That's how men are. As soon as they have you, goodbye flattery! As long as I don't say yes, he doesn't know what to do with me. He can't figure out where to put me. When the sieve is new you don't know where to hang it so it doesn't get damaged. Once it's old: "Crappy old sieve, you're trash, I should just throw you out." That's why marriage has never appealed to me. It's better to do without than to put up with a husband. Alone. I don't need men and I don't like them, in fact they get in my way even if they aren't near me, I wish they hadn't been born! But this tenement house is full of children, they scream so much I feel like wringing their necks. The bad thing is that there are kids everywhere, I can't get rid of them all, but it's not because I don't want to.

Señora Adelina de la Parra had one foot in the stirrup to take off with one of General Obregón's soldiers, and she didn't have anyone to leave in charge of the house. No one wanted to take over because it was a big responsibility. Would you want to be left with someone else's business and have to keep the place stocked, receive clients, pay the help, and be sure to always have friendly girls for the men? Doña Adelina was the kind of woman who was sweet as molasses with the clients and the truth is, I wasn't. She was one of those who were more than willing to put up with snorting men. She took up with a major, and the gullible woman believed everything he told her. I had a different disposition. I didn't let anyone take advantage of me, at least not after I realized what being abused was, which paid off for me in the end. Señora Adelina trusted me and left me in charge of the business; I had to run the whole house as she had. So I was stuck with Netzahualcoyotl.

—I'm going away but I need the house to keep running. I'll leave you an inventory, this is it: tables, chairs, piano, saloon, girls. You have to give it back to me the way I've left it to you. I'm not asking you to improve it, but don't let it go downhill. Sign the inventory list if you're in agreement.

When they saw that I earned a pretty penny, the other girls were sorry they hadn't said yes to Doña Adelina. I had to move from my house on Granada Street, in Tepito, to the Netzahual-coyotl house. I looked after the eight rooms and the dance hall, I paid the ten waitresses and put up with their dirty looks, kept an eye on the kitchen, and stocked the pantry. I bought everything the help needed, wrote down in an accounts book how much money the girls took in and what they spent. I don't know how to write, but I do know about numbers. Each month I divided up the money in the register. One part for me, and then Doña Adelina's share: twenty-four pesos a day after paying the rent. When I started working as a waitress I made a peso a day, but when I took over the business there were nights when I came out with three hundred, four hundred, and up to six hundred pesos. And God willing, it would keep coming! On the first floor of the house there was an extra kitchen, and Antonia, a policeman's woman, asked me if she could rent it. She set up a tortilla shop and paid me eight pesos a month. Since I lived there I thought it would be easy to keep an eye on her and her cop boyfriend who came to spend the night next to the stove.

When Obregón's men returned, Doña Adelina de la Parra showed up and I gave her back her house, she went over everything and nothing was missing; her furniture was all there. I told her what the maids were then making, and the laundry woman, the girls, and the cook, because I had given them all raises. I gave her all the linens she'd left me, and others that I'd had made: sheets, bedspreads, tablecloths, everything that had worn out. The rest I returned the way she'd left them.

—Here are the keys. Check over your things so that you won't say you're missing something later on, not even a hairpin.

—Don't you want to stay on?

—*Pues*, to tell you the truth, no, because I need some space. I stayed because you wanted to leave, but since you're back, I'm moving on. I have a right to some time off. Since you went away I haven't even gone to the movies or anywhere else. I spent all my time taking care of the place so there'd be women and drinks and dancing . . . Ay, señora, before I forget, I rented out the downstairs kitchen that was empty to a woman who makes tortillas. She lives with a policeman, and we're safer here that way.

—That's fine.

I went to see the woman who sold tortillas and told her:

—*Bueno*, Señora Adelina's back and she knows that you've paid your rent; from now on you give her the money, because I'm off . . .

I went on my way. But I didn't take time off like I'd said. I just wanted a rest from all the partying; I was fed up with that dump and all the drinking. There wasn't a lack of places to work, so I started at a dish factory.

AT THE FACTORY on Cuauhtemotzin and Daniel Ruiz streets they separated the good ceramic dishes from the bad. When it came time to fire them, they put them all in the oven together, whether they were good or not, but after they came out of the kiln, the good pieces went to one side and the bad ones to another.

When I left the factory I'd go by a workshop and I'd stay and watch the carpenter, until one day he asked me:

—Do you want to learn?

—Sure, if you'll teach me.

That's how I learned the varnishing trade in my spare time. The varnish is made of shellac mixed with alcohol. You stain the wood with whatever color aniline you want, walnut or mahogany was the most common. I'd take my rag—a little bag made out of a rag stuffed with wool—I'd soak it in varnish and go back and forth, real evenly, not letting the rag stop, so it wouldn't bubble. You have to let each layer dry a little while, and then you give it a light coat of linseed oil so it stays smooth. I learned how to make Austrian furniture from Don José Villa Medrano, who was from Guadalajara. It's the kind that's woven with cane and secured on a lot of little pegs, like the ones on a guitar that you screw tighter to tune it. That's how you tighten the reed, stretching it out straight first and then pulling it across the frame, until it groans and cries like a person. The third layer goes diagonal; I'd add another layer to make it strong. It's meticulous work; that's why cane furniture is so expensive. Back then the carpenter charged twenty-five pesos for each chair, but he did really fine work. He let me use whatever I wanted, but I heard what he charged. And he was right to do that, because it took a long time to weave one of those rocking chairs.

In those days I was really awful. If people bumped into me on the sidewalk, I'd hit them. They'd turn around to ask why and I'd swear at them, I'd say any nasty thing that came into my head; like if they didn't fit on the sidewalk, get off and walk in the middle of the street like burros. Nowadays people still bump into me, but since I'm not the animal I was before, they shove me and step on me, and I take it. I say:

"*Bueno, pues* we're in a crowd." Before, when someone stepped on me I'd smack them with whatever was at hand. I lived the life of a viper.

Back then some people rode in carriages pulled by horses or mules, with a driver in the coachman's seat. For fifty centavos you could ride in a carriage. At one or two in the morning when I came out of the saloons, I'd get into one of those carriages to be taken home.

—Hey, sleepless charioteer, I'd say to them. Drowsy coachman, take me through the city!

And the poor driver would take me all over Mexico City until he got tired of hauling me around and would leave me back at the door of the saloon. By my way of thinking I was back where I was supposed to be and I'd grab my bottle again and continue walking, and halfway through every block I'd stop for a drink of raw brandy, because in those days, even though I liked pulque, there weren't any *pulquerías* open at night. So I drank whatever there was, and when there was nothing else, *pues*, beer. God only knows how I got to Daniel Ruiz Street, but I got there.

That was when they put me in Belén for the first time. I've been in all the police stations, and all the jails, but they only arrested me once in Mexico City.

That day I was coming back from the movies, not from dancing. It was early: eleven at night. I usually left the dances at three,
four in the morning, but from the Rialto movie theater—which
used to be called the Politeama, in front of the Salto del Agua
church—I left early, I was with Guadalupe Escobar. We were almost home when an asshole who had been bothering us at the
movies followed us and pulled my hair. He thought that I'd be
nice to him, and I turned around and whacked him! I slapped
him across the face. I had my hair down because I'd bathed and
he had the urge to pull it. I used to have long, pretty hair, not
these puny braids. So I slapped him. Insolent men, they see a
woman alone and they think she's looking for it . . . They're always
so offensive, like that's just part of being a man. It's the Mexican
disease: they think they're great horsemen because they mount us.
But they're wrong, because we're not all their tamed mares. Of
course, a lot of men say whatever they feel like to women and the
women laugh and go along with it, and then take off with those
rude men. I saw that drunk near the doorway to my house and it
made me mad that he was following me, so I took the crossbar off
the door and hit him on the back. It was almost as big as a beam
and I think I hit him on his side. He turned to run, and I chased
him and hit him again; that blow landed real hard. For some reason he ran into the wall, the kind made of coarse dirt, and a
chunk scraped his face, and I kept hitting him. He was with another guy and they took off down Niño Perdido Street, so I chased
them. Then I thought: "They're going to call the police."

The cops came asking for me and the neighbors said:

—She lives there in that room.

At the movies I was wearing a white dress and had my hair
down. But when the drunk went to get the police I changed my
dress and put my hair up in a bun, so he didn't recognize me
when I opened the door. He said:

—No, she had her hair down and was wearing a white dress . . .
It's not her . . . No . . . It was someone else . . .

Since the neighbors were snooping and saw the fight, they
said:

—She's the one who hit him.

Those sons of bitches turned on me. I said:

—I don't know him . . . I've never seen this man . . .

—You still have to come with us . . .

—*Pues*, I'll go, but I don't know this man.

And that's all they got out of me: "I don't know him."

Guadalupe Escobar was inside my house, since it didn't occur to her to go home, so they took both of us to the Sixth Precinct. There weren't any paddy wagons back then. They herded us through the streets, but no one recognized my face because I covered it with my rebozo. The police brought us up in front of the judge at the Sixth, which is where the Green Cross is set up; it's an organization like the Red Cross, on Independencia and Revillagigedo. Guadalupe said the same thing I did, but the drunk said that a woman had hit him but he didn't know if it was me or not; then they asked him if he knew Guadalupe, and he said no. Around midnight they brought us out and in his second statement he said that three women and two men had beat him.

That's where he made his mistake; it wasn't the same story he'd given before; and then at three in the morning they brought us out again and in his third statement he said there were six women and five men. *Pues*, a few more and it would have been an army, with mistresses and all! They caught him in a lie because he didn't stick with his first statement and he thought that the more people he added, the better off he'd be, but he screwed himself. They didn't believe him. He kept saying:

—*No, pues*, have the men come out too . . .

So they sent us back to the cells, to wait for the next statement! The drunk kept insisting that there had been men!

—*Pues*, where are these men? I asked the judge.

The last time they brought us out I started to argue:

—How do you think I hit him?

Even though I tried to wash my hands of it all, they brought the crossbar in, the splintered stick that I had beat the hell out of him with. That's why his whole back was bruised. They didn't think a woman could have hurt him like that, which is why they listened to the drunk's story! After the last statement they sent me to Belén and they took him to Juárez Hospital. His friend had been with him, but when it came time to give a statement he didn't want to say anything. He told the judge that he hadn't noticed what they had hit his buddy with, so they didn't lock him up, they just detained him in a cell, in the men's section, but later I heard him say to the injured guy:

—You see, man, you're an idiot, you buried yourself . . .

—No, there were a lot of men and a lot of women who beat me. One person couldn't handle me, much less a woman.

—You've screwed yourself. You didn't know how to give a well-connected statement and that's why we're in the slammer. It's your fault; you sentenced yourself for being an asshole. So I don't have to say anything, because it's all written on that asinine list you made up. That's what you get for trying to be so macho; it'd be better to say this bitch hit me and that's the end of it, no way. Your honor, this one just put the noose around his own neck.

The jail in Belén was a big square. The women's section was way in the back, huge wards covered with metal roofs. The jail wasn't ugly inside, or sad. *Pues*, how could it be sad if all those women were there? That was their home; they could sing, dance, and everything . . . It came to be like the men's jail. They had all the festivities too. What was there to worry about? They ate, slept, walked around, they had women, and there was a room for conjugal visits. *Va, pues* they had all the entertainment they could want! You can't call that a prison! The one in my hometown when I was growing up was a real prison! There were real prisoners there. The inmates didn't have any amusements. They didn't even see a shred of the sky! Just so you know, in Belén even the women had conjugal visits, and not just with their husbands, let me tell you! They didn't make us do chores either. You just hung out on the patio or lay down or sunned yourself or whatever you felt like doing . . . The jailers didn't get into it with anyone; they watched us from a distance. They'd just point to you. The only bad thing was that each new prisoner was put in the shower.

—Get in there, said the jailer.

—Let's get in! I answered. Like I was going to take that! And I got nasty.

—You bathe yourself or we'll bathe you!

—Why do I need to bathe? Do I look dirty to you? Wash down the drunken women who come in off the street covered with vomit. You have no right to put me in your filthy bathroom.

—Don't tell me what the law says!

—Don't you try to order me around just because you feel like it.

We were about to grab each other.

—Go ahead, I said. If you think you're that brave, go ahead, let's go at it, let's see how it turns out! We'll end up in the shower together. Come on!

When she saw I wouldn't take it, she said:

—*Bueno, pues* I'll let it go . . .

—There's nothing for you to let go of, because I'm right. I'm not dirty.

And I walked away. Guadalupe Escobar said to me:

—Shouldn't you at least thank her?

They did bathe Guadalupe, because she was always such a dope, she let people take advantage of her. There were showers there and they'd force you into them. But I was like a mad dog and I wouldn't go. Later, they told me to get in line for food.

—I'm not lining up, because I didn't come here to eat your shit . . . They're sending me food from outside . . .

Lola Palomares brought the basket to the door for me. Lola was the woman who helped me, like she did for a lot of the women at the factory.

There was a man in the prison who organized the baskets for both male and female prisoners. He put them all on a cart and then delivered them. They called him *canastero*, the basket man, and everyone really liked him. Lola saw them take me to the police station and she made me food. In those days, since I had a different job than I do now, I had someone do my washing and ironing, and make my food; I just did my job. I went to the dish factory, came home, and the cook had my meal ready. The plates and cups were mine because I've always liked having my own, but I didn't cook for myself.

—Don't be difficult. Just get in line for food. We have kids and we're hungry!

The next day I got in line to get food for the poor women who didn't get enough to eat, since there was such a commotion of prisoners. They gave you a ladle of soup, another one of garbanzos, another one of beans, another one of broth with meat, two little rolls that cost twenty centavos now and used to cost five. It wasn't bad! The prisoners were real poor. Some of them didn't even get that much to eat on the outside.

We slept two to a bed, Guadalupe and I, because we were friends. If not, I'd have been assigned to someone else and God help me. We were always together. She didn't work, because she had a husband, so we just hung around together. Her husband was in the cavalry. He'd given her permission to go to the movies, and when we got out of jail he got mad at her. He said: "When you saw they were taking Jesusa away, why'd you follow her?"

We were in for seventy-two hours, which is the legally required time. I didn't go back to the dish factory after that because everyone knew I'd been in jail.

I had a child with me at the box factory where I got my next job. The boy's mother and I lived in the same tenement, but she couldn't take him to work with her because she made tortillas in a restaurant, but they let me bring him to the factory. I tied him up in a box under the big table where I cut the sheets of cardboard. I left the little one there and didn't think about him again during work. He never cried. The boy's mother was a girl from a village. She wasn't a friend. I don't have friends; I never have had friends and I don't want any. I took the little boy in and I had him with me for three years. His name was Angel and he had cataracts on his eyes.

One night his mother said:

—I'm going to my village for a few days' vacation . . .

—Fine . . .

They'd been out in the sun all day when all of a sudden there was a real cold hailstorm, and since they were far from the place where they had to catch the bus, the boy was already sick when they got back. No, I didn't heal him, I couldn't, I didn't have that power yet. He died of pneumonia on us, and then I didn't have a little boy anymore.

I wasn't sad when he died. Why? Thank God he wasn't suffering anymore! I didn't feel lonely, and I didn't miss the bother either, because no one bothers me. I teach everyone—the kids, the animals, the police, the hens and the chickens—not to be bothersome and to understand me . . . That's why it seems strange to me that children don't obey their parents, but it's because parents don't know how to make them behave and they don't teach them to be respectful.

I was left with three little shirts that belonged to Angelito. I still have them.

I also took in a dog when I worked at a box factory, and he turned out to be a very good watchdog. He was a stray, and when I started to give him bread every day, he got attached to me and he'd come inside and climb up on a chair that I had next to my bed and sleep there. I never knew the dog's name. I used to talk to him: "Yellow, come up here, Yellow." He'd come when I called and fall asleep on the chair. He'd wake up later and take a walk around the area. He took care of me. He wouldn't let anyone get near me. That dog didn't eat meat, just biscuits or rolls. I told the lady at the store to give Yellow bread when he came around and the three of us had an agreement. I'd go to work and I'd remind her as I passed by:

—Give my dog bread.

—Yes, Señora Jesusa.

The dog would show up every day. If they didn't give him all his bread he wouldn't leave the store. The bread was two for five centavos; he ate six rolls or five biscuits.

When I came home from work, I'd go by the store and the owner would say:

—I gave your dog bread.

Yellow would be at the house lying by the front door, waiting for me.

—Did you eat?

And he'd shake his head.

—Have they fed you? Let's go find out.

If he went to the street I knew that he hadn't gotten all his bread. I'd follow him to the store.

—The dog didn't get all his food.

—Well, maybe not . . . There were a lot of people here, so I don't remember, but the dog must know . . .

And then she'd say:

—Look at that fussy dog . . . He knows that I didn't give him all his bread!

—*Pues*, he's hungry, his gut tells him . . .

Animals are real smart. They can't talk but they can make themselves understood. Yellow was an old dog when I took him in. He never bothered with female dogs and he was around for only a short time.

One day, when I got back from the factory, I found him waiting for me behind the door, dead.

To ONE SIDE of the Campo Florido church there was a circus where a Señor Manuel worked. He danced. They called him Robachicos, the boy stealer. He earned good money, but he got sick and moved in with Señora Lola. One time when I showed up to fill my belly, the cook said:

—Poor Manuel Robachicos! He can't work at the circus because his feet are hurt.

—*Bueno*, let him go to the doctor to see what they can do about it.

—How can he see a doctor if he doesn't have any money?

Back then doctors charged whatever they felt like, and bleeding heart that I was, I said:

—I'll give him money to take care of his feet.

I felt sorry for him because all his friends dumped him—they didn't like his peculiarity of taking up with young boys.

I went to the circus every day and I got to know Manuel Robachicos because he'd say:

—Help us out. Come on and dance, because Winged Foot didn't show up . . .

—But I haven't even learned the number you're doing.

—Watch me so you can dance with me. That way you'll learn . . .

Every time his partner wasn't there he'd bring me up on the

platform, which was like a theater stage. The whole roof was made of canvas, like the circus tents, held up by tall poles.

We did the apache dance, which I understand in another country is a streetwalker's dance; a hooker, that's what I figured, because before I went on, Manuel would give me a change purse. In the show the man wants the woman to give him the money and then while dancing he pulls her hair, hits her, squeezes her, he crushes her, he feels her up, and she ends up all disheveled and full of bruises. When he finally threw me to the ground, it was a relief. Then he'd lift up my skirt and take the coins from my stocking. I don't know who invented that dance, but it must have been a savage. Manuel taught me well, and he was so good at beating me that the people would really applaud when they saw me looking like a bruised tomato; they wanted an encore but I couldn't even stand up for the applause.

I had to wear a special outfit and pretty femme fatale makeup. He wore white pants, a black shirt, a checkered cap, and a red scarf around his neck. They gave me something like a silk handkerchief that I danced with, and he'd wrap it around my arm. Sometimes he'd act like he was going to choke me with it. *Uy*, I really liked that move a lot! I liked dancing hard and being really free. Manuel had a lot of artist friends, but he was the only one who danced. He had his own style, a cute butt, he could move his hips like nobody else. Back then there were a lot of circuses, and great artists came out of them. The gold confetti, violet, red, and yellow lights, the shiny curtains dazzled everyone. The master of ceremonies was real polite to the audience. He'd greet them: "Honored guests . . ." And then he'd sing. But the benches squeaked . . . His hair shone just like the curtain, from so much Vaseline. "Ladies and gentlemen, I'll sing you this heartfelt melody . . ." They banged the cymbals between each number. A lot of famous performers crossed that stage. They told dirty jokes, danced on their heads, and sang *cuples* to make names for themselves. I really had a good time. Later, when all Robachicos's friends saw that he had no work and no money and they didn't bother to help him, I felt sorry for him, so I said:

—Poor man, he doesn't have anyone to take care of him!

He had a mother and brothers and sisters, but they didn't want anything to do with him because of the career he'd picked, the bad path he'd chosen to follow, and since Manuel was friends with Enrique, Doña Lola's son, he moved in with them. Doña Lola told me that she was going to take him in because someday her son could be in a bad way and this way there'd be someone to help him out. And I joined them like a pious Martha:

—Listen, Lola, feed him. I'll pay you for Manuel's food.

It cost me one-fifty to eat, and with the dancer's food, it came to three pesos a day that I was paying for expenses. Manuel didn't get better. The sores on his feet got bigger. He was in the fourth stage of syphilis, so he stayed in the house talking to Enrique, who was about eighteen years old.

—Lola, aren't you afraid your son will turn queer keeping that kind of company?

—Ay, Jesusita! What can I say? To each his own. Women now are so filthy that a young man doesn't know which way to turn . . .

Don José de la Luz, who rented the house to us, was really a fag. He told us himself:

—I wear pants but I have the misfortune of being a woman just like you.

Don Lucho was a good person, because effeminate men are nicer than the macho ones. It's as if their misfortune of being half man and half woman makes them better. He had a good heart and he was real decent. At the house he dressed like a woman. He danced in an affected manner. In the evenings he'd dress up for his friends. He put on earrings, his necklace, his stockings, and he was very attractive as a woman. No, it didn't matter to him if we saw him. Why would it if he felt like a woman? He'd dress like a man to go out, but in the evening a lot of friends would come visit him and then he talked like he was a woman:

—Ay, this hurts here! Darling, why are you late?

He was a real clothes horse like us girls—beaded embroidery, sequins, organdy, taffeta, gold and silver embroidery twists—and he could unfasten anything in a flash, nothing ever got stuck. The

powders, the lotions, the unpolished tortoiseshell, the curls. And
so what? That was what he liked. Sometimes I dress like a man and
I love it. I just can't wear pants; first of all because I'm old and second because I don't have any reason to be clowning around, but if
I had a choice, I'd like being a man better than being a woman.
It'd be better for all women to be men, for sure, because it's more
fun, you're freer, and no one makes fun of you. A woman isn't
respected at any age, because if you're a girl they tease you and
if you're old they mock you, everything sags and you're the butt
of jokes. On the other hand, a man dressed as a man comes
and goes; there's no one to stop him. It's a thousand times
better to be a man than a woman! Even though I did everything
I wanted when I was young, I know that everything is better for
a man than for a woman. God bless the woman who wants to be
a man!

Manuel Robachicos wasn't effeminate; he just ruined himself.
Maybe women repulsed him because he had syphilis, or maybe he
was gifted and so he dedicated himself to little boys. He had a lot
of fun with them and said that men were cheaper than women
and more imaginative. Since he wasn't used to paying for things
anymore, it had gotten easy for him to get it out of whoever would
let him:

—Come on, don't be mean, Tehuana. Give me money to buy
cigarettes . . .

—All right, Manuel . . . all right . . . Don't worry, I'll give you
money for your vices.

He always asked for money for cigarettes, but he never had
enough. And I was always giving him more. It wasn't that I liked
him so much or that I approved of his taste, but I had compassion
for him. *Pues*, then he started to put on weight, and it wasn't a
matter of giving him centavos when I could; it became an obligation. He'd send someone to get the money for his expenses in an
arrogant way! Señora Lola's son would come to my room:

—Tehuanita, Manuel wants to know where his money is.

—There it is.

And I'd grab the peso and give it to the boy. It went on for a

long time: the cigarettes, the doctor, the medicine, and the bundle of five-cent candles. Every day he lit a row of candles. That's
when I started disliking him. One day he brought me a little tablet
and said:

—Paint the good friend here.

—Who's the good friend?

—*Pues*, so-and-so . . .

—I don't know how to paint and I don't draw and I don't have
any business with that man, so I'm not painting anything for
you!

—What do you mean? So you don't want to do me the favor?

—No!

When he asked me to paint that face, I realized that he had
started talking with the devil. That day he made his drawing with
black chalk on wood. He painted horns and the bald head and
then he added a tail under the balls and he twisted it around to
the other side . . . He still kept insisting:

—Come on, come light a candle to the good friend.

—Me? Who, me? He's not my friend, I don't even know
him.

Since I didn't do what he said, he became my enemy. I didn't
want to be on his side or help him with that bullshit. But you
never know what the real truth is.

He painted his figure and he lit candles to him. When he
didn't have any money for candles he made a little hole in the
wood and put a cigarette in it and kept on praying for his evil
ways.

On Sundays I was supposed to give him money to go to the
bullfights and to eat with his boy. I liked the bullfights too and
had a friend who was training to be a matador. He made a living
collecting used clothes from people and selling them in Tepito,
but when they called him, he'd go fight bulls. I remember his
name: Jovito, and they called him Bitoque, spigot-head. I don't
know what his last name was. Poor people don't go around asking
each other for last names, because some people don't even have
them. Since I liked the bullfights so much, I could understand

how Robachicos did too and I gave him money to go. The bad thing was I always had to pay for two tickets.

One day I got home in the morning after dancing all night, and my feet were real tired; I lay down at five to get up on Sunday, so of course at eight, nine in the morning I was sound asleep, and that Sunday, Robachicos had the nerve to send Doña Lola's boy to ask me for money. I was dreaming that I was marrying a toreador who had just come from the plaza . . . Wait, I think it was a picador who came riding into my bedroom, horse and all! I didn't know what to do with him because he was bloody with a real long lance, when all of a sudden I hear knocking on my door:

—Who is it?

—Me . . . Manuel wants you to send him his money . . .

—Tell Manuel I'm sleeping, and don't harass me.

I thought: "Let him wait till I get up." I wanted to keep dreaming about that picador.

He came back in about half an hour, acting cocky: Manuel needed the money now because it was getting late for him to make the matinee.

—Who does he think he is? If he doesn't like it, he can harass someone else . . . !

Who knows what Manuel told him, but the boy came back:

—Manuel says that if you don't send him the money you're going to grow horns and a tail . . .

—He can go to hell! Leave me alone and let me sleep!

I went back to sleep, but I didn't dream about anything. I was so mad I didn't eat at the cook's house. I ate Chinese food. Nowadays they don't give you half the amount of food they used to.

Enrique—*bueno*, we all called him Quique—came back that afternoon for money to go to the bullfights.

—Tell Manuel that I don't have any. They don't pay me until tomorrow; he has to wait . . .

—But the bullfights are today, not tomorrow.

—Then he can screw himself . . .

I did have it. I just thought: "I'm not giving him anything." The boy came back later:

—Manuel got mad and said this is going to cost you . . .

—The only thing that costs me is what's hanging on to me trying to bleed me dry . . .

—I warned you, Jesusita . . . That's what I heard him say . . .

I never stopped dancing during that whole time. Every night I was out kicking up my heels. The days I went to the dance hall, I really had a ball: Mondays, Thursdays, Saturdays, and Sundays I went to the big halls. One Monday we got back at around three in the morning. We'd go to the coffee stand on the corner and drink spiked black bulls. Back then there were a lot of corner stands, and we'd put away a couple of shots before going to bed. You sleep great after that and you dream about funny things. We'd sit in the doorway and I'd watch for the police so we wouldn't get picked up. A woman couldn't be out at all hours of the night back then. I don't remember who was president—I think it was Obregón—and he decreed that any woman who was on the street at nine o'clock at night would be taken to jail, even if she was on her own husband's arm. If she didn't have the marriage license, they'd take her away from him and lock her up. So that's why we hid. We'd go to the dance in a horse-drawn carriage; we knew the drivers and they'd come back for us at three in the morning and bring us home.

That night we went to a coffee stand. We set our chairs right next to the stand and I was in the middle chair, when I saw a face look in, the face of a young boy. He was there only a little while. I saw his hair was combed back, curly, he was real young and real handsome. I asked the two with me:

—What's with this one? Is he spying on us?

There were three of us who had gone to the dance, Josefina, Panchita, and me, and we were just killing time. They weren't so young; they were already tough. I repeated what I'd said:

—Is this one spying on us?

—Who?

—That fool that just looked in.

—Which one?

—*Pues*, didn't you see him? He just looked in here.

Panchita said:

—I didn't see anything . . .

And Josefina said:

—Me either.

I kept watching. Then I saw him stick his head in farther, and you could see his bow tie, his white shirt, and his black jacket.

—You two may not see him, but I'm looking right at him.

—You're seeing things!

We were arguing about it when he leaned all the way in. He was real elegant, wearing a coat with tails.

—Look at him, look at him! You can see his whole body.

I ran out to the middle of the sidewalk to try to catch him. I was a fighter and real mean in those days. What did I catch? Nothing. I couldn't find anything. He disappeared on me. I asked my friends:

—Where'd he go?

They just stared at me.

—He looked in here three times. I saw his black tails . . .

Josefina thought it was something bad. She said:

—*No, manita*, you know who he is? He's the good friend.

—Which one?

—Don't act dumb, it's the good friend, the one that goes around taking leave of houses. Don't you see it's four in the morning?

—Well he can say goodbye to whoever he wants, wherever he's been visiting, but not to me. What business does he have with me?

—Don't you understand? Holy Mother of God, it's the devil!

And she crossed herself three times.

—What?

—You saw him yourself, it's the devil. It's four in the morning and he's going around saying good night.

—Why should I care? He can go to hell! Which one of you called him? I didn't call him. Why is he coming to say goodbye?

—He goes to houses whether he's called or not. He knows who his friends are and you're one of the gang, like it or not.

Manuel was calling him to hurt me. Manuel sent Barabbas to

me. The next day the pain started, but I didn't worry much about it. I said: "I get this pain and I get that pain and that's the end of it."

That day I went to the chapel because I wanted to ask about some friends who were traveling outside of Mexico City. There was a spiritist on Luis Moya Street where my protector, Mesmer, worked. I'd met him through those same friends from the factory, José and María Sánchez, who gave me the address.

I went every now and then to find out things that were important to me. Once in a while I took Antonio Pérez, the driver, who also belonged to the Obra Espiritual. I called him through the magnetic fluid and he'd show up. He said all of a sudden he'd have the desire to come to wherever I was. I told him I was casting a spell on him and he'd laugh. I said:

—One day I'm going to turn you into a burro . . .

—Let's see. Do it right now!

—Not now . . . One day when you're not expecting it.

I just said it out of meanness. I couldn't really turn him into a burro. It's only a saying. I was the one who planted the Obra Espiritual in Antonio Pérez. He didn't talk or anything; he just went along and watched. I talked when I had some type of spiritual communication with my protector. I went to ask things, to see what he wanted to know, the kind of answers you give your brothers in space. As soon as I went in, I'd ask the woman who handed out tickets for an appointment; she'd give me my ticket, I'd wait, and when it was my turn, I'd go in. I greeted my protector and asked my question: "Did José and María Sánchez make it to Tampico all right? They haven't written since they left . . . Can you give me any word on how they're doing? I'm worried about them." And instead of answering me the medium said:

—Who did you see? Who did you see at dawn?

—I didn't see anyone . . .

—Of course you did.

—I don't remember seeing anything . . .

I didn't think anything of the question.

—You did see someone . . . Three times.

I sat there thinking: "What did I see three times?"

—You saw something last night . . . Remember?

And the medium kept insisting, she kept saying yes and I kept saying I don't know, so finally I asked her:

—Does this have to do with what happened in the courtyard?

—Yes, that's what I'm asking you about . . .

—Ay, *pues sí*, you're right. The face I saw . . .

—Do you know whose face that is?

—No, I don't. I only saw down to his waist. I was able to see his suitcoat . . .

—That's Brother Lucifer, the one who's watching over you because you've done someone a favor and it hasn't been understood as a good deed . . .

Everything got foggy on me. I didn't remember about giving Manuel Robachicos food.

—You did something good and it was repaid with evil . . .

—What do you mean?

Then she started to explain:

—You did a favor, but you didn't take into consideration who it was for . . . You caused yourself a lot of trouble because that brother wants to take your money from you. Next time, when you do a favor, do it for a woman who needs the help, a co-worker, but no more for this one who isn't even a man . . . who's bad, not a good person at all . . .

Then I told my protector:

—I want him to come back tonight so I can talk to him once and for all; I want him to explain what the hell he wants from me, that's why I need to talk to Brother Lucifer . . .

I wanted to see him. He's a man, and real handsome; young, because Barabbas isn't old. He's about twenty-five. They say he descends to Earth in the shape of an animal, but I saw him as a man. They call him Lucifer or Luzbella, beautiful light, because he's so good-looking.

Then Mesmer, my protector, told me not to get into it with him, because the devil wins a lot of souls through both good and evil.

—Don't be afraid. We're just going to let the devil in partway, so that he knows that he doesn't have power over you . . . He can't do you any harm. On the contrary, he's the one who's going to get slammed. You're going to feel real bad, maybe even like you're dying, but don't be afraid, because I'll be right here with you.

That's why I had that terrible pain. That's why I got peritonitis. From the time they killed my brother, I started having fits, and whenever I got mad I'd get a knot right here. I'd fall to the floor a lot of times, a lot of times. What hurt the most was when people laughed at me when I had an attack. I even hit a woman who saw me on the ground one time and would always remind me of it:

—Here comes the one that falls over stunned from all her screwing around!

She liked being nasty to people, it was her nature; she was a woman with a real bad temper. She was a fighter like me, but real wicked. That day I was on her list, and the fight was with me. She laughed when I walked by—she was real shrewd, real daring—I insulted her, she answered me back, I crossed the street and said:

—Put your money where your mouth is!

That's when we grabbed each other by the hair. After I slapped her and swore at her she laughed and I started to feel real bad, as if I was losing my breath. I know when and how the spasms are coming and I thought:

—Here it comes and they are going to laugh at me if I fall down here on the street.

I ran onto the patio and almost cracked my head on a sink. There was a woman at the faucet filling her jug and I pushed her away and put my mouth on the spigot, turned it on all the way, and drank and drank. I don't know how all that water fit inside me, but I drank a whole jug, like the ones that they used with the old washstands. The attack didn't come. Now I understand that the water dislodged the dead person's vibes and washed them out of my body. Because it was a spiritual being that was beating me.

I got terrible, terrible pain. My gut tied up in knots and I was a living scream. I was sick for about four or five nights, my eyes were almost closed when I saw her come and stand at the foot of my bed.

She didn't speak; she just looked at me. I thought one of the neighbors had come to bring me something. I looked her over slowly; she was standing between a silver piggy bank and a big vase of flowers, all dressed in black; that's why she scared me. Only her hands and her face were white, like white bread. All of a sudden she put her hands together like the Virgin of Solitude. I opened my eyes real wide and there wasn't anything at the foot of the bed and I said: "Who's there? Why did she vanish?" I straightened up and started to scream to all the neighbors: "Death has arrived!" Three women lived next door; they were the first ones to hear me. I woke the whole neighborhood up and everyone came in.

—What's wrong?

I screamed:

—I'm dying! I'm dying! Death is at the foot of my bed!

—What?

—Death just came in. There she is, standing at the foot of the bed!

—What do you mean, Death?

—Death, yes, Death . . . I'm dying, because she was just with me . . .

—What do you mean, she was just here? Don't scream! Don't scream like that!

—She just came in! I saw her . . . I'm dying. There she is at the foot of my bed!

They didn't see anything. But I did.

—I'm dying! Don't be cruel! Don't leave me alone with Death!

They thought I was going crazy from the pain . . . And as I kept insisting, the pain started to ease up and go away; it kept going away and by dawn I felt as if nothing had been wrong. Well, I didn't have epilepsy but I was numb all over. The Virgin of Solitude came to heal me, but since I didn't understand, even though I already believed in the Obra Espiritual, I didn't recognize her and I thought she was Death. Besides, Solitude dresses like Death. The next day I woke up feeling a lot better, but afraid. Everyone left to get back to work when I didn't die. I said:

—I'm not spending another night here, because I don't want to die among good and healthy people . . .

I started getting all my stuff together and Doña Lola, the porter, asked me:

—What're you doing?

—Nothing.

—What do you mean, nothing?

—Nothing . . . Packing my bags. I'm leaving the bed, the wardrobe, and the dresser for Don José de la Luz for the three months' rent I owe him, and all the clothes, so he can sell them. You can keep the night table, the bureau, the table, the basket of dishes, the chair, and the stool.

I started to give things away. I put all my rags in a blanket. I left all the dishes, the glasses, and the table where the piggy bank was to the owner of the house, Don José de la Luz, and I gave Doña Lola Palomares the pig with everything in it. I felt so bad that I said: "What do material possessions matter to me?"

I spent all day giving my stuff to people and then I took off. I gave the key to the porter and I left with just my shawl over me, to go to the hospital. I was like a crazy woman asking for a bed in all the hospitals in town and they wouldn't admit me because they said I was able to walk on my own. No one who's really sick can make it to the hospital walking on their own two feet. That's the deal. You have to be dying so the bed will be free soon. I spent all day going from hospital to hospital. I went to all the hospitals in Mexico City at that time.

When I was completely disappointed after leaving the Campo Florido church, I sat down on the sidewalk behind the circus tent, and that's where Quique, Doña Lola's son, found me. He yelled at me:

—Don't you move. I'm going to call Don Luchito so we can take you home!

I didn't have the strength to leave. I hadn't eaten, and all I had in my stomach was bile. The boy took off running and came back with Doña Lola. That's when Don Lucho got there, huffing and puffing from all the running.

—What in the name of Judas are you doing? Don't you have a home?

—I don't have a house anymore, and since I don't have anywhere to go, I'm going to stay here until I die on this sidewalk.

—Come on, let's go.

They picked me up, one on each side, and carried me like I was a little jug. Then they told me what they had gone through to find me. Every time they'd get to a hospital they were told:

—She just left because there aren't any beds.

They followed me all over the city. I couldn't believe it, really, I didn't know they'd do that . . .

When they had me back in bed, Don Lucerito said:

—There, if you're going to die, die, but don't go moving in with other people! This is where you live and die, not like a dog out on the sidewalk. We'll take care of burying you, even if it's in a garbage can . . . You saw how Chabela left the house and went to stay with María the Chinese woman, thinking she was going to take care of her, and remember how she died. If I buried Chabela, who didn't even live here anymore, I'd be more likely to do it for you, who are still in the house!

I'd thought about Chabela all day. Chabela was a friend of mine from the factory who had also lived at Daniel Ruiz Street. When she got real sick with the same pain I had, from peritonitis, a friend of hers, María the Chinese woman, who was real Chinese from China, told her to empty out her house and move in with her so she could take care of her. It was a pack of lies! She just wanted her things. Chabela moved out of her house and the friend may as well have killed her, because she let her die for no reason. She didn't cure her, or take her to see any doctor, or do anything. She didn't even bother to feed her anymore, and when the pain burned even worse, Chabela twisted up into a knot because she couldn't take it. When the orderlies came to take her body out, they had to pull on her to get her on the stretcher . . . That Chinawoman didn't even leave her a dress to be buried in; she said she didn't need clothes anymore. All of us who were her friends got the money together to get her out of the morgue. We bought a coffin, because they wouldn't give her to us unless we had a coffin. But she was naked. We dressed her the best we could. One gave her a slip, another a dress; someone put a necklace on her and earrings . . .

We didn't want them to do an autopsy on her, because they cut up the bodies. Her whole body was bruised from the pain. We paid the doctor eighty pesos at the police station so he could split it with the police chief. And then we were off to ask for charity for the funeral.

The suitcase with the clothes was still on the bed because Don Lucero didn't take anything out of the room. After I got better, the friends from the factory asked me:

—Where's the piggy bank? We want to feed it and we can't find it.

—I gave it away.

—Did you take out what was inside it?

—No.

They started to do the calculations, because they were the ones who decided to fatten it up for me. Whatever change they had they'd put in. It had three hundred pesos. It looked like a real pig, huge, one of those white ones that they sprinkle with silver dust. The owner of the house returned the suitcase with the clothes just like I'd left them; everyone gave me back what I'd given away, but the piggy bank came back empty. I asked Doña Lola:

—What happened to what was inside it?

—There wasn't anything inside it, it was empty . . .

—Well, isn't that something! Thanks for letting me know!

What else could I say? If I gave everything away because I was crazy from my illness, she took advantage of it. I started to think that a moral person would have said: "*Bueno, pues* you need the centavos because you're sick . . ." But she didn't even give me back part of it. I didn't say anything. I was so sick that I thought I was finished. When you're young and suffering, it happens, you get meek. Now when I get sick, I lock the door to my house.

I didn't give Manuel Robachicos money again, not even for his gangrenous feet. His spells didn't work on me; in the end he couldn't hurt me. My protector had warned me: "He will come back to you and will want to be your friend, because he will be repentant and ask you to forgive him. Don't hold a grudge . . . You have to be friendly with him."

And that's how it was. He came to see me three months later and said:

—What are you up to, Tehuanita?

—Nothing. Just hanging in here.

—I came by to say hello and to ask you to forget the setbacks we've had . . .

—You haven't done anything to me and there's no reason for you to ask me to forgive you. For what? I'm not upset.

—Yes, Tehuanita, I have offended you and I beg you to forgive me . . .

—*Bueno*, forget about it . . .

He was quiet and then after a while he said:

—I also wanted to ask you to do me a favor and take my St. Ciro to be blessed.

It was an all-black saint.

—Yes, of course. Just bring it to me . . .

I already knew that if he was asking me to be the godmother for St. Ciro, he was doing it to be free of guilt. I took the saint to be blessed at the church. I gave it back to him, and that's how we left it. As friends. But it was at my protector's orders. I'm spiteful and hold a grudge forever. Anyone who messes with me pays for it, with interest, because when it comes to hating I'm the best at collecting on debts.

I MET DR. RAFAEL MORENO at a pharmacy in Cuauhtemotzin. He lived in the San Antonio Abad neighborhood with his wife. He waited on customers in his small drugstore, but he had to work at the hospital to make ends meet. I went in one time asking for Dr. Bell anti-pain medicine and we became friends. Dr. Moreno was dark-skinned, thin, and wore a white coat, as all doctors do. He left for the hospital at eight in the morning, and in the afternoons he treated families. He wanted me to be his nurse at Morelos Hospital:

—Do you want a job? You probably won't like it, because you have to look at people and touch them. But if you come with me and you learn, I'll arrange for you to stay on as a permanent employee . . . I'll teach you what you need to know . . .

—All right. I'll go.

—Okay, but I warn you, they're not nice women . . .

—What do I care? I just want to work. It doesn't matter to me if they're bad or good . . . I'll go.

I went over to Alameda. The entrance is next to the church of San Antonio, the saint women pray to so they'll get a man. You walk to the back of the little garden and there's the door. It's still Morelos Hospital, though they call it Women's Hospital now, for women who have a husband occasionally. When the agents catch them, they force them to be examined at the Public Health Department on Tolsa Street, and anyone who's sick ends up at the hospital. The agents make their rounds at night on San Juan de Letrán, 5 de Mayo, and 16 de Septiembre streets, looking for the hookers who work the streets, especially the tough old ones who rummage around, grabbing men.

—Hey, honey, let me sharpen that little pencil for you!

The guys from the Health Department seize them and take them away. The other ones have to get checked every week if they want to keep their permits. The hookers are real careful, they hide in the tenements, but they still get caught and taken away in cars.

I was a hard worker at first and I saw so much stuff; Dr. Moreno would say:

—Look here, this is such and such and this is whatever . . . Go ahead, hold the irrigation tube.

He showed me a lot of the sicknesses women get for devoting their lives to love and then they pass it on to all the other johns: gonorrhea, all kinds of scabby and soft sores, syphilis, from the first stage to the fifth, infected sores, white discharges and clots. And that's without counting the critters, the lice, the ones they call crabs that everyone has and are so hard to get rid of, you have to pull on the skin to get the lice to let go of the crotch. In those days they used calomel powder and Soldier's ointment a lot to help treat that.

I did it for about two months. When I'd go home my stomach would be so upset I couldn't eat:

—If other women saw the things I saw, I swear they wouldn't offer their tamale so freely . . . !

Even though I washed my hands and put lotion on, they always felt dirty . . . One woman had green pus oozing out; the doctor told me she had a yellow discharge and that's why she had marbled clots coming out of her. I washed her with permanganate solution, then swabbed her with iodine and put a medicated tampon inside her: a piece of cotton this big soaked in a solution of glycerine. The next day they'd take out the tampon and put another one back in after they washed her and treated her. The woman got better just from that plugging and unplugging, and was free to go back to her ways. There was another one who was covered with sores, her whole crotch was a big red circle. A lot of them had that same infection. Dr. Moreno treated them with something that looked like a pen. First he washed them real good and then he touched them with that infernal pen. That's what they called it, because it was connected to an electric cable. That woman I was talking about would get zapped all around with the tip of the pen to burn the rotted flesh. And she screamed because it burned everything away and left raw skin. She'd twist up and down and back and forth like a wave. Then he'd put iodoform on to deaden the pain. He got rid of all the nasty stuff with soap and permanganate solution, and after he dried her off he put on powders that smelled real bad.

—That really stinks!

—We'll just use a smidgen!

—Just a little, please!

—I promise.

At night I made them a liter of lemon water and let it sit overnight. The next day they drank it on an empty stomach. Sometimes the disease would move to their butt hole and the doctor would stick them real careful back there with the pen. They'd scream like crazy, but they had to put up with it if they wanted to get their permit card back.

I only talked to them when they came in for treatment. I'd ask:

—Did you wash yourself?

I'd give them warm water and they'd go to the bathroom and clean up so they wouldn't be indecent when they climbed up on the table. I'd wash them again with hotter water and boiled soap. I got the razor ready and put their legs up in the air so I could shave them. I was always amazed that Dr. Moreno still liked women, because he was a real playboy.

—*Ay, dotorcito! Ay, dotorcito! No, dotorcito!* Not like that!

And he'd pat them on the butt.

—It'll feel better, it'll feel better!

After work I'd go from saloon to saloon to forget. The truth is, I feel sorry for the poor men. That doctor was a good man. As I followed him around, he'd say to me:

—Come over here and look, so you'll behave and not go

around believing what all the poets say . . . Come see what happens to the ones who get into this kind of stuff . . .

The hospital was packed full every day. We didn't have sufficient supplies, there weren't enough nurses, and there were always women waiting for beds. Sometimes we lay them on the floor next to the ward that faced Alameda Street. There was a separate room for pregnant women. After a few days of recuperating they were back out on the street. Those women didn't have husbands; that's why they were on the street. They were all poor women: cheap street women, the ones who will sell themselves for whatever they can get. The ones in the ward had friends come by. The men didn't come in, but everyone brought fruit and other kinds of food, and a young man took the stuff at the door and would deliver it: "Bed 12!," "Bed 23!," "Bed 41!," and they'd hide their little packages under the mattress, so they wouldn't get stolen. The women visitors could come in on Thursdays and Sundays. In the hospital we'd give them soup, stew, beans, coffee, milk, and bread, so they'd get better fast.

One day there appeared a bunch of women and a few young men who claimed to be teachers from the Department of Education. They took down a lot of the orderlies' names, including mine, and they enrolled us in classes. I expected them to teach us letters or numbers or something, but they just asked us things like how many trees were in Alameda Park and what do you call the skin between a duck's toes, useless crap, and no reading.

When we finished our work in the hospital they got us all together in the dining room. They tested us right there sitting on the benches, and we talked nonsense because we didn't know anything about that kind of stuff. I put an end to that immediately. I didn't want them laughing at me. If you think I'm cranky now . . . this is nothing, I used to be a lot worse. I told the teacher, a skinny old woman with a bun who wore a long black dress that reached the floor:

—No, thanks. I'm not playing this game. I'm interested in having you teach me reading and arithmetic. If you can't, then don't make fools of us. Thanks a lot, but you buzzards can take off. I'm not doing this bullshit!

The teacher told me that I was very rude.

—I'm real rude and you're real dumb because you're only asking us idiotic things that don't matter to anyone. Teach me the names of the letters, and if I don't answer you, then you have a reason to make fun of me, but you aren't teaching me to read, you're asking me about . . . ducks . . . No way! You teach us to read and we'll learn. If not, then you're better off looking for another job; this isn't going to work out for you, because you'd never be able to handle me.

—Listen, don't be so dense. Make an effort. Let's see, how many trees are in Alameda Park?

—If you've counted them, then please tell me, because I go back and forth and in and out of that park and I have no clue. I don't have time to go around counting trees. If you're so interested, count them yourself!

Can you believe they'd ask such a question? If that's how the Department of Education teaches, then it's just a school for baboons . . . Several teachers got upset with me for being so outspoken. "I've had more than enough. If you're not going to teach me, take me off your list. I can't be wasting my time on the shit that your majesties ramble on and on about. So fly away, you buzzards!"

Those teachers wanted to have fun with us, because we were grown-ups. Who knows if it was a new education system, but I didn't pay attention to them! What do you call the seven-colored birds? What do you call the fish under the water? Fish . . . right? And what about those flowers that they say are both male and female? I said: "Not with me, you don't. I'm not interested in looking for tits on snakes. So this is where it ends for the illiterate one." I left the hospital for rotting women because, first of all, they paid me very little and then there were these teachers who were pulling our legs with tests in comparative biology, or whatever they called it, and I told them all to go to hell. I never went to any school after that. And I stayed dumb as a mule but very content. I'd rather bray like a donkey than pretend to be a scholar.

I went back to Netzahualcoyotl and that's when I ran into Antonio Pérez again. We hadn't talked in about two years. He was real sick, but he didn't want to be hospitalized because he didn't want his mother and his wife—he'd gotten married—to know how bad off he was. He took care of changing the dressing himself, but according to his friends, his member was falling apart. I spied on him from the balcony windows, because he came by to eat every day. God only knows how the poor devil could work, because when he got out of the car he'd have to swing his body out before he put his feet on the ground. Oh my God! He had to go through that cleansing because of his quarrel with me. We'd been at a dance and one of his girlfriends wanted to take him away from me. When we finished a number, she came up to me and said:

—I like Antonio, so I'm taking him away from you.

She took him by the arm and then turned to me and said:

—If you want him, you'll have to fight for him.

I had no reason to, so I said: "It's his choice!"

She grabbed him and took off with him. I thought: "*Bueno, pues* let them have fun and best of luck. I don't give a damn."

I already knew that Antonio had a girlfriend, but since we thought so much of each other, we went everywhere together:

—Do you want to go to the dance?

—Sure, let's go.

We'd go anywhere, without saying things to each other—well, nothing that wasn't just what one friend would say to another. Since this woman offered it to him, he couldn't tell her he couldn't. Because of course he could do it, he was a man and she asked him in front of everyone. And if he ended up sick from her, it's because he behaved like a man. María was the one who told me she was sick, you know, between friends. She was a whore and a blabbermouth; everyone knew about it. We called her La Puerquitos, the Piglet, or María Snout-face, because her mouth was like a pig's. Back then she had crusty venereal sores, which are the worst kind.

—These things really itch a lot.

Since she supported herself by going with different men and was in love with Antonio, she took him to stay with her. I understand that he didn't see me anymore because he was embarrassed about leaving me in the cantina and making me pay for the beers. Then I got mad. I couldn't tell him not to get involved with her. No, not even to save him from getting venereal disease. If he'd been involved with me, I'd have grabbed her and slapped her. But he was just my friend, and if I'd said, watch out or you'll catch what she has, he'd probably have thought I was jealous. All things considered, something stopped me.

Later my friends said that he was really sick.

—What do you want me to do? He asked for it.

We didn't speak. I saw him because he lived close by on Netzahualcoyotl Street; I lived at number 16 and Antonio lived at number 11. Of course, I'd look out the balcony. I knew what time he came for dinner and when he left for home. I could tell things were real bad for him. So I locked myself in my room and really concentrated and I asked my protector to heal him.

—No, let him suffer, he said.

—But it isn't his family's fault. The poor things. They don't know and he's really suffering . . . I can see it . . .

—Okay, I'll make it three months to cure him . . .

—*Ay, no, ay, no,* in three months death will have taken him . . .

—You want it to be quicker?

—The sooner the better, if you could . . .

—*Bueno, pues* a month . . .

—Less, less, please . . .

By insisting and insisting I got him down to two weeks. And there I was counting the days. Yes, I loved Antonio Pérez, it's the truth. And every day I'd go out to the balcony to see him come in: "They aren't helping him." I was disappointed when I saw how he got out of the car. Because of the heat from the gasoline, the jostling from the engine, and all that, his thing got so swollen he couldn't drive. I screamed at the spiritualist brothers:

—Please, heal him as soon as possible!

On exactly the fifteenth day, I didn't see him leave his house. I said:

"They didn't do it." I waited for his friends to come by.

—Where's Antonio? What happened to him? How's he doing?

—He's in bad shape. They sent for the priest.

I ran and found the medium and put her into a trance to call my protector:

—You didn't cure him . . . He's gotten worse.

—He has to get worse . . . Don't be in such a hurry. Tomorrow he'll be fine when he wakes up.

I saw him leave for work the next morning, on the sixteenth day. When he came home, he got out of the car as happy as a clam, his legs moved just fine. He didn't know anything about the cleansing until my protector appeared to him dressed as a priest. He insisted that Antonio come and ask for my forgiveness, for leaving me in the middle of the floor at the dance hall, with the bill for the beers. My protector told him:

—That's how you pay that woman back for all the help she's given you? That's why we subjected you to all those purifications.

Antonio came over to number 16 and whistled for me, because we even understood each other's whistles. When I came out he said that he was going to go back to the Obra Espiritual, and wanted to know if we could go together. Antonio didn't marry me because we were from different classes. He was respectable, more educated than I was. There was no way. His family, his brothers and sisters, had already picked a wife for him from a better class. She didn't work. They knew that I was a poor factory worker, that I liked to dance and to party, and that I didn't fit in. That's who I was, so that was the end of it. I liked to dance and so did he. His brothers and sisters knew that I drank a lot with Antonio. They wanted him with a lady, a señorita! A señorita, give me a break! Well, whoop-de-doo!

JOSÉ G. SÁNCHEZ and his wife, María, used to come to Netzahualcoyotl to dance and drink and we got to be good friends. Guadalupe Escobar, the one who got sent to Belén Prison with me, who was married to José G. Sánchez's brother, came too. All four of them were in the cavalry. They'd traveled by train to Tampico, and had covered a lot of track; they'd seen a lot of places, a lot of the country. They talked about the snow and the seashore, about the flooding of the rivers, about the lagoons and the chachalaca birds and the maguey groves and the fields of prickly pears, about the jacaranda trees and the royal poincianas in the temperate zone. As they talked, it felt like my eyes had filled with dust, all the dust of Mexico City, and that it was time to head for the countryside.

We talked about shooting guns. I really like that. I love battles because the sound is so nice. You hear the first shots, but once the fighting gets going you don't hear them anymore, you just see the smoke coming from the different places. Just remembering it made me want to go back to the Revolution. That's why I told them to let me know when they were leaving Mexico City, so I could go with them to the first battle. I wanted to get out of the city.

We left the Peredo barracks with the first squad of the cavalry. My friends José and María, and Guadalupe Escobar, we all took off. If it had anything to do with firing a gun, I was ready. And I'd go again if there was a good fight, as long as there was shooting, a lot of shooting. I love to trick fate.

The Cristeros had a passion for shooting. The fighting was heavy. They hanged men from trees and left them swinging in the wind. When the battles were over it was pretty hard to find a priest anywhere around. The soldiers were just dumb Indians who shot the hell out of anyone who raised a gun to defend the Virgin of Guadalupe. What did those assholes really think they were defending? The Virgin was well protected in her glass case. They'd shout: "Long live Christ the King!" while they shot at each other. The priests were hiding behind the saints, sipping their chocolate and nibbling on biscuits. That's why the government threw them in jail. Everyone who got caught causing trouble or carrying a weapon was blown away. The Cristeros were hungry peasants, wearing huaraches on their feet, looting all over the place, while they crossed themselves and prayed. "Blessed Holy Virgin, conceived without sin"; that was their greeting, their rallying cry. I never saw a cassock anywhere; just barefoot Indians walking the countryside with muddy hands that couldn't aim a gun. But they say the priests were right there with them, stirring up the villagers, guarding the Holy Book, the hosts and the chalices, blessing people as they passed by. We returned to Mexico City as common soldiers after that. The cavalry was disbanded and I went back to Netzahualcoyotl, where Doña Adelina welcomed me with open arms.

—You're back?

She'd missed having me around because she never picked up after herself. If she dropped something, she'd say:

—Leave it there, I'll pick it up tomorrow.

There was nothing you could do about it, that's just the way she was. I went around collecting the things she left all over the place.

In the city the government soldiers went through houses looking for statues of saints, while the rich people bragged about being so pious. The more they pursued the issue, the more emotional the

214 ~oo~ *Elena Poniatowska*

situation got. That's when priests started wearing civilian clothes, and pants. I don't really think they're priests anymore; they're just making fools of everyone. Before, you could tell who was a priest and who was a monk. But during that period they all moved into private homes so they wouldn't get caught all together. People who were closest to them spread the word to let others know where they'd be saying mass. They'd walk along the street and check you out, and if you looked Catholic, they'd whisper real careful:

—There's going to be a mass at so-and-so's house at such and such address, and they're giving communion.

They took a lot of risks, but since most Mexicans are Catholic, a lot of people went.

I don't believe in priests, because I've seen them in action. When they're saying mass, they're fulfilling their mission, but once mass is over, they're just men, like any other man on the street, with the same faults, maybe worse, because they're hungry for women. When they say mass they forget about the world and women and other temptations, because they have opened themselves up to God and salvation. But once they finish their work, they're like all other men, and it'd be better if they were only that normal, because some of them . . . well, I don't even want to talk about what they're into! That's why the first thing Benito Juárez did when he went back to Oaxaca as a soldier, as governor, as the all-powerful, was to empty out the convents. He knew about the priests' comings and goings. He knew their signal codes because he'd gone to the convent every night with the priest who raised him. He waited until the last priest went in and when they were all inside he knocked on the door five times in the special way he'd heard since he was a child. They honk the car horns that way now when drivers are mad at each other. The priest had taught him to read and to eat meat (because before that Benito ate only mountain grass called *quelites*). The priest never imagined that the little Indian boy was craftier than he looked and that he'd paid attention to everything that was going on. That was the reason he was one of the best priest-catchers, and if he hadn't died, there wouldn't be a cassock left in Mexico. When he knocked, the padres all looked around at each other to see who was missing, and no one was, but they still told the youngest priest, the most humble:

—Go ahead and open the door, because they're using the password . . .

—Maybe it's someone who wants to harass us.

The young friar opened the door and Benito Juárez entered with his guards and caught all the priests red-handed and hauled them off to jail. He threw the nuns out and ordered them to dig up the patio of the convents, because even as a young child he'd noticed that one day the nuns had real big bellies and the next they were flat. Since he wasn't stupid, he thought: "Where did all these babies go? There's no way they could all have had miscarriages."

That's why they found lots of little skeletons, little bones that were still soft when they dug up the ground. What other choice did the nuns have but to be the priests' mistresses? How could they sleep alone for so many years? Benito Juárez opened everyone's eyes and forced them to face the facts. He got all the priests and all the nuns together and told them that he wouldn't let them continue to deceive the masses. He wanted them to get married and stop the lies and deceit. But since they wanted to keep things the way they'd been before, he pursued them and took away all their belongings, their houses and their treasures. How many girls have been raped in the confessionals! A little confessing and a little touching, they start manhandling them and then take them off to the dormitory, as if they were in a whorehouse, and to get to it faster they do it in the vestry. That's why I don't like them. It's even come out in the newspaper here in the Federal District. About thirty years ago in the very Basilica of the Virgin of Guadalupe they excavated a whole graveyard of little dead babies, like little newborn calves.

I can't stand the sight of nuns, even if they aren't pregnant. I've seen them, so I know what I'm talking about: hypocritical daughters of Eve, don't be stupid and do it the right way, in the light of day. Besides, priests and nuns, how disgusting, behind each other under their skirts! I've seen them, there are women who love black robes and the smell of priests. I've heard them squealing myself, or I wouldn't be sticking it to them. I may roast in Hell for saying this but it's the truth. The priests eat well and have women and are as fat as barn rats. Before, the nuns were their mistresses. Now they don't let the nuns get mixed up with the priests, but when they were locked up in their convents, the Daughters of Mary and the Sons of Joseph all blended together like guacamole. And that's not right. That's a nasty trick to play on people. I don't think there are any good priests. I don't. That's my only fault, that I don't believe in them. There aren't any good men or women anyway. All of us on this earth are bad. There's bad yeast in humans, and God our Lord said: "I'm going to burn you like the damned fig tree."

I went to the town of La Piedad because there was a detachment of Cristeros; at least they thought they were Cristeros, but they were really just common bandits. They were starving peasants who got rounded up and drafted. They didn't even know what to shoot at. It was a real mess. The government named them the 2nd Artillery Regiment. I knew that they were in the town of La Piedad because I kept in touch with the soldiers, and the War Ministry gave me passes to catch up to them. That time we spent about twenty days on the plains near the Puebla highway, waiting for them to give us orders to leave. I didn't want to go back home anymore, not because I was afraid of the police, but because I thought: "Any minute they're going to move out of the barracks in the middle of the night, and I'll be home asleep in my room . . . !" From the plains they sent the 2nd Artillery Regiment to Oaxaca, and I went along with the woman who cooked for them.

OAXACA IS FARMLAND. I wouldn't say it's any big deal. It does have a *zócalo*, a square, and the Cathedral is like the one here, but I don't particularly care for it, even though they say it's a pretty city. People who don't know any better will be impressed by anything. But I've been around, so I can tell the difference, and to me it's just a hill with houses perched on top of it, like goats clinging on so they don't fall off. For all I know, they may have leveled the hills and it's all flattened, but the place where they founded the capital city of Oaxaca was a hill covered with gourds. Who knows what it looks like now. I haven't been there since 1926, but it probably isn't any better, because the cities in Mexico always get worse. The houses in Oaxaca are just like the shacks around here. What's so great about this slum I live in? The walls are peeling, dirty, old, and the trees have only two branches, and don't move because there's no wind to sway them. There were trees in Oaxaca like anywhere else, but very few because of the dryness. I probably just didn't notice. Since I didn't like to go outside, I didn't look around much. What was there to see? I never went to the ruins; no one even talked about them. Besides, it was like it is here in the city where everyone wandered around like stray dogs. During the time that I was there, people didn't hang out in the streets; when it got late, at eight o'clock they were inside their houses, so who'd even notice what the place looked like? I'd shut myself up in the room I rented. I lived in a tenement just like this one; a room here, and a room there, and a room over there, all in a row. Since I wasn't raised there, I don't have much to say about it or have anything to praise it for, because no part of me is Oaxaqueña.

I looked after the soldiers in the 2nd Artillery Regiment but I never lived in the barracks. I washed and ironed and made tortillas because I was the cook's assistant. A lot of the soldiers were my friends and still are. I just don't see them, because in the first place I'm old and what the hell would I do with them anyway, and in the second place there aren't any real soldiers left. I have no clue how many years it's been since the 2nd Artillery Regiment left for Huateca Potosina or what happened to them. But if there ever was another revolution and I had the opportunity to go to war, I'd be there in a second. I want to travel again.

The Puerto de Cádiz was a store the size of a block where they stored coffee, sugar, beans. They had everything, even hardware. Here they think that those holes in the walls are stores:

—I want so much of this or of that . . .

—We don't have any.

That's not a store. They used to call them stalls but now they're stores, even if they don't have anything to sell. I went to the store once with Señora Santos, the cook, to help her get groceries. The salesclerk asked me where I was from.

—Where am I from? Guess, if it's so important to you.

—Don't take it the wrong way, but I can't tell where you're from because you don't talk like the people from up there.

—Where is up there?

—Where Señora Santos and all the other outsiders that came with the troops are from . . .

—And what do you call this here?

—This is down here.

I shot the breeze with the shopkeeper, just to pass the time.

—Well, then I'm from up there, if you must know!

—No, you're not, no way . . . You're from down here . . . Come on, tell me where you're from . . .

—To tell the truth, I don't know where I'm from.

—The truth is, because of the way you talk you don't sound like you're from up there, you sound more like you're from down here.

I started to think: "Well, what does he see in me that makes him think I'm one of them? I've been out of this state for a long time. How does he know?"

—You're close but I'm from farther away . . .

And I laughed. In the meantime the clerk's wife had come out and was leaning on the counter and said to me:

—How would it hurt you to tell us that you're from Oaxaca?

—I'm not.

There was no way I was going to say yes or no. I'm not very trusting, and besides I was running away from the police, who wanted to arrest me. Then Señora Santos turned around and asked me:

—Why don't you just tell them?

—Because. What business is it of theirs?

And really, what did it matter to him if I was from down there? There was nothing for him to gain or for me. After all, I really have no country. I'm like the Hungarians, the gypsies: not from anywhere. I don't feel Mexican nor do I identify with the Mexicans. If I had money and property, I'd be Mexican, but since I'm worse than garbage, I'm nothing. I'm trash that the dog pees on and then walks away from. A strong wind comes along, blows it all down the street, and it's gone . . . I'm garbage because I can't be anything else. I've never been good for anything. My whole life I've been this very same germ you see right in front of you . . . When I was left alone I intended to go back to my homeland. I'd have had a better life in Salina Cruz or in Tehuantepec and I would have seen my stepmother, but the years went by and I was never able to get the money together for bus fare. There's even less chance of that now. I'm older and can't do as much, but that was always my dream. I've been a lot of places, but I've suffered more here in the capital than anywhere else. Living day to day has been real tough for me here. But I'm not sad, I'm not. Just the opposite, I'm happy. That's what life's about, being happy. And that's the end of it. You live. To get through it. Because you can't run. I wish you could run to make the journey end faster! But you have to go at the pace God dictates, following the procession.

Then the shopkeeper started in with it again:

—You know why we're asking? Because you favor a family from here.

—Okay, I'm from a ranch . . .

—What's it called?

—Miahuatlán . . .

Then he said:

—It's not a ranch, it's a district of the capital here, and I know a family there named Palancares. The father was a councilman for the market . . .

—Really? You know him?

Like it or not, I had to tell him:

—I was born in Miahuatlán, and my parents were Felipe Palancares and María Hernández.

—I'm going to tell Señor Palancares, Don Cleofas, who's a friend of mine, that you're his relative . . .

He took it upon himself to let everyone know and the next day when I went to the store he said:

—They are your relatives. They want to meet you. Here's the address . . .

When I went to Uncle Palancares's house no one was there with him, no wife, no daughter, no one. It was a big house, old, with a hallway and a fenced-in patio with flowerpots. He met me in the hallway:

—You're Jesusa Palancares?

—Yes, sir, I am. I'm Jesusa Palancares, Felipe Palancares's daughter . . .

My uncle was a grouchy old man, just like I am now, of average height, not tall or short, not fat or thin, but old already. He was my father's eldest brother. He had a deep voice. Instead of answering my greeting, you know what he said?

—Well, if you are a member of my family you've come at a bad time, because everything that belonged to your father was lost! The government took it all during the Revolution!

—A bad time? Why, señor? I'm not coming at any time. You said you wanted to meet me and that's what I came for, to meet you and so you could meet me . . . I'm Felipe Palancares and María Hernández's daughter . . .

It made me mad. I thought he was going to say "Good afternoon," and I would have said "The same to you," but seeing that he was so tense, I said:

—I haven't come to make a claim for any property. I've come because you say that you're my father's brother, but I'm not so sure I believe it, because my father never talked about you!

He kept rocking. I got angrier and said:

—I grew up poor, I'm still poor, and I'll die poor. What do I need an inheritance for? I don't have anyone to leave it to anyway.

He didn't say a word. He relaxed back into the chair and told me to come back and visit.

—I only came by because you sent for me. I'm not asking for a handout.

From that conversation I figured out that my grandparents did own property; my uncle made that real clear. When he said that I'd come at a bad time, I realized that there probably was something for me to inherit; otherwise, why was he so anxious? But you need proof to make any kind of a claim; papers are proof. Besides, if my father had a right to whatever it was and never claimed it, I, who was twenty-four years old when I went back to Oaxaca, had even less of a right to it. It made me angry, but what was the point of fighting for something I never had or even knew about? And after all, why would I want land? There was no way I was going to stay there and farm.

The uncle didn't even offer me a glass of water, nor did any of the other relatives who started peeking out when they saw me leaving. I thought: "What the hell am I doing here?"

—If you'll excuse me, I'm leaving now. And you'll never set eyes on me again.

My grandmother was Indian and my grandfather was French. My guess is that this Palancares was a French soldier who stayed in

Oaxaca. He'd have been a fool to go back to his country when he could make a living here. I imagine he must have deserted. He was probably a peon over there in France, and he thought: "I can get some good land here!" And since he was a virile man, he started out farming his small plots of land the same as the other farmers; they lent him their land and he planted it, and since he was such a hard worker and went the extra mile, he eventually took it all over. He planned ahead and was always ready when opportunity knocked. When the dry season came, his wife taught him to make cheeses from goat milk, from cactus fruit, butter, cream cheese, and who knows what else. He had all kinds of ideas. In the mornings he'd say to his wife:

—I'm off. If you haven't finished by evening, you're going to get it.

I heard my father say that there were lots of tracts of land, and since they were cheap, everyone got some. In 1915 the vacant lots in the Federal District around Narvarte were being sold for two centavos a meter. Now they cost an arm and a leg, but at one time they were a good deal. My father said each plot of land in Miahuatlán would yield a load of corn; which is two overflowing bags, one for each side of the pack animal. So they had to be good-sized pieces of land to produce so much corn. His grandfather raised pinto cattle, the black ones with white spots, lots of cows and bulls. He always said:

—You have to be ready for winter.

My father was the son of that Frenchman and an Indian from here in my homeland. My father was white with a thick beard, and he had hair on his chest in the shape of a cross, and a full black beard that was real curly, and curly hair, a wavy head. My mother was short, and my father wasn't much taller: around five one; at night he'd talk about the land, reminisce next to the stove, and I'd listen while I made the tortillas.

In the olden days the daughters went to live with their in-laws. None of the brothers had gotten married except my father, and my mother was the only woman in the house. She took care of my grandfather, fed him when she was supposed to, took care of his clothes, and looked after him real well, as if he were her own father. She was raising the four of us at the same time: Petra and Efrén, who were the oldest, and Emiliano and me. But she still always managed to find a way to make some kind of treat that my grandfather fancied. And he started loving her more all the time. One day he told his other children that everything in the house, the land, the seed, everything, belonged to his daughter, meaning my mother. Of course the unmarried sons started to hate my father.

—He's going to give the land to your wife!

—You know that all I've earned the whole time I've been married is this pair of burros. That's my whole estate: two burros. And it took a lot of hard work to get them.

—María owns everything!

My mother was just getting around after the birth of the baby, it hadn't been forty days yet, she hadn't even been through the bathhouse ritual, when my father came back from the woods and said:

—Get your things together and keep your mouth shut.

He tied baskets on his burros, and put my brother Emiliano on one animal and me on the other one. He loaded the metate, some pots so my mother could cook on the road, and some odds and ends, and that was all he took. My older brother and sister walked and so did my mother, carrying the newborn in her shawl.

We crossed the entire sierra until we got to the Isthmus of Tehuantepec, which is what I know as my homeland. My mother carried the dead child the whole way and we buried it there, we didn't even know when it died. The poor thing was already smelling bad. It could have been from sunstroke, the difficulties of the trip, or the dust, he was so little, maybe he just got cold. That was life, and my uncles were responsible for that child's death, because it wasn't even forty days old.

I washed and ironed clothes for an elderly man in Oaxaca: Captain García from the artillery company, and one day he said to me:

—I got two tickets to the bullfights but I'm on duty now. Here's your ticket and another one for the kid to go with you. Don't go off alone like a crazy person . . .

Since he had to take care of the reserve guard, Captain García sent the young son of one of the women who traveled with the troops. When we were leaving the bullring, I was walking in front of the kid, talking, and as we crossed the park a soldier caught up to me, grabbed my arm, and spun me around. As I turned toward him, he jammed a gun in my stomach, without saying a word. The gun got tangled in the fringe of my shawl. God only knows how it got stuck, but as he pulled and pulled, struggling to get the gun out, he stopped suddenly and stared at me:

—I'm sorry, señora. I thought you were my wife!

I heard the gunshot, because the gun went off at that very instant, and I felt like I was growing, like someone was stretching me upwards. I grabbed the soldier around the waist, by his pants, and I was so strong that I dragged him half a block to the corner, where he grabbed on to a pole to stop me.

Since nothing hurt or felt funny, I didn't check myself out. It wasn't until the next day when I went to get dressed that I noticed that my undershirt, the very bottom one that's right next to the skin, was burned. And all of a sudden it occurred to me: "Only my protector could have saved me." It made me understand that I wasn't alone; the spiritual world was with me and that was what tangled the gun up in the fringe of my shawl. I asked around the neighborhood to find out where there was a temple and a woman said:

—A spiritual oratory? That's an easy one! On such and such street, there's a place where they do that kind of stuff . . .

I went to the market and bought some flowers and a bottle of oil. My neighbor went to the doorway of the chapel with me.

—Knock and go in here . . . Ask for Brother Loreto.

From the minute I went in I liked the temple. I got a good feeling in the oratory. There was only one candlestick with three lit candles, and when I saw the triangle of light I liked the place. I thought: "Yes, it's real." It was about ten in the morning and they were already working. A young man was looking at me and asked:

—How can we help you?

—I'd like to speak to Father Mesmer.

—Just a minute, I'm almost finished with this session. I'll ask Brother Loreto to call him for you . . .

I was one of the last ones he admitted, because the line was really long. At the Obra Espiritual they don't call it a line, but a chain. We lined up to the right in a small square room and we went out to the left. Dr. Charcot worked from inside Brother Loreto, the human vessel. He was a foreign doctor, I don't remember what country he was from, if it was Germany or France; I think it was probably France. He was speaking in his own language. I've seen Dr. Charcot work on Indian flesh like mine and his work is divine. There's no one like him when it comes to massages; he's a very high spiritual being. He takes regular flesh, kneads it, and speaks like he did when he lived in Paris. He speaks French from inside Indian bodies and I understand him, really I do . . .

After quite a while Brother Loreto spoke to me:

—Sister, this is the first time you've been here. Welcome to the Fountain of Grace . . . Sister, I greet you in the name of the Almighty in this holy and blessed temple.

Then I answered:

—Brother, I return the greeting in the same name.

He said to me:

—Are you here for a private consultation?

—Brother, I just wish to speak to my protector. I ask you to allow me to see Mesmer.

Spiritual beings can go anywhere; they have human vessels everywhere. They're healing people in China, in London, and here in Mexico all at the same time . . . Since Dr. Charcot was working through Brother Loreto, he called Mesmer himself. The two are fellow countrymen. Dr. Charcot told me that my Mesmer was a very revered holy being, the doctor of the sick, and he was working on another continent at the moment, but he was sending a messenger to go get him:

—Don't be afraid, sister, my spiritual brother will be here in a few minutes. I'm saying goodbye because your protector will take charge of you from here on and I congratulate you because you are in very good hands.

And with that Dr. Charcot left the vessel and ay! when my revered Mesmer entered my flesh I felt a chill between my heart and my back. I recognized him the instant he penetrated me. He has a real special way. He puts his hand on my lung and goes like this. Each spiritual being has their own style. I told him:

—I came to thank you for helping me out yesterday . . .

—Child, even the leaves on the tree don't move without God's will. The responsibility that my God and Lord has given me in watching over you is great. You aren't alone, although it may feel that way sometimes.

—Thank you, Father . . . Thank you . . .

He also made me see that the scorch mark on my blouse was the manifestation of an invisible protection. So I was not abandoned. And then I understood that this wasn't the first time he had watched over me, because Pedro tried to kill me several times but it was never allowed. So I started to believe that my protector had been looking after me since the day I was born.

A few days later I got into another fight at the market, with one of the women who had a stall there. I wanted to buy a cheap white plate, and when I asked her how much it was, she tried to charge me a peso or one-fifty—I don't quite remember which—and at that time those plates cost twenty-five, thirty centavos at the most . . .

—No, I told her. It's not worth that . . . Is it china?

She had the nerve to tell me that I was a beggar *soldadera* who never had anything but clay and pewter dishes. I stayed calm and said:

—Watch what you're saying, because you're probably more of a beggar than I am. You go from market to market stealing from whoever will let you, while the government supports me on a captain's salary. So stand at attention and click those heels together!

—Do you think I'd give away my plates even if you were a general, you two-bit tramp?

—Thief! Shut your mouth before I break it.

—What a shame the government spends so much money on whores like you, battalion woman . . . !

Since the insult made me feel so bad, I grabbed a stack of plates and started breaking them on her head one by one. Then I climbed up on the stall and did the apache dance on top of the dishes, breaking them to pieces, and that's when we grabbed each other. I left her almost naked, thrown on top of her broken pieces of pottery, bleeding like Christ on the cross. The councilman for the market came and picked both of us up. Once we were at the jail she started demanding the price of the broken plates at the top of her lungs. As they locked me up, I kept saying:

—I'm not paying, I'm not paying, I'm not paying.

—Then you'll stay in jail.

And I stayed in jail until they got tired of feeding me for free.

WHILE I WAS LOCKED UP, the 2nd Artillery Regiment came to Mexico City, because Plutarco Elías Calles was being sworn in as president and the troops had to be there for the takeover, to keep the situation under control. The soldiers got me out of jail, but while I was packing my things to go with them, the train left. When I got to the station, the switchman told me:

—The engineer was waiting for you, but there was no way he could stay any longer.

I went back to the disbursement office to get a pass for a freight train, one that was slower than molasses. God only knew when we'd get there.

One of the men there who was also arranging for a ride challenged me:

—I'll wait because all the rest of you are waiting, but if I were alone I'd walk.

—If you walk I'll follow you and we'll see who gives up first. Just don't stop in the middle of the road! We can leave at five in the morning, if that's not a problem for you.

There were six of us who had missed the train: two women, the twelve-year-old boy who had gone to the bullfight with me the day I got burned by the powder flash, the man who had dared me, and a dandy in white linen and a bow tie who wouldn't tell us his name. He wrote poetry and supported Vasconcelos. We were all from the same barracks except for the dandy. We took off at five in the morning and after the second day the braggart was tired. He didn't handle the trip well.

We walked along the highway and sometimes we cut across the roads and went through the woods. We'd stop wherever we could at villages or railroad stations. In Puebla, everyone started to complain: "If this keeps up there'll be nothing left of us but hunger . . ." I told the women and the dandy, who were really exhausted by then:

—There's nothing to discuss. We've gone more than halfway, so it's better to keep heading straight to Mexico City.

By the time we finally got to there, the 2nd Regiment had already left for Tuyahualco, so the women and the boy went off after them.

I went by the carpenter's shop to see José Villa Medrano, the man from Jalisco who had taught me how to make furniture. He was an older gentleman, about sixty, and he looked like a gringo, with very white hair and blue eyes. He also owned a barbershop and told me that he was moving to Guadalajara, and if I wanted, he'd turn the shop over to me on the condition that I send him money orders. And that's what we agreed to.

—There's a house in the back, he said. So you have a place to stay if you want it.

It was a pretty big place right in the center of town with eight chairs and a courtyard that opened out onto the street, so a lot of people came by. There were five full-time barbers and three who only came in to handle the overflow on Saturdays and Sundays, when it was busier. All kinds of people patronized the shop. They'd like the way one of the barbers cut their hair and they'd keep coming back. When we closed at eight at night, the barbers would give me their slips. They really ran the business. They made about twenty pesos a day and I got half, which was ten pesos from each of them. Back then it was so cheap to get a haircut; it only cost fifty centavos for a shave and a haircut. Now it's about six pesos and that's in a second-rate barbershop; you don't even dare set foot in the first-class ones. Barbers make good money now. We raised our prices ten centavos when we started: so it was thirty centavos for a shave and thirty for a haircut. But then everyone kept raising the price until it had gotten to be a big headache to get a haircut. And that's my fault for starting with the ten-centavo increase when I was trying to help the boys out.

I didn't do anything. Since I was the owner, I simply took the money. The barbers had a different-colored slip for each service they provided: one color for shaving the head and another for shaving the face. When they finished a client they'd tell me:

—It was a double service.

And I'd give them two slips. The money they earned was based on the number of slips they'd collected at the end of the day. I just supervised.

At night I put away the tools and supplies: the trimming shears, the aftershave lotion, the razors, the combs, the shaving brushes, and everything else. I bought alcohol, lotion, shaving cream, and especially the powder they put on the customers' cheeks after shaving. If someone asked for special powder, they got powder, and if they wanted talc, they got talc. If they had dandruff and they wanted to get rid of it, we'd do that too, but it was a bother. I was bored because I was cooped up there all day, walking around, tending to the clients. Out of what the barbers paid me I had to cover my own expenses, pay the taxes, the rent, and the electric bill, and send a check to Don José Villa Medrano in Guadalajara.

I got rid of the barbershop. I told the boys:

—I see hair everywhere, even in my soup. I can't stand it anymore.

So I sold it. Besides, by then I was tired of the aggravation from the unions. I'd belonged to several unions at different times, but when I realized that they were all users I told them:

—Take back your violin, I'm not playing this tune anymore.

I was in the carpenters' union, the barbers' union, and the box makers' union at the different factories where I worked. It was more disorganized back then. In the May Day parade I usually marched with the carpenter-cabinetmakers, but then the barbers wanted me so they'd have more people, and it was total confusion and I was pulled from one group to another. Then they started asking us for money, and that's when I didn't like it anymore, because we earned so little as it was, and then we had to hand it over to the union. Not anymore.

—No, thanks, I told them. I'm looking for someone to support me, not someone else to support.

Back then factory workers had a good life. When the clock struck one in the afternoon, you'd leave to go home and eat; you'd have soup, a little rice, some meat. But not now, they don't do that anymore; those shitty unions ruined everything for everyone. If employees happen to go out, they're in a hurry to eat tacos filled with germs, right on the street in the middle of all the dust, or at one of the hundreds of filthy taco stands. The unions screwed those that had and those that didn't have. It's no joke! They don't even help you out! Just the opposite; they destroy you. And it's not just two or three people who get hurt; it's everyone who lets them, all the poor people who don't have any other choice but to steal. Anyone who doesn't join the union can't get work, if you can believe that! So you have to go hungry, and if you're in the union, they take your money: there's a fee for this and a fee for that. The whole mess is a bunch of crap. And then there are the speeches: "Fellow workers, in the agreement that was reached at the meeting this past month of October . . ." So that's another screwed-up situation. Don't be including me as a fellow worker.

Before, work started at eight in the morning and ended at four o'clock sharp. Then the next shift started and went until midnight. Then another group started. And you could work two shifts, if you were up to it, to make extra money. Not anymore; now there're just morning shifts. The work and the workers are drying up at the same rate. I didn't want to support those loafers anymore and I told the union leaders themselves:

—This is as far as I go, Ministers of the Interior and Agreements. And you, Mr. Treasurer, say goodbye to my dues and find yourself other members who are more gullible than I am.

And I handed in my resignation.

One day I ran into Madalenita Servín on the street:
—You're back? she asked.

—Yeah, I've been here a long time . . .

—So you've left the troops?

—For now, but I'm ready to go again . . . I have a barbershop.

—You're kidding me!

—And I'm looking for a place to live . . .

—Why don't you come to the street where I live.

Madalenita was a good friend I knew from back when I worked in the factories. I met up with her again when I came to Callejón de los Reyes. I hadn't seen her for a long time:

—I went to Cuernavaca, that's why. I was out of the shoemaking trade because leather was hard to get, so I went back home. I sold everything.

Madalenita sewed the upper part of shoes. People took the cut pieces of leather to the tenement house and she sewed the outer part with a special machine that had very strong needles for sewing leather. She worked at home so she could take care of her kids. Sometimes she'd put together as many as three dozen shoes a day. She also trimmed them and sewed the lining—because they used to line shoes; they didn't make them the shoddy way they do now—then she'd sew them up at the heel and they were ready for the cobbler to put the soles on. Those shoes were sturdy with real strong stitching.

—Nicanor asks about you a lot . . .

Nicanor was her son. He and I had worked together at the factory.

—What's that?

—I said, Nicanor asks about you . . .

—There's no reason for him to be doing that. What the hell is he asking?

—He just wants to know when you're coming to visit . . . He says: "If you see Jesusa, tell her to stop by . . ."

Imagine that!

I rented a room on San Antonio Abad Street, or rather, on Los Reyes and San Antonio Abad. I took my rags with me and that's when I met some of Madalenita's friends, Sara Camacho, my *comadre* Victoria and her daughter, little Sara (who was named after Sara Camacho), who became my *comadre* too. I had a big room with a kitchen and all, and at first, Nicanor would come and stand in the doorway and talk to me, but when I found out that the soldiers were leaving, I told him I was moving to the de la Garza neighborhood to be closer to the soldiers and know what they were up to.

—If I stay here, I won't know what time they leave and they'll go without me. It's happened before! They're in the barracks on Chivatito, there in Chapultepec, and the de la Garza neighborhood is right next to that!

Nicanor turned white and said:

—Get out of here, Jesusa, and don't ever come back.

I left my things with Madalenita Servín.

I lived in the de la Garza neighborhood for about three months waiting to leave, when they told me the company was on its way to Tampico and the detachment to San Luis Potosí, San Ciro, and Ciudad del Maíz. If things were still done the way they used to be, I'd go back to working with the troops in a heartbeat! These days the men are just puppets. They ride around in cars, coming and going, here and there. They wear soldier uniforms, but they're not real troops. Before, the cavalry rode day and night and the infantrymen pounded the pavement carrying their things on their backs! But not anymore. They don't even have women now. They don't allow them in the barracks. The men sit in classrooms, studying about advancing and retreating from diagrams on a blackboard, and they don't even seem like men to me. They're stuck in their cement boxes in the middle of a field and the hospital is nearby because they're almost always sick from lack of exercise . . . Even though they have their own houses they only go out on their day off, like the maids do.

Now, if there's a war, the enemy will cut their throats, chew them up for lunch and dinner, and spit out their bones, because Mexican soldiers have become worthless since the fighting stopped. It's all a sham! Just fake bullets! White umbrellas they call parachutes! Smashing each other's faces in because they don't have anything else to do!

I left twelve pesos for three months' rent with Madalenita Servín and was on my way. Since I didn't have to answer to anyone, I just said goodbye and left. I could take off without any set plans and follow whatever path I came to. That's what I was like, the daughter of life, used to going from one place to another, pitching my tent wherever I felt like it.

I set up a hog-slaughtering business in Cuidad del Maíz, which they now call Ciudad Valles. I bought the hogs and hired two boys to help me with the slaughtering, carry water, and all that. I killed the hogs, cut them up, and cleaned them.

You have to strike a pig right in the heart. If you know how to do it correctly, the animal doesn't even have time to squeal. If not, let me tell you, the noise will break your eardrums! Pedro showed me how when we were up north. When I got into butchering I had to buy all the tools, platform scales, ladles, knives, weights. I sold raw meat by the kilo and I fried the pork rinds in the pots: crispy browned rinds.

On the road between San Luis Potosí and Ciudad Valles I found a child. He was a big boy about ten years old, one of those vagrants who wander the streets. He asked me if I'd give him a five-centavo piece:

—Why are you begging?

—For food . . . I haven't eaten in a lot of days . . .

—Don't you have a mother?

—No.

—If you don't have anyone to look after you, I'll take you in.

He didn't say anything.

—Do you want to live with me? I'll take you in as my child, I'll dress you, I'll buy you what you need, but you'll have to help out butchering hogs . . .

—Butchering? Okay, I'll go with you . . .

And that's how I took him in. That boy's name was Rufino. He was like most kids, a walking disaster. I taught him how to butcher hogs. When I picked him up he was barefoot; I fed him, dressed him, and bought him shoes as though he was my own son. I didn't give him money, because he had everything he needed and he started acting sneaky.

Since he'd been a vagrant and didn't stay in one place for longer than three days, he had the itch to move on. Rufino was born to wander, and who could change that? Certainly not me. I was always a wanderer myself, although I was a real hard worker. That's all he could ever be, like those stray dogs that roam the streets. In the butcher shop an older man sold the meat to the customers and helped with the heavy work. Rufino carried water, went for wood, and put the pots on the fire.

They sent a division to Rancho del Guajolote, and even though the main group stayed in Ciudad Valles, I followed the division because all the boys I sold meat to were in that group and since they bought from me on credit I had to follow them to get paid. That's how we ended up in Rancho del Guajolote and why I bought cattle—eight- or nine-month-old calves—to butcher. I started selling beef but I didn't do well, because the soldiers couldn't pay me if they didn't get paid. I bought the cattle on credit, and I paid for them when I sold the meat. But I couldn't make it. I got rid of the calves and said: I've had enough debt and foolishness.

I had compadres in Rancho del Guajolote, because Pedro and I had crowned Refugio Galván when he had died a long time ago. When I got to the ranch the same family asked me to baptize their newborn son, in memory of Refugito. But the company received orders to move out right then and I told them if they wanted they could bring the child to Ciudad del Maíz because we couldn't do it at the ranch. They agreed and we became compadres for the second time. I turned the celebration into a big party with mole and everything. The lieutenant colonel came, the general and his staff came, they all came for mole. That's when young Rufinito asked me:

—Where did you leave the knives?

—You know where we keep them, I said, half buzzed. Buzzed like the sound flies make when the cow swats them with her tail.

We kept celebrating until ten o'clock the next morning. I was sleeping like a blessed baby, when one of the soldiers woke me up and said:

—Listen, so-and-so deserted!

—Who deserted?

—One of the soldiers deserted and they saw him running away with your boy . . .

—How could it have been my boy? I just sent him to get firewood.

—That may be, but he was seen with the soldier at dawn . . .

—I saw him lying down next to me on some sacks. I saw him sleeping!

—Maybe he did lie down, but the neighbors saw him when he left with the knives and some ropes.

He took the scales around the back by the wall and the soldier caught them on the other side when he threw them over, waiting for him to come out with the rest, but the neighbors, who always get up early, saw him and he couldn't come back for the other stuff.

If he could have, he'd have taken my suitcase with the money and all my things. Rufino stayed with me for two years and then took off. That's why I said I wouldn't raise anyone else.

Since things didn't work out for me in Ciudad del Maíz, I went to San Luis Potosí, through the towns of San Ciro and Río Verde and Cerritos to get to know the area, and I was headed back to San Luis Potosí, where the troops were stationed. I walked with the feeling that things had gone bad on me. I wanted to find Rufino to give him what he had coming. One day I decided: "Enough of this, I'm going to the capital." Once I said: "I'm going," I felt better about things.

I left at ten in the morning on the Saturday before Easter Sunday. With the little change I had I sent my suitcase on the express, the one I carry my rags in, it's up there on top of the wardrobe and I keep it for the day I decide to leave. I threw some dishes in a wicker basket: cups, bowls, knives, a stone mortar, an empty milk bottle, and I carried it on my head. My traveling companion was a white dog everyone called Jasmine. This Jasmine belonged to the troops, but in the barracks he always followed me around. He left me halfway through the trip because he found a dead animal along the road and he decided to stay there and eat. I heard he went back to San Luis Potosí after that, but if he'd wanted to he could have caught up with me. I walked and walked until I got to a station. If I found out I could make it to the next one, I kept going. I just drank water and walked all day without resting. It's a habit I picked up when my father was a peddler. We traveled from one town to another, with him herding me and his burros. My father sold cane, bananas, brown sugar, pineapples; he bought from the ranches and traded it in the town for butter, grease, and things they didn't have on the ranches. He always dragged me everywhere, and even though I was just a kid, I learned to keep walking.

The only blanket I had was a red scarf I wore on my head. I walked along the railroad tracks starting at three or four in the morning to avoid the strong sun. When it got really hot, I'd sit down and rest in the shade, but I always gauged it so I'd be close to a station by five or six in the afternoon, no later than that. I never stayed out in the middle of nowhere. I'd approach the houses next to the station and say:

—I'm coming from such and such place . . . Would you please allow me to stay here tonight, and tomorrow I'll take off real early? I'm going to such and such place.

And they'd let me stay in the kitchen next to the fire. If I didn't have money to buy coffee or sugar, I'd ask them to lend me a pot to heat something up; if not, they'd say:

—Don't worry about it, you can eat with us.

Peasants are like that, real generous. I slept on the floor in the kitchen. Sometimes they'd lend me a *petate*.

Since people outside of Mexico City get up really early, I'd try to leave then too, like at three in the morning. I'd have some coffee and then keep walking until I got to a place where there were other people. Even now, when it looks like the situation is lost, when I can't work, I'll sell all the dirty old things I have, and I'll take off down the railroad tracks, without any set course, to see where God has destined for me to die.

WHEN I WAS ALMOST TO MEXICO CITY a Flecha Roja bus gave me a ride, for free, but I got disoriented. At the terminal the driver asked me:

—Where are you going?

—I have relatives in San Antonio Abad.

—I can leave you here in La Merced.

Since it was ten at night when we arrived, I thought to myself: "Which street do I take here? It's so dark." I asked the driver:

—Which way do I go?

—It's real late. It'd be better for you to stay in a hotel.

—But they're too expensive.

—I'll talk to them so they'll give you a place to sleep for a peso . . .

They took me up to a little room way up above the attic. The driver didn't leave.

—It's a cot for two, little one . . .

—What?

—Yeah, we'll share dreams . . .

I cursed at him. I'd paid the peso for the cot. The hotel owner came up and yelled at us to stop arguing on the stairs, and to get the hell out. The driver threw up his hands. I think the people at the hotel knew him because when they said: "Go on, get out of here and go get drunk," the guy did what they told him.

The next morning when I woke up, I opened the window, and

oh my God, I still didn't know where I was. It might have been
from weakness or Lord knows what else. I was hungry so often because all I ate was whatever taco someone gave me, so when I took
off early in the mornings my head would spin.

I went downstairs and asked the people outside the hotel how
to get to San Antonio Abad. While I was out in the fresh air and
walking the streets, I started recognizing places, but all of a sudden I got dizzy like never before.

—Why didn't you write us? Why didn't you let us know? We got
the ticket from the express for your suitcase and we were worried
that something had happened to you . . .

—What about Madalenita Servín?

—She moved.

—Where to?

—She didn't say.

—What about my things?

—She sold them . . .

—The cane furniture, the Austrian furniture?

—Yeah, that and the two tables and your brass bed. She sold all
of it. But you never wrote . . .

—And now?

—Now you're without a place to live.

My *comadre* Victoria, Sara Camacho, and little Sara just stood
there staring at me. Then little Sara said:

—Come sleep with us, right, Mama? You can't be all alone
with just your soul.

About three days later I went to look for work and I took
the first job that came along. I worked as a maid, on Abraham
González Street. I was off on Sundays at one in the afternoon and
I had to be back the next Monday at five in the morning. I'd leave
the dance hall and go straight to work, to light the fire in the
kitchen and stir it, scurrying around like a dazed rat. They paid
me fifteen pesos a month and I started saving up to buy furniture.

—I wonder how Madalenita's doing? I said to my *comadre* Victoria.

She opened her eyes wider.

—Don't you know about Nicanor?

—What about Nicanor?

—That's why she sold your furniture, to pay for his medicine.

—Really?

—Yeah, Nicanor was dying from grief.

—Because he loved me so much?

—Ay, Jesusa, why are you laughing?

—How's he doing now?

—The poor guy, he's getting by. He moved to Cuernavaca. I went to visit Madalenita.

—You finally came back, she said.

She always said the same thing to me. No matter what happened, she'd shake her head and say: "The world is the world."

The woman I worked for in Ribera de San Cosme really made my life miserable because she was so demanding. She followed me around all the time, and every now and then she'd say:

—Stop doing that and go over to such and such.

I couldn't finish the ironing before she'd be ordering me to peel potatoes or to clean the toilet. Then I'd go run errands and she was so scatterbrained, it took me twice as long to do everything. "Hey, you, I forgot the onions. You have to go get them!" She didn't know how to run a house and it was too late for her to learn. She constantly interrupted my routine of chores. And her house was like that too; nothing was ever in its place. After that when I went looking for work I'd say:

—If they're Mexican, don't bother giving me their address, because I won't work there.

They may be my fellow countrymen, but frankly I don't want to deal with them. It's not that foreigners don't order you around, but they have a different way of doing it; they aren't such tyrants and they don't meddle in your life: "Have you gone to mass yet? What time did you come in last night? Don't go talking to any men, you hear me, because we won't be responsible if something happens, you know what I mean?" Back then there were no placement agencies. I'd go to the houses and knock on the door to look for work. There was one house here on Roma Street where I started one morning and by five o'clock that afternoon I walked out because I couldn't take it. Back in 1917 when I went to work for the blond Spaniard, she made me drink tea, which I didn't like, but the Mexican woman said to me:

—There are leftover grounds there. Go ahead and boil them so you can have some coffee.

I thought: "No way. I may be real poor but I don't drink grounds. Excuse me, but you can keep your grounds, and shove them up your ass and enjoy them yourself."

She started lunch at noon. They brought filet from the butcher shop. She pricked it and put it in the oven. When they finished eating at the table, she put all the leftovers from the serving dishes in a soup tureen and told me to stir them together. I said fine. "If she wants me to stir them, I'll do that. She can eat it with her bread." Then she took a piece of rotten meat out of the refrigerator; it was slimy green and hard. She cut two slices off, one for the chambermaid and another one for me, and she put a leaf of lettuce on each side. I thought: "She can eat that herself, because I'd rather go hungry."

I hurried to clean up the kitchen and mop the floor, and when I was done, she said: "You can go get your clothes."

—Yes, ma'am. And you can wait for me right there in that chair.

—What did you say?

—Just what you heard, ma'am. I worked for you today for free.

And I left. I went to Madalenita's house because whenever I visited her she'd say:

—Go ahead and have some bean soup.

—Ay, no, I'm not that poor that I have to eat beans.

I don't eat beans. I know how to cook them, but they aren't food to my stomach. But that day it was six in the evening and when I saw that pot of beans boiling they looked so good. I said:

—Ay, Madalenita, give me a little bean soup with a bunch of those bullets in it because I'm starving to death. I didn't even have breakfast.

—My Lord! What do you mean, you haven't even had breakfast?

—I'll tell you later.

So she gave me the bean soup, and she sliced onions on top,
and cilantro, and cut up a chile, and I started to sweat just watching her, because I was so hungry. After I ate I told her the story
and she said:

—Rich people are really cheap.

After that I went to a house on Lucerna Street, where the
kitchen was bigger than this room with a white tile hearth, and all
the walls were tiled. You had to wash them with a rag and soap so
they wouldn't be dull, and when I rinsed them with a hose the water got all over me. I started at five in the morning. My feet swelled
up so much from the dampness that I had to buy shoes two sizes
larger than I usually wear. My legs swelled up too. I had to walk
even though it hurt, but if I tried to sit I'd scream because I
couldn't bend. I ate standing up. I did everything standing up,
but I couldn't walk either. If I sat down I wouldn't be able to
straighten up.

It took a lot of effort to go up to the roof to sweep, to hang the
clothes out in the sun. One day I heard an organ grinder playing
"El Señor de Chalma." In my own denseness I said to myself: "If
there really is a Señor de Chalma, I want him to heal my legs."
Every day my legs got worse, and the organ grinder played the
song over and over: "Señor de Chalma, it's you I must see . . . I'll
bring the candle that my wife sends thee." At night when I'd lie
down to sleep I'd cry out:

—Lord, please help me out here. Come heal my legs, because
I don't know what will become of me if I can't walk.

I didn't know anything about that saint from Chalma. I'd just
yell to him. I'd wake up at four in the morning and in those wee
hours I'd say: "What do I have to do to be able to get out of bed?"
It took forever for me to get feeling back into my legs. My bones
were like iron rods . . . One night I dreamt a doctor came and said
to me:

—Don't rush it, the pains will go away.

I told the woman I worked for:

—I'm sorry, señora, but I have to leave, because my legs can't take it anymore.

—What's wrong with you?

—It's your tile walls, señora. You'd be better off calling the firefighters to come hose them down . . .

None of the homes paid more than fifteen pesos for housework, which included washing, ironing, cooking, grocery shopping, scrubbing floors. Maids earn several hundred pesos now for doing one thing, but back then there was no such thing as a chambermaid, a downstairs maid, a kitchen maid . . . you did it all.

Walking all the way back to San Antonio Abad felt like I was doing penance. I was almost crawling on all fours by the time I got there. I had to really stretch those fifteen pesos to buy a cardboard box to sell cigarettes, candy, chocolates, gum, marzipan. "I'll just sit here and sell my stuff because that's the only way I can support myself now." I set up my stall behind the Tres Estrellas factory. Since I couldn't pay rent, I'd go stay with my *comadre* Victoria at night. My *comadre* Sara, the little one, met a widower who set her up in a small store, to help her and her mother out.

—Listen, Jesusa, Victoria said to me. My little Sara will probably marry that respectable widower . . .

—When?

—Well, he has a son and he lives with his sister. Since he supports them he can't marry my Sara right now . . .

The widower said that when God came for his sister he'd be free to do as he pleased, but as long as she was alive he wouldn't be able to leave her. He had all of us waiting for God to remember about the sister!

I slept on the floor inside the store. They gave me pieces of cardboard; Sara Camacho slept there too. I'd leave early in the morning with the cigarette box to set up my spot. The holy doctor kept visiting me at night. I'd see him in my sleep and he'd put his lips close to my ear:

—I'm here with you. Can you feel me? Do you recognize me?

He came with his assistant, who was dressed in white because all spiritual doctors have an assistant in a white jacket.

—Don't you have eyes to see me? Can't you feel me healing you?

I must have lost consciousness, because I couldn't tell if I was lying down or not. I just remember that it took a lot of effort to kneel down and pray and when I woke up at four in the morning I was lying down, so I assumed it must have been my protector who laid me down on top of the cardboard and put the serape over me.

I don't know how it healed me, but he smeared my whole body with divine ointment. It felt real soft, gentle, especially on my joints. It just didn't last all day. The relief was only for a little while and by the next day I was gnarled up again. A woman named María passed by on Lorenzo Boturini Street on her way to sell used clothes at the market. She lived in the same tenement and even though she wasn't a friend she asked me:

—What's wrong? You look terrible.

—Why are you asking? You can see I'm in bad shape . . .

I already had a nasty disposition, and then with the pain on top of it . . . But she kept insisting; she was real concerned.

—Child, who's taking care of you? Why aren't you getting treated? I'll take you to a place where they heal people on Tuesdays.

On Tuesday she stopped by for me and we went to number 5 Chimalpopoca. There was a whole world of sick people, men, women, children, a lot of people. They were going in one at a time. The mediums or the priestesses, the pedestals and the columns, their helpers, stood in rows next to the stairs that had a lamp lit at the very top. First the priestesses would go into a trance, and once they were asleep, each one would grab a sick person; they laid their hands on them and started to cure them with the power of their minds.

That day I met Trinidad Pérez de Soto, the woman who would later become my godmother; she was the guide for the place. She went into a trance, and the protector who came through her started to remove the evil I'd picked up. She cleansed me with a bouquet made up of seven herbs: St. Mary's, lavender, rue, mint, eucalyptus, fennel, and cloves, slowly, slowly, sweeping it over me from top to bottom, breathing out hard through her mouth so that the humors would leave. Then she rubbed Seven Machos lotion on my forehead and told me to stay warm.

The cleansing took twenty-one days; the first seven times she used bouquets, then seven with fire and seven with cloud flowers. For the fire cleansings you light a eucalyptus branch covered with alcohol. After the twenty-one cleansings I could walk. That's when Trinidad Pérez de Soto singled me out. One evening she ordered me to help her.

—On Monday you'll start working with me. You'll sit to my right.

—Why? the other ones complained. We've been in the chain being massaged for four or five years. She's new.

—She has a very high-level protector. He's worked her enough spiritually and she's more than ready for it.

—We go into spiritual trances too. Our protectors put us to sleep too.

—Yes, sisters, I've seen that. You sleep like logs and snore like sawmills. You go into a natural sleep, not a trance. Those of you who can't sleep at home come here to the Obra Espiritual to catch up and that's not the way it's supposed to be. You have to choose one or the other; either you follow the right path or just keep treading on the same old patch of dirt.

They lowered their heads, but that's when they started to get jealous of me. They gave me dirty looks as I walked through the vestibule to go into the temple. I had to be at the chapel every day at five-thirty. We started working at six and ended at nine. I bought a thick bunch of cloud flowers on the way to the temple to make the cleansing bouquets. Tomás Ramírez, the spiritual child who manifested himself through Trinidad Pérez de Soto's flesh, healed people with white flowers and if there weren't any white flowers, he used alfalfa.

He was a spiritual being, but anyone with eyes could see Tomasito. He was a boy from Xochimilco who died young; he must have been about three years old when he left his vessel, because in his second or his third reincarnation—who knows how many he'd had—he materialized as a girl and he hated it, so he choked himself on a mouthful of beans. He told us that in other reincarnations he'd been a different type of child, but this time he got real poor parents and he suffered because all they gave him to eat was beans. Since he didn't like being poor or a girl, he stuffed his mouth full of beans until he couldn't breathe, so he returned to the spiritual world. There aren't any pictures of Tomás Ramírez. He was Indian; no one would have taken his picture. On Tuesdays and Fridays the spiritual child came down to Earth, and since Trinidad Pérez de Soto worked with her eyes closed, I had to hand her the little brooms of herbs and flowers and I never left her right side.

I needed physical guidance, so I sat next to her like a monkey to learn the ceremony, until the other sisters' and priestesses' spirits got all worked up. Since they couldn't get off the ground, they were Earth-bound, and they got even more jealous. Maybe they didn't have good protectors or they just didn't pay enough attention to them. The spiritual massages felt like you were getting the chills because your flesh trembled so that the being could come through. Their bodies never even moved. That's why they fasted.

I suffered a lot and felt like slapping them to get rid of their hiccups. At one sermon the Lord told me that I had to be calm, because that calm would allow me to step from the dark into the divine light, where none of those jealous girls had been. But I was flesh and blood, and I'm still flesh and blood, and I don't like anyone telling me what to do. I still feel things physically and I defend myself.

THE SPIRITUAL BROTHERS made me lose my business to make eternal salvation easier for me. They sent the workers from the Tres Estrellas factory to ask me to give them my merchandise, and I did. I say I gave it to them because they bought on credit but never paid me back a centavo. When Saturday came and they were paid, they took off for home, forgetting about me, until I had nothing left to sell. I just handed out all my merchandise; give me this bag of peanuts here, how about some cigarettes, I'll take some candy, let me have it on credit, everything was always on credit. Selling candy is a good business, if you're paid in cash. At first I'd buy my candy at the stores of La Merced and I made a lot buying wholesale. But after a while my money ran out and I couldn't compete with the retailers that go around stealing from you. And soon I had to declare bankruptcy because I was broke. It's been the story of my life, because when I had a big clothing stall in San Juan—to make a long story short—I gave the clothes away too. They'd say:

—I'll pay you such and such day.

—Go ahead and take it . . .

I'm not good at sales because I can't say no to the customers.

I arranged to work in the Castillo drugstore on San Antonio Abad with Señora Ester for a while. I cleaned vials and mortar dishes like when I was in Tehuantepec and I liked to tell the customers what to take for chills, spells that had been put on them, headaches, sadness, fear, bile, jaundice, indigestion, heartburn, a head cold, or terror. I'd tell them to put a glass of water out to steep or to drink virgin honey, or toloache elixir on an empty stomach, or basil, green tea, or nettle or willow, or peace flower or peyote or marijuana or spearmint or damiana or camomile or St. Nicholas. The old fogy, Señor Castillo, couldn't stand to hear me prescribe recommended treatments to people:

—Do you think you're a doctor? You're here to sell, not to be chattering with the customers.

Whenever the line of people who came to consult with me got too long, he'd raise the roof:

—I'm going to send you and your prescriptions both to Hell!

It wasn't a live-in job and Señora Ester treated me well. I guess I increased her clientele. She gave me a lot to eat and by eight at night I'd be on my way to Victoria's. Someone always stopped me on the way:

—Good evening, may the souls in Purgatory rest!

—Good night.

—Jesusa, listen, can I have a word with you?

They spoke to me so respectfully.

—What do you need to know about? It's getting late . . .

—What do I do for a sharp pain that I get here on my side? Do you think it could be my liver?

—I'll give you the address of the Midday Temple . . .

—Okay . . .

—Have a good evening . . .

—Good night, may the souls in Purgatory rest!

I'd get to the tenement house and we'd put the coffee on to heat. We slept in the back of the store, like chickens without coops, Sara Camacho, little Sara, her daughter Carmela, and my *comadre* Victoria. When the widower stopped by he'd get irritated with all the mess: "This looks like a pigsty." I finally told Sara Camacho:

—You and I are fifth wheels here. We're taking in their air.

That's when she and I rented a room on a backstreet in Magueyitos for three pesos a month. I took the mattress I'd just bought and threw it on the floor to sleep on. Sara paid me one-fifty, but since all her friends were drunks, just like her, she'd bring anyone who was passing by into the room. I got mad.

—We're real poor, but there has to be some respect for each other here in the room. I don't want people coming in and out of here. We may share the rent but visitors aren't allowed.

It had been years and happy days since I'd had a drink. When I decided to quit I just watched everyone else, because you don't have to pay for that. And it worked; my will was strengthened. And then I told myself: "I'm not going to drink anymore," and I just stopped drinking. One time I saw a young girl lying out in front of a *pulquería*. She was holding her child, but she was so drunk she vomited on her daughter. I said: "God, have mercy, help me stop drinking." The truth is, I have real strong willpower! If I decide not to do something ever again, I never do. I've been stubborn that way since I was little. I see men who can't control themselves: "This damn vice won't let go of me!" and it really makes me mad. They stay hooked on drinking and that's a crying shame; it's a sickness the weaklings can't overcome. It does take a lot of work, of course it does. Like the Obra Espiritual, which is really beautiful but real hard. I can't seem to tame myself, but I do have some control. It took a lot for me to stop fighting, stop drinking, but having a strong will takes away vice.

Sara kept bringing drunk men into the room, until I put a stop to it.

—I can't take any more of your lepers in here . . . I can't even sleep with all the shrieking . . .

Since I didn't get anywhere by talking, I took my mattress, which they'd probably crapped up with their juices, and I went back to live with Victoria. Sara came back after a while too, because she couldn't afford the three pesos' rent alone.

When I met her, Sara Camacho was a poor woman who didn't know how to do anything. People paid her fifteen, twenty centavos to write letters for them, and that's how she made ends meet; she wrote them out real careful, in nice handwriting. That's what she did for a living because she didn't know how to work. She had a sister who had a good job, and she was the daughter of a military colonel who fought with Porfirio Díaz, but since she went down the wrong path, her relatives didn't have anything to do with her. In those days women didn't work except in their homes or as maids. Now women outdo men with all their liveliness and partying. They don't stay home anymore: "I'll go one way and you go the other, and see what you find."

Sara Camacho drank pulque every day like it was water. She didn't fall down drunk but she did get tipsy. I decided to clear out, so I took a live-in job with a Cuban woman, Belén Caridad.

I'd been working at the Obra Espiritual for almost six months when Sister Trinidad Pérez de Soto said to me:

—Do you have money for the bus fare to Pachuca?

—Well, not really. I don't get paid until the last day of the month . . . So I don't have the money to go.

—The First Seal is in Pachuca.

—Since I haven't even been working there two weeks, I can't ask for time off.

—Well, if it's God's will, you'll get the money and permission to leave.

One morning, out of the blue, the Cuban woman said to me:

—Listen, we're not going to be here for Holy Week. We'll be back Sunday night. I'll give you three days off.

Imagine, the sisters at the Obra Espiritual would have been green with envy!

In Pachuca they started the prayer, and when they were saying: ". . . give them, Lord, an atom of divine light," that was when Vicentita Islas, the priestess, and Trinidad Pérez de Soto received the message that I should be marked.

At that baptism the priestess applied a triangle of light, first on my forehead and then on my head, my ears, in my mouth, on my feet and hands, with my palms facing up. That's the triangle of divinity. And that triangle can stop storms, wind, tidal waves, tornadoes, and it calms the turmoil inside of you, evens out the precipices. That day they marked thirteen men and women. After that, most of the people there told about their visions. We were all standing around a small well. I was staring at some pipes that formed a cross inside it, when all of a sudden a white hand appeared on the surface of the water and stirred it up. When it was my turn I told everyone what I'd just seen.

—I just saw a hand make the sign of the cross over the water . . .

They explained that it was Brother Jacob's hand, the one from the Bible, because the water in that well at Rancho de San José comes from the river Jordan.

After saying grace they spread out the tablecloths and sat down to eat.

I cried a lot there at the well, God only knows how hard I cried. The feeling was so strong, I didn't know what was happening to me, why so much water came into my eyes. I wasn't sad, it was like feeling full. Then they called me to come and eat. I told them I wasn't hungry, for some reason. After eating, the whole brotherhood went to the well to gather water. Sick people were healed when they drank it; by the time they got back home they were cured. The Messenger Elías, otherwise known as Roque Rojas, dug that well himself. When he was five years old he had the ability to perform wonders that Jesus Christ was only able to do as an adult. He mastered twenty-two trades but he practiced only three. He studied to be a priest but couldn't be admitted because his parents, who were Spanish, died and left him with a tutor who also died. So he went to work in a jewelry shop, got married, and had a daughter or two or three, I can't remember now. When he reached the right age, he heard a voice that said:

—Roque, your time has come. Go out into the streets and look for a trustworthy man to dig a hole, a big well . . . You draw the circle.

He lived in an old, old house over near Arena Mexico, where I went to the bullfights.

—Have the worker leave. It's your turn to dig now. When it starts to get dark, put three candles in a triangle on the ground. You and your wife and your daughter will form the other carnal triangle. Then you climb into the hole with the pickax!

Everything is written down in the First Volume of Geography. That's why I'm telling you this. They undid the carnal triangle and Roque stayed there alone. He struck the ground once with the pickax and a stream of water started filling up the well. When it got all the way up to his neck, and had completely bathed him, the water receded on its own. He was completely dry, and he heard the voice again:

—Have you been bathed? This was your baptism. Your name is Elías. Elías the Son of Mary . . . Roque Rojas no longer exists.

He didn't respond. Then the voice asked him:

—Did you see the angel that gave you the scroll?

—Yes.

And he wasn't the only one who saw it; his wife and daughter did too: a messenger on a white horse, an angel with wings, a messenger from the Lord, with a scroll in his hand.

From that moment on, Roque Rojas was able to devote himself to fulfilling what was written on the parchment, now that he was Elías. He covered the Earth with his mysteries. He performed more than the fifteen you see on the Boulevard of Mysteries that leads up to the Basilica of the Virgin of Guadalupe. Have you seen those lumps of stone that they call monuments along the street? That's where Roque Rojas left his miracles. They're sacred cloisters.

The time came for him to be raised from Earth. But he scattered the seeds so that people could follow his path. He's buried here in Dolores. They brought him from Pachuca, and every year on the sixteenth of August the believers go to the cemetery to join Father Elías, also known as Roque Rojas.

One night Sara Camacho stopped by little Sara's stall:

—I'll be right back. I'm going for my pulque . . .

She crossed the street with her empty bottle. When she didn't want tacos, she bought a tamale, but usually she ate a special kind of beef—I don't know if it was brains, or loin, or flank steak, or testicles, but it was some part of the bull—and she made tacos with a lot of salsa; she bought her meat and washed it down with her pulque. That day they didn't have the kind she wanted and she had her tamale in her hand when she went to cross the street. She avoided the train that was coming up, but she was blinded by the light and was hit by the train from Xochimilco that was coming from the other direction. The train locked up almost right in front of the door and they came running in to tell us that some-one had been killed. Sara Camacho wore men's ankle boots and she cut her hair like a man. I recognized her by the boot and her head, because the train cut it right off. The only thing that was left whole was her one foot that came off at the ankle, and her head, which rolled to one side.

Sara Camacho liked hanging out with men. She was macho. By five in the morning she was out drinking spiked coffee with the streetcar drivers. All the people from the depot, the old drivers, were her friends. By the time the motorman was finally able to see her in his light it was too late to brake. He didn't run away; he got down and stood guard next to her head. When they came to check it out he told them:

—You figure out how to lift the car, because I'm not moving this thing forward or backward.

They got a jack to lift the train. When they finally got her out, you could hear the sound of the bones inside her skin and her clothes. She was all in pieces. They took her to the Fourth Precinct, on 5 de Febrero Street, on a stretcher in an ambulance. We waited there, but they wouldn't let us see her. Pieces of her were left stuck in the tracks! The train smeared her all over the rails. You couldn't even recognize her head, because the electric-ity from the train turned her face to ashes. They gave her to us to bury, but we never knew if it was really her, although we never saw her again after that.

Victoria said that Sara Camacho had to come back; that she wasn't the one that had been crushed, but I'd recognized her.

—It's her, but I hope I'm wrong, and that God will bring her back.

We're still waiting for her.

My friend Sara Camacho the fighter and Victoria were insepara-ble. When I went to live in the tenement on Callejón de los Reyes, they made friends with me and asked me to take their saints to be blessed. That's why they became my *comadres*. I'm always the godmother to one saint or another. Sara Camacho wasn't into women, but she did everything just like a man. They called her Sara What-a-macho, to insult her, but she wasn't a dyke. Dykes have lovers and start to act like fags. I've never seen it, but they say that they switch back and forth, one month they're the man and the next month they're the woman, because they have both a man's thing and a woman's thing. There used to be a lot of them in the city. When I was young, I liked long-sleeved blouses with a man's collar and a tie, but since the dykes wore them I started to detest them. One day the police raided Alameda Park and took them to jail. Many years ago you could walk through that park and you'd never have guessed who was a man and who was a woman in the dark behind the trees. And the police would catch the women in the act. That was when they started to arrest a lot of homos. They call them homos and lesbians. They rub their pussies against each other and butt heads like sheep. That's not legal. I'll go along with things that are legal, but that's a whole different thing, it's shameful. If they want it so much, why don't they go for a man? It's been like that throughout history, for centuries, that's the way it has to be. If it's considered bad if a man is with a woman, then imagine between a man and another man or between women; that's just pathetic.

It's been about ten years since I ran into Victoria's daughter—Sara the little one—in San Juan de Letrán, but I didn't recognize her. She saw me and spoke to me, but just real quick:

—You never came to see us again after my mother died!

—No, I didn't. Everyone has to go their own way.

Since she'd had good fortune and was in a better situation, she never bothered with me again. She was real conceited, putting on airs when she spoke to me that day, like she didn't remember being poor.

—My daughter Carmela is married, and so is my son, so it's just my husband and me now.

—Where do you live?

—Along Villa Avenue; I own property there.

She didn't say: "I'll have you over," or "Come by," or anything.

That's why I've lost touch with a lot of people, because I've had friendships like that one with my Sara. But they move from one place to another, they get to be real arrogant, and I don't see them again. That's what'll happen with the porters where I live; the day that I leave this tenement they'll throw dirt at me, and I'll never hear from them again. God only knows where I'll end up.

A LL THE WORKERS from the Tres Estrellas factory ate at the Torres family's stall, on the corner of Tlalpán Avenue and Lorenzo Boturini, where they sold both beans and rice with chile sauce. I set up my box with the candy on top and went to the stall to fill my belly. We were sidewalk neighbors. The Torreses lived in a tenement on Alfredo Chavero Street, but they got thrown out because they couldn't pay the rent, so I told them about a lot in the Magueyitos section, where there were buildings that were falling apart. The person in charge would rent them an empty piece of land. For three, four, five pesos for the walls and the floor they'd have a house to live in.

I'd like to find myself some land to rent now, one of those with half-fallen-down walls, but that's like asking someone to bring me the Virgin's pearls!

When my *comadre* Victoria left, the Torreses told me not to be in a big hurry to find another place, because I could move in with them. I thought it'd be a good idea, but I wasn't even living under the roof. I slept outside, up against the wall, on the street side. I borrowed some boards and arranged them so I'd have a place to sleep under the eave that sticks out from the roof, where the water runs off.

The Torres family was really poor; there was the mother, Doña Encarnación, Candelaria, the daughter, and the two boys, Domingo and José. They had to take down their stall because they couldn't afford to keep it stocked; no matter how much they watered down the soup or how much dirt they put in the coffee, they couldn't make a go of it. Since I wasn't working at a private home at the time, they asked me if I wanted to wash mattresses at the hotels with them. I'd do ten or twelve mattresses, depending on how many there were; then we mended the covers and beat them to fluff up the stuffing inside. They were cheap mattresses like the one I have; with the stuffing all bunched up, not the kind with springs.

Domingo was a real braggart but he had a good heart. When he said: "There's work in such and such place," we knew that there'd be enough for everyone. He took his daughter Juana and his niece Antonia, his mother and Candelaria, and asked me along. José went somewhere else; he liked selling clothes at diners, in cabarets, wherever, and when he wasn't selling dresses, he raffled off chickens in the cantinas; but the money he made wasn't anything to shake a stick at. They paid me half a peso a day, and if things went well, a peso and a half, depending on the number of mattresses I washed. On the way back home it was "Come on, Jesusa, buy us candy." I bought whatever they wanted along the street and then I had hardly anything left out of the money I'd earned. So they ended up getting the candy free. With the little that was left I had to buy dough, tomatoes, chiles, coffee, and sugar. Bread was three for ten then. I ate ten centavos' worth; otherwise I just drank my coffee with the small thick tortillas I made . . . I've swallowed a lot of bitter drinks, but lately they've been so bad that I don't seem to taste them anymore.

When Lázaro Cárdenas became president he ordered everyone out of Magueyitos, and he promised to relocate them somewhere else. There were a ton of families that had settled on that land. It wasn't long before they were fighting over what wasn't even theirs; people like that are users. Tres Estrellas bought the land that used to be Magueyitos and now it's a truck stop for shipments coming from Cuernavaca and Acapulco. It was an old hacienda, but there wasn't anyone to claim it, because everyone from the original Spanish family that had owned it had died, and after a long time the farm became government property. The people who had moved in near there, looking for warmth from all the bricks scattered on the ground, used the walls, made adobe, and with the intelligence that God gave them built little houses with cardboard on top for a roof. The government took over the land and sublet the small plots: an employee would collect the rent, which was five or six pesos, and they gave out little receipts that looked like bus tickets. Big Snout Cárdenas decided the place was too good for the poor people and had us thrown out. The people of the neighborhood divided up into political parties and commissions; everyone took a side, and a woman named Micaila started the movement to fight for the land, so they named her president. She got a big group of people together to go to the Zócalo to fight for the property. She did all the arguing; we went along to make a bigger crowd. We didn't even know why she was summoned, but we followed behind her like animals. Frogs, keep quiet, the toad is going to preach! I don't know if she was smart or not, but she talked with all the government people; who knows what she was working out, but she fixed things her own way. Nobody really wanted to leave the land, because they were happy there, and since the authorities didn't pay any attention to her, Señora Micaila ordered us to protest at the Caballito statue, so we stayed there all night long. We were like beggars trying to get them to give us the land. That Micaila was real forceful, a real arguer, real shrewd, and she never left us alone. We were like a battalion of soldiers and she was our general. A lot of people didn't think much of her, because they said she was puffing herself up with importance, like a toad, and she'd end up handing us over to the enemy.

At night in Magueyitos, they'd buy their liquor, get drunk, and start yelling. They'd go visiting from house to house, men and women, and in their drunkenness they played one dirty trick after another. Then they'd get into fistfights with people from the other party and during one of those fights they said they were going to blow up Micaila's shack. Since it was our duty to guard her, we took turns, and one of us was always there to make sure no one got near her shack. When it was Señora Encarnación Torres's turn, I told her that I'd go in her place.

Micaila never spoke to me about her business, because I had

no value. Like an ass, I just went to watch out for her. We weren't paid to keep an eye on her; at least I wasn't. When it was my turn to guard her, I never got five centavos; she didn't even turn around to look at me. It was all about political games; this one wanted a higher position than the other one, and the other one wanted more than the next one.

One morning they came and told us that Lázaro Cárdenas had given our land to the traffic police, so we tried to catch up to the president. He divided the neighborhood up himself. He told the police to build homes on the empty lots. Yes, I saw Cárdenas. Of course I did! And I was furious at him, because I'd met him when he was an ordinary soldier back with Carranza's troops, when he wasn't so flashy, with a big staff, or whispering orders to his people. But we clearly heard him say: "You have to get this element out of here . . ." He didn't recognize me, because the bosses can't pay attention to the ordinary people and even less when they're poor like me. Lázaro Cárdenas walked everywhere, even after he became president. On September 16, Independence Day, he walked all the way from El Ángel to the National Palace. The crowds threw confetti and streamers at him, wrapping him in colors. He's the only president I've ever seen in profile, parading through the streets on foot.

When he left the Traffic neighborhood—that's what they named it—we ran behind him to try to catch up to him, but he was too far ahead. We yelled: "No, we won't obey. Why should we? We're staying right here." And nobody moved.

José Torres was attending the temple by then and spoke to my godmother. He didn't have the balls to talk to me face to face; instead he went and told my godmother, who wasn't really my godmother yet, that he wanted to marry me. He addressed the Ser Espiritual and received this answer:

—Brother, this isn't something for you to arrange with me. Work it out with Sister Jesusa. If she says yes, we can marry you here at the temple. But you need to convince her in your own human form.

That's what the Ser told me later . . . I think José fell in love with me but didn't say anything to me because he wanted to arrange everything through spiritual mediation. He was ugly as sin and I wasn't any better; besides, why in the hell would I want to get married? In the first place, the poor thing is horrendous to look at, and although I do have bad taste, I'm not that hard up . . . I said: "Not me, sweetheart, what would I want you for? I had a real man, and you think I'd be interested in a completely worthless scrap like you?" José is very short, with a big mouth, and he's quite black; I'm dark and he's dark, we'd look like a pair of salamanders . . . Besides, he didn't even court me, he didn't come to see me in person, he went and talked to other beings. He knew that I was involved in the Obra from his sister Candelaria and through Doña Encarnación, so he asked them to pimp for him. But the poor man really made a mess of it. I had no problem answering him face to face, but he went and embarrassed me.

Georgina Valencia, who was a Spiritual Being who manifested herself through the medium, asked me:

—Do you want to marry him?

—Not him or anybody, not for the Virgin's pearls.

Spiritual children handle love issues. It was always either Tomás Ramírez or Georgina Valencia, a little white albino, who was real white, like covered in flour, with snowy eyelashes and cotton-ball hair, a pretty little thing who died from a sunburn when she was small—one of those little ones who are white like milk and can't be out in the strong sun.

How could I let someone tell me what to do? No way! He was a lost drunk, worthless. Since he'd addressed the girl, she was the one who communicated with me, and it made me really mad. When I got home I thought: "If he mentions anything about it I'll let him know what I think of him." But José didn't say anything to me. He went back to the Spiritual Girl to find out my answer, and he'd have been better off if he hadn't.

One day José showed up with a woman, a poor girl named Epifania who worked as a waitress at a cantina over on Candelaria

Street. She made a living serving drinks, and José picked her up and brought her home. He started making her life miserable. I heard it. First he'd hit her and then he'd take off, slamming the door, and when he got back he'd say, real threatening: "What's up, Chula, let's rub our crotches together . . ." Poor girl, he really put her through hell! It didn't matter to me, since she was his woman . . . but I was angry about what he'd done to me and I wanted to get even.

I suffered through downpours, the heat, and the cold under that little board out there under the eave when I was with the Torreses, because I didn't have anywhere else to go. I didn't want everyone to know that I was all alone, like a corncob, so I put up with all of it. When José came in drunk he'd be nasty to me, he'd say horrible things, so one day I gave it back to him good. He yelled:

—Shut up, you kept whore! What are you doing here?

—I'm not what you said, and if I were, what would it matter to you? It's none of your business. I can make a kite out of my asshole if I feel like it!

—You cover yourself real good with someone else's gut when you sleep, and that's some kind of blanket!

Then Epifania pulled him away and made him go inside, but it didn't stop me from wanting to belt him. I said: "You won't be the first man I've hit where it hurts. I have calluses from all the jerks I've beaten." He shouted:

—Whore!

That's when I thought: "It's time for me to get out of here, right now." And the next morning I left real early. There were a lot of mattresses that still had to be washed, full of lice, but it was their problem to work things out so the hotel wouldn't get mad.

About a month or two after I left Magueyitos, the government ordered the firemen to run everyone out of there. Lázaro Cárdenas sent in the red fire trucks.

—Get them out of there with the hoses.

They connected the hoses to the hydrants and with watches in hand they gave everyone half an hour to load their things into the trucks that were lined up. They dumped everyone out in a field the same way they'd rounded them all up. They were given the chunk of dirt they landed on. That's how this neighborhood they named the Jewel was established. It was an empty field, like almost all of Mexico City used to be. It was all plains; there weren't any houses. It's been built up over the years.

Cárdenas did give them the land. They just don't have the right to sell it. So if they're starving to death, they can't sell, because the land still belongs to the government. As long as they're alive the house is theirs, but if they die, or there isn't anyone to represent the family, they lose it. The government owns it.

The women stayed in little caves around the empty lots and the men went to the United States to work and send them money to build their houses. The Torreses were bricklayers, but they needed money to buy materials and what they were paid for the mattresses wasn't enough. They were ordered to build or lose the land, so they didn't have any choice but to take off for the United States. Now they're landlords and live off the rents. They never come visit me. Domingo says hello to me once in a blue moon.

He built a three-story house and he has a lot of renters there. They all built good houses to rent out. They got big plots because they even put the name of their niece Antonia on the list so they'd get more land. And fool that I was, I ended up with nothing.

If I'd waited a month I'd have my own land, but that's the way it goes. I was born poor and I'll be poor when they throw me in the hole, if I even get a hole.

If you're meant to be a tamale, the leaves that you are to be wrapped in will fall from heaven.

The money went to the Torreses' heads. Doña Encarnación was pretty old by then, but she was falling down more from pride than from age. I don't visit her because I don't want her saying I'm after her riches. I did go to see Epifania. She and José ended up getting married in the church and legally too. I went to the wedding.

Epifania said to me:

—I'm real grateful to José for marrying me, but he's so mean to me.

—Well, you're the fool, you're responsible. You already knew he made your life miserable, and you went and made it worse by marrying him.

—I had to get married so I could visit my parents.

—I'd never have married José, even if my parents called me a whore.

She lowered her head. I think from being hit so much. I'm sure, from all the times he kicked her, that poor fool Epifania came here to the Jewel to die.

The day I left the Torres family I went to see Madalenita Servín, the tall, fat, real good woman who had always helped me out. I told her how I was living.

—You don't have anywhere to live? she asked me.

—No, I don't . . . I have my things piled up there on a wall outside.

—Oh, my Lord! We'll look for a place for you to live. I'm going to send Nicanor to help you look for a house in another neighborhood.

She was always pushing me toward Nicanor. He'd come back from Cuernavaca and worked running errands at the factory. When he got off his shift, Madalenita asked him:

—Do you know of anyone who has a house that Jesusa can rent?

—I don't, but if she likes I can take her to look around . . .

He took me through all the neighborhoods, like Rastro, the slaughterhouse, and Bondojo, asking at the stalls. I'm no good at finding a place to live. He'd ask around and we'd go in and look, until finally we found something in the Felipe Angeles neighborhood, named after the guy that Goat Beard had killed. The Vidales family rented me a big empty room, about four meters long. They owned land and they rented out rooms too. That was twenty-nine years ago.

FELICITAS VIDALES had ten children. Nine are living; Rutilio died from that illness that kids get that's like smallpox. Zacarias is the oldest, and then, in order, Fidencio, Pascualina, Lola, Julio, Rutilio the deceased, Perico, Hilaria, and Blanca. Oh, no, Rosa's missing. She comes before Julio, and after July comes August. I messed it all up. I don't even know what day it is anymore. Is today Tuesday or Thursday?

Besides renting out rooms, Felicitas Vidales sold hats. She bought them wholesale in the big factories in La Merced; but before she sold them she'd sew decorations on them. Everyone in the family was involved in the hat business; they didn't know how to do anything else. To this day none of them know how to work. The mother was the only one worth anything; she dealt with the bricklayers and built the house. She did all the buying because her husband, José del Carmen Vidales, was useless.

Every morning I left for work. I was a washerwoman, not a maid anymore. I earned a peso a day, and the employers paid for my transportation and my food. Then there were commuter passes on the buses that were twenty-five centavos for three rides. I got to the houses at about seven in the morning and I left when it started to get dark. After the Santa María neighborhood, I went to San Cosme on Alzate Street to work for an Arab woman, I ended up on Luis Moya with Señora Corcuera, a native of

Guadalajara with real pretty eyes. And from Luis Moya they sent me to the Liverpool Building where a newlywed couple lived.

In the evening, when I was on my way home, Señora Felicitas would chat with me. She was always happy. She'd sing in the kitchen in front of the fire, she'd sing while she decorated hats, she sang all the time. Her mouth was always open with a laugh ready to come out. When people would ask her how she knew something or other, she'd say: "A little birdie told me . . ." and she kept giggling. She talked to her kids all the time too, about clouds and mockingbirds. She told them they'd be princes on golden thrones, a bunch of bullshit. She was like a parrot! When she was done telling stories she'd say:

—Are you all happy? . . . Yes? Then I'm leaving . . .

—No, Mom! Don't go! Tell us another story . . .

And she'd turn around and leave . . . She was always coming and going in her permanently starched slips, chattering away. And she wasn't just surrounded by her own kids; all the kids in the neighborhood laughed with her. Perico, her youngest son, followed me a lot because I'd bring him, in a lunchbox, the leftovers they gave me at work every day, and since he had a hard time holding his head up because he was weak, I'd say:

—Do you want a bread roll?

—Yes.

I'd give him a roll. When I got home he'd come out to meet me. I'd say to him: "Stinking Blondie," and he'd answer: "Rabbit's foot." He trusted me. He called me Jesutiti, I don't know why. He'd run to my room and I'd let him in and give him rabbit stew. The newlyweds were Spaniards, and they loved rabbit. They had rabbit every other day, and sent the leftovers home with me; otherwise they'd go bad. Perico would ask:

—Will you give me a centavo so I can bring you water?

—Go ahead.

He'd go back and forth and back and forth bringing water. He was three years old at the most, and he carried water all day long, a little bit at a time, in a little pewter pan. Most of the time he spilled it along the way, but since his mother had taught him that you have to laugh at everything all the time, he'd sit and laugh at the spilt water. Then the kids on the street would hit him, but he never hit back, he just moved out of the way. He was never an aggressive person.

One night when I came back a little early, Felicitas was sitting on the patio and said to me with her wavy-shaped mouth:

—Listen, I have bad news for you. The roof in your room fell in and I got scared because one of my boys was running around up there and he almost fell through . . .

Oh well. The roof fell in on top of the bed like there'd been an earthquake . . . She was still talking to me and playing with the kids who were climbing all over her. She'd pinch them:

—This little piggy went to market, this little piggy stayed home, this little piggy . . .

Until I said:

—I'm going in now.

—Me too, I'm going to make dinner.

She went to her kitchen with her kids hanging off her skirts like bells, and I went into my room to check out the situation: "Ay, what a mess to come home to. I'm so tired and I still have to sweep dirt off and shake out my blankets just to be able to sleep!"

They'd already put boards up and covered the hole the best they could, but I still had to clean up all the dirt. I was trying to figure out how to carry out the rubble when Lola came in and said:

—Jesusita, Jesusita, my mother's calling for you to come make her better.

—Don't be bothering me! What's wrong with your mother? I was just talking to her. Don't be telling lies. Leave me alone so I can pick up all this garbage . . .

The little one left but she soon came back:

—Come on, don't be mean, my mother's in really bad shape.

When I went in, I looked her over. I could tell it wasn't good. She looked like she was already dead. The children's father was in the doorway, smoking one cigarette after another. I warned him:

—Listen, you need to get her a doctor, because she's real sick.

—No, she's not sick. She has pain in her head . . . Put some ointment or something on her and she'll get better.

He kept talking to the other people there. That dick made me so mad that I yelled:

—You're not going for a doctor?

—What for? She just feels a little sick.

—I'm not responsible if she dies. I'm washing my hands of this.

And my hands really were dirty from the mess in my room. I turned around and left. A little later Zacarias and Fidencio showed up and went to get the doctor. He gave her medicine and a shot, but she didn't get any better. Nothing changed the look on her face. She was real, real bad off.

And that doctor charged them a fortune! Then the doctors all got together to talk about her case, but it didn't do any good, Felicitas was dying. But another doctor, who lived on Platinos Street—who knows if he still does—figured out what was wrong. He said she'd had a stroke and gave her strong medicine to bring her back to herself, because it was like she'd gotten stupid. She got her speech back but it wasn't clear. After three months, she still talked like babies when they start saying dada dada. The doctor warned the children not to make her angry, to feed her well, but bland foods, no beef, just fish and chicken and rice, and give her her shots, and he said that they had to force her to drink the tonics. Felicitas was worn out from having so many kids, one right after the other, five girls and five boys, like reloading a shotgun. I guess it just exhausted her. No matter how well she ate, that was still a lot of children for such a little mother, because before they're born, boys feed off the mother's lungs, and little girls are nourished from her stomach. The males from the lungs to have air and the females because they'll need a womb, that's why they eat from the stomach.

One day Zacarias came in to see his mother:

—How do you feel?

—A little better, my love.

—Then I'm going to the United States to work on farms, because we're really in debt from your illness . . . My brothers and sisters can keep the hat business going . . .

At that point what did it matter to Felicitas? She didn't say a word. Her happiness had withered away a long time ago. No, I don't know what Zacarias did in the United States.

There was no reason for me to stay around once Felicitas died. I moved from the Jewel neighborhood to this shithole where I am now. But I didn't stop dropping in on the Vidaleses. Felicitas left them the house, which was paid off, and a lot of work to do, more than five thousand pesos' worth of merchandise, but the father started drinking and between him and his sister-in-law they went through every single peso. It broke my heart to see the little ones suffering.

I always made beans or something so they'd eat. The little girls wanted to be on top of me all day, and when I got back from work they'd climb on my bed:

—Give me a little kiss, Jesutiti . . .

—Come on, a little smooch.

—A little kiss on the mouth . . .

That's how Felicitas raised her kids. She'd kiss them on the mouth, on their bottom, wherever.

Their Aunt Rogaciana would take the kids to live with her as they grew. As soon as they looked strong, she'd put ideas into their heads. She told them that I took them in for my own convenience, so they could work to support me. She took them away from me one by one. She was a fat-bellied woman, all bloated from drinking. Rogaciana was always walking the streets wearing flapping sandals, with a filthy rebozo and a greasy apron. The kids went with her because she let them do whatever they wanted. She'd even jump in bed with them and tickle them and that kind of stuff . . . So I ended up with just Perico.

At first I left my Perico locked up in the room. I'd lock the door and leave him inside, just like you do with animals. I'd take off at seven in the morning to do laundry and I'd get back around five or six in the afternoon. That little boy was alone, without his brothers and sisters, crying and crying and crying:

—Why didn't you eat? I left the food there for you . . .

—Because I'm not hungry.

—Then why are you crying?

—Because I was locked up.

—Then you come with me.

Since he was so needy and helpless, it took a lot of work to raise Perico. He wouldn't eat just any kind of food. His mother made him lemon tea or black coffee, or tortillas and beans. In the midst of all my poverty I've been in so many different houses that I've learned to eat different things, and it was really rough with Perico because he couldn't tolerate much. I thought he was dying on me, so I started giving him watered-down soup and oatmeal and coffee with milk and chocolate, when I could afford it, and that's how I strengthened his little stomach. Pico had pale skin and red hair. He was born like that. Felicitas was blond and he came out like a match head. One time I punished him because he went outside and stood in someone's doorway after we had just finished eating breakfast. The family was having lunch and they gave him a taco. Imagine that, they gave him a taco! I looked out the door and I saw him with the taco.

—What're you doing?

—Nothing.

They said:

—We gave him a taco, señora.

—Yes, thank you very much.

And I brought Perico inside.

—Come over here! You eat your taco now and I'll get down the pot. Come on, either you eat all these beans and all those tortillas or I'll wallop you. I don't want you to go stand in other people's doorways like a beggar. Weren't you full? Since you didn't eat until you were full, you're going to right now. *Ándile,* finish your taco and gorge yourself with what I'm giving you!

—I can't.

I sat him there and I stood with a stick in my hand.

—If you don't eat the rest of that I'll beat you. Which would you prefer?

—I can't.

He started crying, because he couldn't eat all those beans.

—Come on. There's the spoon. You swallow it one bite at a time or however you want, but cram it down.

I made him finish them. I thought: "It may send him to his grave but he won't be a beggar!"

And by God, it worked! He never stood in anyone's doorway again.

Sheets are real heavy work for a laundress because they have to be scrubbed and rinsed three times; then you put them out in the sun, bring them back in, scrub them, and then rinse them again. I washed sheets every day. I'd wash them four times. The first time I'd just use water to get rid of the dust; I scrubbed them good to get all the little hairs and the body odor off. Then I'd soap them and throw them in a tub to loosen the grime; once they were soaked in soapy water, I'd take them out one at a time and scrub them in the laundry tub, separating them. Once I'd finished scrubbing all the whites, I'd throw the colors in to soak in the leftover soapy water. Meanwhile I'd put all the white clothes in a pail and put them out in the sun with clean soapy water. When they were dry, I'd take them out of the sun; I'd rinse them with clean water and soap them again. Once I was sure there was no dirt I'd scrub them again on the washboard, rinse them out good, hang them up, and go on to the colored clothes. You always wash the whites separately. Some people are so dumb that they wash them with colors and permanently stain them. I did a lot of sheets every day. Sometimes I'd just wash them once, because they looked real white and had come right off the bed, but when I turned them over I'd see that they were all black with big grease stains. The body betrays you that way. Then you have to wash them completely and put some elbow grease into it; otherwise it's not worth the bother. Laundry is hard work, but I think it's harder to take care of kids. I've never liked kids. They're real annoying and mean. I had Periquito not because I liked him, but because he was a child without a mother. And he was already used to me. What could I do? Throw him out in the street? I had to fight with him like a bullfighter, just as if he were my child, my very own, because it was like he had dog's blood; everyone really loved him. Not just me, everyone liked him; he was a well-behaved little one, real obedient. No one ever complained to me:

—Listen, your boy did this to me.

If I was washing, he was right there next to me, playing with whatever he had, but right there next to me; he never hung out in the street. He never destroyed things on the patio, or ran around, nope, none of that. When he got tired, he crawled under the laundry sink and went to sleep. And when he saw me taking the clothes to the roof, he followed me and then got back under the sink. He didn't give me any trouble. Just the opposite. I'd say to him:

—Go to the park and play ball with the kids.

—You won't go away . . .

—How can I leave if I have so many clothes?

—No, I better help you.

He'd take the buckets of clothes to hang in the sun. If the whites were rinsed, he'd take the colors up and then help me hang them. Otherwise he'd pick up all the napkins and wash them; he scrubbed the socks real well and he'd ask me:

—Are they okay to put out in the sun?

He'd take his bucket to put the wash in the sun. Handkerchiefs. Perico would wash all the handkerchiefs for me, and once they were real clean, he'd put them in the sun, then he'd go back to get them and rinse them out.

—Should I hang them? Do they look all right to you?

I'd look them over and tell him:

—Go ahead.

He helped me a lot. He was different, that little boy; he was a good kid. And I never let him run wild; he was always on a short leash. From the time he was little he was shy. He didn't like to be alone, always hanging on my skirt. He didn't play marbles or anything with the others, he played alone. If he did go out, he didn't go far; he stayed in the doorway, watching the games and keeping an eye on me, because he was afraid that I'd lose him. He'd rather leave the games and stay with me. The men in the building would infuriate him; telling him that they were going to take me dancing, and invite me out for a walk, and he'd bite his nails real hard, I think from nerves. I put him to sleep between two chairs: I put a piece of wood on top and a mattress on top of that. He'd hug my arm, he'd grab both my hands and put them in his hands, like this, and say:

—That's how I feel when you let go of me.

—Oh Lord!

—You might leave me when I'm sleeping!

I'M NOT AFFECTIONATE, I don't like people. I've always been distant. I never really got close to anyone. I'm a real scolder, I talk real loud. "Stop that . . . leave that alone!" So when children follow me it's because they want to, and not because I cuddle them or anything like that, Lord help me. I'm real straightforward with everyone, even my animals.

Perico was affectionate. He'd say to me:

—Go lie down, lie down, I'll soak the beans, I'll clean up, I'll mop.

In the morning he popped out of bed like a spring:

—Stay there! I'll go get groceries!

I still had to get up anyway because while he went to run errands I'd put the water on to boil; otherwise there wouldn't be enough time to get everything done. If he left early to get dough, I'd make him half a kilo of tortillas so he'd have food whenever he got hungry.

Perico always called me Jesusa. When people would ask him:

—Where is the señora? he'd say:

—My mother? Inside.

But he never called me "mother" to my face, because I never let him:

—I'm your mother because I'm raising you, but you weren't born from me, just so you know.

And I reminded him that his mother had died.

The saying that the one who raises a child is more its mother than the one who bears it is a complete lie. It's not right to take other people's children as your own. My stepmother never told me to call her "mother" either, ever. I called her Señora Evarista. I won't deny that she was a mother to me, because if she hadn't taught me everything she did, what would have become of me? But I knew that I had another mother.

I took Perico to the Obra Espiritual on All Saints' Day and on Mother's Day so he could say hello to his mother. He talked to her several times; I did what I should have, and of all the nine brothers and sisters he's the only one who received his mother's blessing.

His mother gave him good advice at the spiritual temple on Niño Perdido Street; she told him to take good care of me and to do whatever I told him. Perico didn't recognize her voice, because he was so little when she died that he didn't remember it. She died at dawn when he was sleeping. He got up and went out to play with the other kids in the neighborhood like always. They were putting drains in the streets in Felipe Angeles and the kids were all sitting around watching. Perico was looking down into the drain when we went by with the coffin. We left him there and buried her, so he didn't really know what death was all about.

I don't like to talk to people. When I'm home I'd rather talk to my animals: "Inside, come on inside!" or "Get down off there!" or "Go to sleep!" or "Be quiet!" so I can hear my voice, but I don't talk to the neighbors. I'm very strange. But there was no way not to hear Transito. She lived in the building where I worked; was she ever a chatterbox. She'd come up to the wash area to talk, wound up like a clock, and keep going on and on, even if no one was listening. She'd say to me:

—Come on, honey, let's go here or there.

—What about the boy?

—We'll take him with us.

Her *comadres* lived across the street, at number 20, so we went over there to eat, but I'm real funny; I don't like the taste of food at other people's houses. Transito insisted that she always got lost in Mexico City, so she wanted me to go everywhere with her. That's why we went out together, her in tight skirts, chattering constantly; honey this and honey that, and I barely said a word except when I had to. I have a different personality, she was happier, friendlier; she talked to Mr. So-and-so, and with this one here and that one over there. I'm choosier. When I was young I liked to sing, I was real lively, but now I don't like to talk to anyone.

About twelve or thirteen years ago, on his saint's day, Transito's husband—the current one, because she replaced them as often as you change a mustard plaster—asked me to dance, and my legs stiffened up on me after only one dance.

—I can't dance another step . . .

—But we're just getting started! Why not?

—No, señor, please excuse me, but no.

To remind me of my promise, my legs completely refused to move. The Spiritual Brothers allowed me to dance one dance, but not two or three. I went and sat next to my Perico.

Transito loved men and she loved fooling around. She'd get so excited. There are women like that, horny, who always have the itch. Transito was real obvious too. Whoring around was the only thing that made her happy. One day she told me:

—I have a Spaniard, I have a Spaniard, I have a Spaniard, a Spaniard . . .

She was dancing around like castanets. *Uy*, did she ever brag! Once when I was sitting there looking at him, I said: "This man looks anything but Spanish. He's one of the darkest Indians I've ever seen."

I told Transito:

—The Spanish aren't so dark, you've got to be kidding me. That man's not Spanish!

—He came from Spain.

—He must have just been passing through.

Since he wore a beret like the Spanish grocers do, she figured he was Spanish.

The husband she had then was the son of General Felipe Angeles. From all her talking and talking it came out who this Rafael

Angeles really was. He came to Mexico with a Spanish woman who took care of him in the hospital because he was injured when he was fighting in the Civil War in Spain. He met up with Transito in the city because she gets into everyone's business . . . As long as she gets laid she wouldn't trade places with the Queen of Spades! Angeles lived with Transito for a while, and he was bold enough to bring his innocent Spanish woman with all her children to Transito's house for dinner, and that really upset me. Transito was interested in having Rafael toss her money and wine and dine her. That woman is a piece of work that Satan pawned and never went back for.

In spite of being a partier, Rafael Angeles was a good man. He got Transito's son a job working on those big billboards that have lights on them, the kind they put on the roofs of houses. And he adopted him, even though he wasn't his son. He was the son of the Mexican Revolution. Well, at least he was born in the middle of all the fighting . . . Angeles gave Transito and her son money and his name. So that's why the boy was called Miguel Angeles.

Between one somersault and the next, Transito would scream, terrible screams, because there's nothing worse than the pain of an abortion.

—What's wrong?

—I went to see the doctor and he stuck a probe up me.

—Why?

—Because.

—You're hemorrhaging too much.

And she fainted and fell down from losing so much blood. I thought: "This woman's going to die and her parents are going to say that no one bothered to let them know."

I really got scared that time and I called her mother and father:

—You must come. Transito's in real bad shape. She could die!

They came, real concerned. That was the last time I saw her so bad off. The next day when I stopped by to see her I asked:

—Hey. Why didn't you tell me you were sick earlier? I could have heated you up some tea.

—No, it was pointless by then; it was time to get rid of it.

She has just one son, but she got rid of a bunch when she was about three or four months along, when the little one was already formed. A lot of women get rid of their babies. When they're sure they're pregnant, because it's been two months, three months, and nothing, then they go to the doctor, the man with the big old ears who always says: "Someone else puts it in and I take it out. You'll have to pay me so much. All these dead babies keep me well fed." The woman would pay and then he'd stick a hose in and unwind and unwind it for who knows how many meters inside her and that would make her lose it. Transito got rid of eight or nine, just during the time I worked over there. That's why she got fat. She didn't have a bad body; she was thin, shapely. Today she's a big ham, ugly, with huge arms that look like Jell-O. And she's always slimy because she puts so much cream on.

Women get fat because they suck in too much air and that's what damages them; it blows them up inside. A pregnant woman's pores open up all over her body to take in good vibrations, but Transito didn't have a baby inside her; so she filled up with air because of all the children she killed.

Perico was ten, almost eleven years old, and he didn't want to go to school because he was afraid of losing me. He didn't want to let go of me, but one day I said: "You have to learn something in your life. I don't want you to end up like me." I hit him real hard and made him go off to school. I forced him. That was the deal. I didn't want him to be a loader. I wanted them to teach him something worthwhile. I bought him books, notebooks, everything he needed. Now they don't have to buy books, but when Perico went to school, I had to pay for them.

I'd drop him off at about two in the afternoon, after I bathed him, combed his hair, put clean clothes on him. I'd take him and bring him home, and his classmates would make fun of him:

—Here comes your maid.

He'd get red, real red:

—It's not my maid, it's my mother.

They didn't believe him. They thought: "How can that dark old woman be his mother?"

I'd console him:

—Come on! What they say can't hurt you!

—They should mind their own business; they're saying that you're my maid when you're my mother.

—Let them say what they want! That's their problem!

—But you're not my maid. You're my mother!

—That's what you say.

Perico didn't drink coffee anymore because that was the first thing they told me at school, that it would turn him as dark as me. So I was careful what I did with him, and I made sure to get him milk from the stable. I sat down in front of him even though I didn't understand a thing, and I made him do his homework. Every single day of the year, even during vacations, he had to go over his books so he'd know the answers at exam time.

I gave him an education and I hit him a lot.

—You behave like decent people. When you greet people, say: "Good afternoon or good morning."

One day I went to Transito and insisted:

—Do me a favor and don't give Perico any more money. I don't want him to get used to having women give him money. If he wants spending money he can earn it.

—Jesusa, all the kids get a little money on Sundays.

—So? Perico knows I'll never let him go hungry. He always has a full belly, I buy him fruit, I give him ten centavos, not much, just enough so that the boys don't think he's broke, but I can't let you give him money.

Then she was hurt:

—Man, don't be so proud! Sometimes he carries my groceries for me.

—He can go grocery shopping for you or whatever you want, but not for money. Don't be paying him anything!

I'm sure she didn't like me talking to her that way, because later I found out from the neighbors that she started giving Perico bad advice. She'd ask him why he put up with me. After all, I wasn't his mother. And Transito turned the boy against me.

The last year, when he was almost out of elementary school, they asked me for his birth certificate. I asked his father, but he said he didn't have it; he said I had to go all the way to Texcoco, where the little one was born.

—I'm willing to sacrifice my time and money to go to Texcoco, but you have to come with me.

My boy felt sorry for me, and when I got back home he said:

—Why are you going to Texcoco if my aunt has my birth certificate?

—Then go ask your aunt for it.

Rogaciana couldn't find it anywhere. She never could keep track of any of her papers. I think that when Perico asked her for the certificate, she said:

—Why do you need it now that you can finally support yourself?

His aunt pointed him in the wrong direction. She asked him why he was still with me if he already knew how to read and write, and why he didn't go get a job of his own if he was old enough. She put ideas into Perico's head, because before that the boy went everywhere with me, every day of the week, and all of a sudden one morning when it was time to go to work he started acting funny.

—I'm not going.

I figure he had already arranged to leave and that's why he got so cocky on me. When we got to the building he said:

—I'm going to the park.

Other times he went to the park and came back when it was time to eat, but that day I ordered him:

—Stay here.

I started ironing. After a while he said:

—I'll read you a novel.

—Go ahead, sit right here.

I really liked the way he read. It reminded me of Pedro. I always liked it when he told me about how the bread was broken to feed many. After a bit, he stopped reading and went outside. I kept ironing. I thought he'd gone to the bathroom. He'd spend hours in there. He came back and after a little while he disappeared again, but I knew he wasn't far away because I could hear his voice.

I finished ironing at ten that night. When we were leaving for home, Transito was there all covered in her perfumed lotion, leaning on the outside of the door to the entrance of number 17 and she said:

—Wait a minute. I'll pay you.

—No, not now. I'm leaving now . . . You can pay me tomorrow.

—Now, come on in . . . Yes, right now.

I went back with Transito, and Perico stayed on the sidewalk. When I went out I saw him half a block away. Then he turned the corner and I was following him, way, way back. I said to myself: "He'll wait for me at the bus stop." He didn't wait and I didn't see where he went. I didn't find him hiding in any doorway. I thought: "Maybe he walked . . ." After a while I took the bus. I got home and was waiting for him, it struck eleven at night, twelve, and then one, so I went to bed. "He'll come soon," I thought. But he didn't. The next day I got up early and went so see his sisters, but none of them knew where he was. I went to see his brothers and they didn't know anything either. I said: "Since he isn't with his sisters or brothers, I'll go over now to see his aunt." And he was there, with her.

—What're you doing here? Is this your home?

—No, it's not my home, but it's going to be.

He talked to me with such smugness, he was so arrogant that it made my mouth dry.

—Why?

—Because I'm staying here.

—You're going to stay here? And? You can afford to pay for school?

—I'm going to work.

He was swinging his legs on the bed like it was no big deal. I got so mad I felt like beating him, but I said: "No, I need to control myself."

—So you aren't going to study?

—Yes, I'm going to night school. I'll work during the day and study at night.

—All right! Then you're staying here?

—Yes.

I thought: "I'm leaving, I'd better get out of here . . ."

Then his Aunt Rogaciana noticed how upset I was and said:

—I'll bring him back to you tomorrow.

But tomorrow never came.

I KEPT WORKING as a laundress. What good would it have done me to be sad? He was having a good time. Should I fall apart? No way. I put all his clothes together in a suitcase, and I said: "If he doesn't want to be with me anymore, let him go." I sold his things little by little. What would I want them for? They were a dead person's clothes. "He didn't come for them, and when he does there won't be any." His brothers and sisters tell me how he's doing. About a month ago they told me he was in Acapulco. I found out from one of Felicitas's godchildren that he's sorry he left me, because things didn't work out for him. But it's too late to be sorry. Here he'd have had a good job and would have gone to school, because I'd have done without for him. He didn't want it, so I don't bother with it anymore.

He left his Aunt Rogaciana and went to pick coffee beans in Veracruz with some friends. From walking in and out between the coffee plants he came back all pockmarked, a wreck, he had to hold his arms over his head because of the sores in his armpits. It was really rough trying to get over that, but he never called me or anything. I found out about it from friends I ran into on the street.

A few days after Perico left I found a lump here and my whole left side swelled up, leg, arm, face, and I had this big inflamed flap of skin hanging from my back. My hands were so yellow they looked like I'd stuck them in yellow congo, so I went to a clinic about three blocks from Balderas Street, over there by Bucareli. A little old doctor made me take my stockings down, and when he just touched the backs of my knees, scales fell off. My skin got dry from the swelling and that's why my legs shed like snakes do . . .

—You need to go over to Tolsa Street and get shots every other day because you're in the fourth stage of syphilis.

—I don't know where I'd have caught syphilis.

—Take off your dress, but keep your slip on, because we're going to put you through a machine.

Later someone told me that they see your whole body naked in that machine; they can see your skeleton, even your soul. A few of the nurses said my voice sounded like that actress that works on the radio: Prudencia Grifell. They gave me twenty-two bismuth shots over there at the clinic on Tolsa.

Finally I got tired of the whole thing:

—I've had enough, I don't want to have any more blood sucked out. I don't care if I'm well or sick. Let me die in peace. I'm not coming anymore.

I boiled rosemary at home and took seven sitz baths and the steam from the rosemary lessened the pain.

I didn't go back to Transito's neighborhood so I wouldn't have to see her again. I still did laundry at the other houses and I got a job scrubbing overalls in a printshop. At night, back in my room, I'd think about Perico, but in a natural way, not like when you go over and over sad memories, like a dog that scratches a wound until it gets infected. You could turn into a bundle of sadness, a ball of grief, without eyes to see what's going on around you. I had no reason to be sad, I knew Perico was with his family. I never went looking for him. What for? He'd already told me not to.

I don't know what sadness is. I've never been sad. You're speaking Chinese to me. Ah, crying is one thing, but sadness is something else! It's bad, worthless, it doesn't matter to anyone but you. I cry when I'm mad, but I've never been sad. I cry because I can't get someone back and tears spring out from pure rage. I have to get even somehow, biting, kicking, however. But to cry like

I've been abandoned so people can say "poor thing," no way! I'll swallow it first. Sad people don't think of anything but their own sorrow. I never told you I was sad. I told you that the life I've led has been sad, but not me. Life, yes, life is tough, but me sad? I really like to sing at the top of my lungs; when I was young I was real happy, always dancing—now that'd be a good laugh—but if it were up to me I'd sing all the time; actually, I do, but just to myself. Sad? I'm happy here all by myself. I bite myself and I scratch myself, I fall down and I get up all alone. I've never liked living with anyone else.

That's how I spend my time. When I finish doing chores at home I lie down and sleep. Sometimes the pitiful radio's on, talking and talking and talking, and I'm asleep. I have to be at the workshop early tomorrow. I get up at six in the morning to feed my animals: birds, chickens, pigeons, cats. I'm nuts about canaries again, I have this need to take care of animals—like a craving—I think because of what I did to Duchess. But I warned her . . .

I had her for nine years and I loved her. I said to myself: "Poor animal, at least when I die she'll drag me out and throw me in the field." But instead I killed her. She caught me in a bad mood and I thought: "The dog isn't going to change. She's just like a slut." Duchess wouldn't raise her pups, she ate them. Two weeks after they were born, she was back on the street stealing again. That damned dog! She stole eggs from the chicken ranchers and the neighbors fought with me because she was always into something. I took her over here to a drugstore on Inguarán Avenue to get poison:

—Why are you going to kill her?

—Because, sir, I can't take it anymore. Sell me something so she'll die.

—Only on the condition that it's for the dog.

He told me to pour some on a piece of meat, and he sold me a little bottle of "The Last Supper." I said: "What do I need the bottle for? One day I might forget what it is and chug it down myself." And I gave it all to her on a piece of bread because I didn't have meat. She didn't even finish it. As soon as she swallowed the first bite, she fell over like a stone in a well. She was real fat; my dog ate a lot but she made me so mad. Any day now I just know someone is going to poison me for poisoning the dog. She went wherever I did. If I went to work, she'd be outside on the street all day, and she wouldn't leave until I did. I took the bus and she walked, wagging her tail the whole time. She knew her way around. She was so tired when she got home, from her own stupidity; no one asked her to follow me. I'd order her: "Stay!" I'd hit her. I'd tie her up and she'd untie herself. You have to pay for everything during this lifetime, because you can't in the next; they send you back to Earth to purge yourself of your sins.

Duchess left me an eight-day-old puppy from her last litter, Blackie. Ungrateful dog, just like her! He left as soon as he grew up. First Perico left me and then Blackie went away. He's still wandering the streets. Sometimes I see him. The last time he came by I yelled:

—What're you doing here? Get out. If you're leaving, get lost for good. Otherwise, stay put.

I didn't have to say it twice. Blackie turned around and took off.

Every home has to have some kind of animal, any kind, because according to ancient legends it protects the owners. If it's a dog, his hair stands on end at midnight and from then on he fights with Barabbas, because Barabbas wants to possess his owners and the dog says:

—Let's make a deal . . .

He puffs himself up and his hair stands on end like a sea urchin.

—Count how many hairs are on my back from my head to my tail. See how many there are.

—All right, Barabbas answers. I'm counting.

He starts to count, one, two, three, four, five, six, real slow, because there are a lot of hairs, and when he's almost to the tail, the dog shakes. Barabbas gets real mad and yells:

—You made me lose count!

—Then start over, the dog answers calmly. Start over. What have you got to lose?

Barabbas starts counting again. And they go on like that until four in the morning. When the clock strikes four, dong, dong, dong, dong, the devil says:

—You've tricked me.

—No, I haven't, Barabbas.

—Yes, you have. I've got to go because dawn's breaking. We'll see each other tomorrow.

The sun comes up and the dog has saved his masters. But it's an endless battle with the devil that goes on all three hundred sixty-five days of the year. Cats do the same thing and chickens too; each one takes care of their masters in their own way. Every animal that survived on Earth after the Flood has a mission to fulfill. They're not here for free. They complete their mission just as we Christians do. But the animals may even do more than us because we're selfish, and at a certain age we choose to do whatever suits us. The animals are more obedient.

One day Perico's father, José del Carmen Vidales, came to the house.

—I've come to let you know Pico's in jail.

I got mad:

—What do I care? I didn't put him there . . .

—I'm telling you because he's your son.

—If he was my son, he'd be here with me and not in jail. But since he isn't my son, he went where he thought was best. Go tell the mother he has now.

He left the way he came. I kept thinking about it, but my heart didn't flinch. If Perico didn't write to me, why should I go and beg for him now that he was in the clink? That's why I told his father to tell his Aunt Rogaciana, since that's where he ended up. But the aunt never went to see him in the penitentiary the whole year he was there. She treated him the worst of anyone.

I've had some beautiful revelations that I don't deserve, visions that perfume the air as if someone was burning incense. Sometimes it smelled like orange blossoms, other times like verbena, or like fruit, like musk, and a rain of violet light, real faint, would fall in the room. But revelations fly by real fast like a filmstrip. I even tried to open my eyes, but they're there one minute and gone the next. I haven't been able to see more than a little piece of sky this big, about the size of a postage stamp. That's why, on Wednesdays, when the brothers stand up at the temple to tell about what they'd experienced, I don't believe them when they say they saw a real, real tall mountain or a great waterfall, I don't believe them. I can't believe that you can see things so big from the huge immenseness of the Otherworld. I think they say that to impress the rest of us, but I think they're just lies. A lot of mediums brag about their visions and say that they see Him shepherding His flock . . . I don't believe them! Because if He's in that great immensity of space, how the hell can they see that far? There's no way. That's an exaggeration about the Obra and I don't go along with that.

Here in Canal del Norte there's a man like that named Manuel Alcalá. God has never allowed me to stand at Alcalá's door, even if he's from the same Obra Espiritual, because he exaggerates a lot. When I ride the bus I see him sitting at the entrance to his chapel in a purple gown, wearing a crown and a sash that he ties at his waist so it hangs down to one side. I think he's out of his mind, because people in control of their senses don't put on such a show. Yes, the Obra is real sacred. Eight or nine years ago I heard that Alcalá had gone to a lake to walk on the water like our Lord Jesus Christ. That's what I heard, and he sank straight to the bottom and they had to pull him out because he drowned from all his clowning around. But about three years ago I went by Canal del Norte and I saw him sitting in the doorway:

—Was he resurrected or what?

I don't believe anything he says, not even his blessing. It's one thing for our Lord God to give us a mission during our life and another thing to make such a mockery of things.

Now, when I close my eyes at night to sleep, I get comfortable, and I just barely close them when I see a cloud pass by, or I feel like I'm riding in a stagecoach with a leather top and everyone greets me with respect and when I wake up I hear the clue. At least that's what it seems like. I've clearly seen our Lord walking in profile at the foot of a ravine, suffering with His cross, His cape, and His thorns. It's a revelation I don't deserve. I'm unworthy of it, but God has granted it to me no matter how much I pray, saying to Him:

—Ay, Señor, I'm not worthy of Your greatness and riches because a woman as bad as me shouldn't contemplate such marvels!

But He insists and I continue to see the visions until I beg:

—No, Señor, let me sleep now or I'll wake up dazed from all Your wonders.

I was told that when the time came to fulfill the mission that was entrusted to me, I'd see three roses. One night I saw tiny roses like baby's breath, a yellow one, a pink, and a white, but real small. I thought: "They told me three roses but those are awfully little . . ." I expected to see normal roses like you'd cut from the garden. That's why I didn't mention it to the Guide of the Temple. But on the third day of teaching he forced the words out of me and I told the brother that I'd seen something real small, itsy-bitsy; a pale rose, another faded yellow one, and a misty white rose, but they were specks the size of baby's breath.

—Yes, you were expecting a natural flower, but that's not what I sent you. I sent spiritual flowers from the farthest reaches of space.

That's why I say that the immensities are contemplated real small, and that people who say: "I see a huge river," well, it must be like a little silk thread crossing the heavens. That's the reason I didn't see big roses, but just sparks. Every time the Lord has allowed me to contemplate His divine greatness, it's been my size.

One day around the time of Holy Week, during spiritual teachings when I had my eyes open, I saw a little armchair surrounded by a red light appear above the brother's head, and it came over to where I was standing and I watched it without blinking. It stood about half a meter away from me. When I saw it get so close, I closed my eyes, and when I opened them, it had moved back over the brother's head again. The chair came to me three times, but I didn't understand what it was about, and the third time the Lord spoke:

—My child, I have given you my light three times. That's why

I'm touching you again now; I've spoken to you spirit to spirit, but you pretended not to hear. Listen to me. I have come toward you spiritually and I have called you, but you're deaf because your headphones don't hear the word that I've given to you. Although you haven't answered me, today your filthy flesh serves as my speaker.

—Sir, are you talking to me?

—To you, my child, to you . . . The time has come for you to fulfill your duty. You can tell your brothers what you've seen.

—Lord, with Your divine permission I will share with my brothers what You have allowed me to see. Half a meter from the skull of the flesh through which You manifest Yourself a small armchair of red light has appeared that moves forward and back, and a white bead is seated in the very center of the chair. That is what You have granted me to contemplate and what I can give to my brothers.

Then He said to me:

—Now fulfill your misson on Earth.

I went into a trance. Only God knows what I must have talked about. The sensation was so strong that when I came to, I wasn't in my right mind and I didn't even know where I lived.

Zanaida, one of the sisters, took me home:

—This is where you live, Sister Chuchis . . . You're still feeling the effects.

I was willing to fulfill my mission, but everyone looked down on me. They're all real selfish. In the first place, I was poor; I didn't have nice long white robes that came down to my ankles like the rest of them and they stared at me like I was a germ. But that's not Jesus's teaching, because to Him, the rich man is just as much His child as the beggar. They're all His children, but here, the way they treat you is based on the clothes you wear. I had my little Christ statue, candles, a scepter, the Seven Machos lotion, and all the things you need to work a cure, but they were cheap, even though they worked real well. In the second place, I stood. I didn't work sitting down but standing, because the other mediums at the temple took away my desire to sit. When I'd get ready to go into a trance and we were all sitting so the beings could penetrate us, other mediums would show up as if they had bought the chair. They'd elbow me out of the way:

—Sister, move farther back.

They'd move me, shaking with anger, to another chair. If I was, as they say, already in a trance to receive a spiritual being, they interrupted my energy flow and strength. I'd feel pins and needles all over my body and I'd have to fall asleep all over again. I'd concentrate again, and when I was massaged back into a spiritual trance, Sister So-and-so would say to me:

—Sister, move over a little for Sister Guillermina. She's one of the chosen ones because of her visions. If you don't mind.

So it meant that all the chairs were for Sister this and Sister that and there wasn't even a stake for me to sit on.

—Well, take your chairs and slam both of your cheeks down on them.

I thought: "What do I need them wrinkling their noses at me for? I won't come back anymore . . ." But that seemed wrong to me because God tells us: "I've given you my light so you can raise it up, not for you to hide it." So if God gave me the torch I have to pass it from hand to hand and wait for each of them to enter. They sat at the front of the congregation next to the divine stair and when all the powers were seated I stood up next to the door. I said the prayer standing, I closed my eyes, and I asked God to help me. I was all tense, cramping up all over, my whole body hurt and my mouth was full of saliva, and that's how the Spiritual Power came through me. So to this day, when my protector penetrates me, I stand up because I can feel that it's him and we do it well standing. And it makes the rest of them mad:

—Sister, you're drawing attention to yourself.

—I can't go into a trance sitting down, sisters. You have to accept that.

Mesmer, my protector, saw that they never saved me a chair anywhere and saw the contempt they had for me and that's why he taught me to receive the divine powers under any circumstances. Of course, that's how he dominates me now. He lifts me up, puts me on his knees, he does whatever he wants with me, and the peo-

ple there pay more attention to me than to the other mediums.
People who have seen me work can't take their eyes off me:

—Well, of course, because you walk around on your knees.

—I can't see myself.

—You don't work like the others.

—It's my protector's orders. I don't command myself. So let
the protector do whatever he wants, through my vessel. I can't
contradict him.

At the Obra Espiritual they don't ask us to fast or to do the
crap they ask you to do in the Catholic Church: "Don't eat meat,
eat fish." It's all bullshit. Usually people don't even have enough
money for beans. How are they going to eat fish? Look at me. I
was a big dancer, a big drinker, and a big fighter. To stop drinking
and fighting—that's the kind of fasting the Ser Supremo asked of
me.

It's been a long time since I've been with a congregation because everyone where I used to belong has been taken to eternity.
I still have the same faith, but I don't go anywhere, because
they've turned the Obra into a business. The whole world has become materialistic! In this city they don't have sewers or dumps.
Everything smells, everything rots, there are only stinking streets,
like stinking women. It's all one big swamp. And this is because
the world has turned a deaf ear to the Lord. We're wearing His patience thin, and one day He'll say:

—Well, that's enough. This is the end.

And let's hope we've been to confession that day.

THE COYOTE may catch me once but it won't a second time. Some people fight and then speak to each other again, and then fight some more and make up again. I don't go for that. To hell with them! I had this friend Iselda. She's Casimira's sister-in-law. Casimira owns the tenement house. I shared a room with Iselda and we got to be real close. Her children called me Gramma. We were inseparable friends: whatever I had to eat I took to her and whatever she had she shared with me. Who knows what people told her—I never found out—but she changed completely. Her sister Faustina was a big gossip. A lot of time went by, and one day after many years of not speaking to me—it was May 10—Iselda said to me as I walked by real early on my way to get milk:

—Listen, the girls have a Mother's Day gift for you.

—For me? Why? I'm not their mother.

—No, but they really love you.

After so many years of friendship. At about noon, the oldest one, who had real big ears and always made funny faces—I'd known the girl since she was a little thing—brought me a little cup and saucer and said:

—This little gift is for you.

—For me? Why?

—Because it's Mother's Day.

—And why are you bringing me a present? I'm not your

mother. I'm nothing to you. Take this gift to your mother. I don't need it. I can drink water out of a chamber pot . . .

Faustina, the blabbermouth who lived in the pigsty across the street, *uy*, she got real nasty:

—See, Prisca, that's what you get for trying to be nice . . .

—I didn't ask her for this. She's not being nice and she has no reason to try to be nice! From the looks of it, you're the one who needs it.

I turned around to the girl:

—Take it to your aunt. Go on, take it to her.

And Prisca left with her gift. I would have accepted it if they'd brought me stuff before, when they were little girls, even if it was a banana, anything, a kernel of corn. But after so many years . . . The girl was already twenty-two when she thought to start sucking up to me, and on Mother's Day no less. To a mother who was as barren as a mule!

Prisca never came back. I'd carried the little pisser around when she was just a spinning top. I saw the other ones being born because I was the one who took them out of their mother's womb, like I do with my cat, so they don't suffocate her. Doctors are useless because they don't tie their belly button off good. You have to make the knot tight, real tight, pushing it down close to the newborn's skin, and then you measure four fingers of cord and you cut it. If it's a female, three fingers; if it's a male, four. It can't be any less than four fingers for a male, and then you cut it with scissors that have been heated over the fire. Here in the city they don't burn it. But with Iselda, I buried everything that came out after the baby, the blood, the placenta, the cord. I dug a hole in the ground and buried it in a field. You can't just throw it out, because it's part of the child; it's living flesh. I dug a hole in the ground and I buried it there. In hospitals they just throw out the afterbirth; sometimes they even toss out entire babies. That's in the city, where they don't seem to be very Christian. Besides, they charge three hundred, four hundred pesos. I went by a garbage can one time that was filled with roasting placentas, and you can just imagine the dogs hanging around there! The doctors don't give a damn about anything! Here they just laugh at the faces the women make and at their screaming. They won't let them squat down or cover them, they just pull their legs open: "Come on, come on, don't scream so much, think of your honeymoon . . ."

I really loved Prisca's mother—Iselda Gutiérrez a lot, and now when she says hello as I pass her on the street, I say good morning, good evening, but not with the same respect we had for each other before. I've missed her all these years and I still do, but we'll never be close again because I can't beg for friendship. I still don't even know why we split up. She never tried to clear things up and that's not the kind of thing you leave for another day. I don't need her. If I'm sick, I lock myself in and roll around in here, all by myself. I'm not one to go say:

—Come rub something on me to make me feel better, even if it's just spit!

No way! I've been this way my whole life. I still do my chores, even if I'm in a bad way. I complain because I'm flesh and blood, I'm all callused, with my soul hanging by a thread, but I don't give in. When it's my time I'll just lie down on a hill so the vultures can help me die. In the meantime, I'll keep going to the workshop and cleaning. I can hardly get on the bus, the backs of my legs hurt so much, but I've never stopped working, not even when I'm falling flat on my face. Never. That's how I was raised. Ever since I was little, there hasn't been any sickness that can keep me down. I'll keep my *ay, ay, ay, ay* to myself, and no one will hear me. I'm not a bother to anyone. I'm still here in this world, washing overalls, cleaning the metal on the presses with gasoline, picking out the good book covers and throwing the defective ones out, cleaning my house, walking to the stable for milk, even though I know I can't change anything. There isn't even a little piece of me left that's any good. I'm old, old, old, it's old age, just old age. If Jesus complained because He couldn't take any more, imagine how I feel. I'm only garbage.

In other times, in God's world, life went by quiet and slow, and people lasted on Earth a long time. Now, whenever you're in pain, it's slice, slice: "Cut him open." And they turn people into idiots because they cut things they shouldn't and they leave nerves frayed like those electric cables outside that aren't connected to anything. They get to be dim-witted because so many little threads inside their brains are unplugged. Look what they did to me instead of healing me. Don't you think they ruined me taking that liquid out of my spine? And then they wrote me prescriptions like crazy. If your head hurts, you lie down.

Surely they must have taken out my marrow and that's why I'm all wrinkled, because my vitality shrank down.

At the beginning of time our grandparents ate vegetables and fish. Their ancestors drank milk and honey from the rivers and food rained down on them from Heaven. They didn't work; they just walked slowly so they wouldn't get tired. Years passed but they stayed strong, their bodies didn't stoop, they had energy. In pictures you see they have white beards, but they aren't wrinkled or hunchbacked, because the food was good, and it went straight to the marrow. Now, with modern refrigeration, how many months old is the fish when you eat it? Before, they took the fish out of the sea and they multiplied right away. They cut them open while they were still moving, they cleaned them on the beach and fried them up, fresh. Cattle were slaughtered and eaten the same day and they drank the warm red blood. And lamb was also eaten as soon as it was sacrificed and sanctified by the Omnipotent Jehovah's hand. That's why the years didn't pass for our ancestors. I know from revelations. I've seen the desert and how the waters open to let the chosen ones pass; I know because it's written. But since they wanted to have more than He did, more than the very Eternal Father, He sent Adam and Eve. First there were the primitive ones who walked the face of the Earth, the old, and from that descent came Adam and Eve. No. There were no monkeys! Maybe over in France they believe that monkey business, but here in Mexico we're Christians and we're more open-minded. There weren't any monkeys! Adam and Eve were pieces of clay and the Eternal Father made a hole in them and blew them up and gave them life. But they didn't have to work for anything. They didn't need anything. They didn't worry. When they got hungry they ate with pleasure. What did they have to worry about? They lived under the trees protected by the infinite power of the Eternal Father. There wasn't cold or hot, neither light nor dark. There wasn't anything. It was always the same and they were well fed. They were never hungry. And that's all that matters, not being hungry. Until Lucifer, in the form of a serpent, wrapped himself around the tree of knowledge of good and evil. They hadn't noticed it before. And the snake called to Eve:

—Eat. Look how good it is . . .

The serpent had bitten the apple before Eve did. He could speak because he'd made a pact with Barabbas. The serpent transforms itself into different animals—a hog, a goat, a turkey—and he nests in women's wombs. Eve ate the apple, and when she did, she developed a bust, because she didn't have a bust or curly hair either here or there. She was just a doll, flat, one piece, smooth, without breasts or that mishmash of hair. And at the very instant she bit the apple, her breasts came out and the hair here and there started to come out thick, like chives. She didn't realize it, so when she bumped into Adam she said:

—Take this. The serpent gave it to me and it's real good.

She couldn't see herself and she still looked the same to him, but when he put the apple in his mouth he noticed the change and it scared him. When he tried to swallow the bite of apple, it got stuck in his throat, and that's where the Adam's apple comes from. When she saw him choking she said:

—What's wrong with you?

And he yelled at her:

—Ay! You have hair and tits!

And she yelled too:

—Ay! And look at what you have!

And she ran.

A cross of hair came out on his chest, and all the men that come from the creation of Adam have the apple and the cross of hair. They were trying to figure out how to cover themselves when the Eternal Father spoke to them. They didn't know how to appear before Him. That was when Adam broke a leaf off the grapevine and covered himself and gave her three leaves. But before that they'd walked around stark naked. They didn't feel cold or heat. The Lord scolded them and then Adam said:

—I didn't do it, Lord. Eve gave it to me . . .

And then Eve argued:

—The serpent gave it to me.

The two of them kept blaming each other. Without another word, the Lord raised His arm and threw them out of Paradise. He told them to find their way to Earth and leave. The angel came for them, I don't remember what its name was, if it was Mercury or Gabriel, but they assured me at the Obra Espiritual that, no matter what had happened, Eve wouldn't have lasted twenty-four hours in Paradise. Adam, on the other hand, was a different story. He lived the best years of his youth there, while he was alone. The angel pushed them to the door and that was the beginning of Earth. They struggled, worked, slept, and woke up. That was when they had their wedding. They were a couple, but not married, because they'd never seen each other with earthly eyes. Now they saw each other for the first time and started creation. It wasn't the Lord's world anymore, but theirs, mankind's. They had a lot of children. You can imagine how many children it would take to form all of creation . . .

One Thursday last month, the eighteenth of August, the prodigal son showed up. He asked Iselda and the girls in the doorway if Señora Jesusa Aguilar lived there:

—Yes, she lives here, but she's not here now.

And since I'd told them about him, that he was a redhead, they stared at him.

—Are you Chuchita's son?

—Yes, I'm her son. Do you think there's a chance my mother will see me? I've come to ask her to forgive me for everything I've done to her.

—Yes, she'll see you. Wait for her here, she'll be back later.

—I can't stay now because I'm going to see my sister, but I'll come back tomorrow.

The next day, Friday, he knocked on my door at seven o'clock at night. When I saw him I didn't feel anything, just anger. He said to me:

—Don't you recognize me?

—No, sir, no, I don't recognize you.

Of course I did, but I told him I didn't.

He started to stamp the ground with his feet like a calf:

—I've come to ask your forgiveness for what I've done to you.

—To me? You haven't offended me . . . So since you haven't offended me in any way, there's no need for us to talk.

—But I'm so-and-so . . . I'm Perico.

—That Perico left years ago and I don't know and don't want to know anything about him.

—You don't want to recognize me, so I'll leave for good this time. I'll never come back to the city.

I didn't want him in my house, but I remembered I'd left the grill on, and whether I wanted to or not I asked the boy to come in.

—I have an egg on the fire for the canaries and it's going to burn.

He talked to me for a while. It was getting dark and I turned around to look at him.

—I don't have anything to give you . . . If I make a cup of coffee, will you have some?

He answered me real humble, always looking at his shoes.

—Yes.

I made him coffee, I fried him some potatoes and an egg, and I gave him bread. I didn't have anything else. He ate every bite. When he squatted down to eat I noticed that he'd lost a lot of hair; it wasn't pretty anymore, red. Things hadn't gone well for him. Then he asked:

—Will you let me come visit you every day?

—You can come.

Within a week he bought supplies to make picture frames and he walked the streets with his frames hanging on one arm, the kind people buy to frame religious pictures like the Sacred Heart or the Virgin of Guadalupe.

He told his father and his brothers: "I went to see my mother," because everyone knows that he thinks of me as his mother. "She's forgiven me and I'm going to visit her every day from now on." And he came every day.

I liked it and I didn't like it; I was embarrassed to have people see him coming and going. The only ones who knew he was my son were the next-door neighbors—from the picture I showed them, from his red hair, and from what I'd told them about him. But most people would think the worst. They'd say: "Useless old woman, taking up with a young man!"

Perico told me that he'd gotten into some real tight spots. He had a bump here on his head and the little Jesus child statue that I bought to protect him has all the same injuries that Perico suffered in Nayarit, in the north, in Acapulco, wherever he was. The statue has its head split open, its back and ribs are cracked, the arm is dislocated, and one of the feet too. Perico still sells frames in Acapulco, and they've assaulted him so many times on the beach. Now that he comes to see me he tells me all about it. He lives real far away but he's here every day at five in the evening, six at the latest, and he leaves at about nine at night. We reminisce about when he was young and he says he's sorry to see all I've had to go through with the owner of the tenement. He says:

—So, Casimira got mean?

He knew her when she was different. Every time the sink in the hallway would get stopped up she'd have it fixed; in the dry season, two masons would come to patch the roofs, and in spite of the fact that water would still leak in, you always appreciated the effort. But not anymore. Now she's always threatening to sell the place on us, because she says they're offering her a good price for this pigsty. She even put a sign on the roof that said: "Empty Lot for Sale," but the wind blew it down . . .

Perico had realized he missed me because he needs help. So he comes to visit me for his own convenience. Do I think he'll look out for me? No. Quite the contrary. He'd like me to die real soon. That's why I've thought about getting rid of the few odds and ends I have; it won't be the first time I've slept that way if I end up having to lay a piece of paper on the floor. What do I need things for? Let him work to get what he wants when I die; I've broken my back to get the few sticks of furniture I have. That's what Perico's after, to get hold of my things, I'm sure. When he left, I didn't have a sewing machine, or a radio, or a wardrobe, or a crescent-moon dresser, or a nightstand, or little chairs. I didn't have anything, because I spent what I made to feed him. I got what you see here when he left. If he came without a cent, he's screwed from head to toe. What did he come here for? He couldn't have made it any clearer. Don't be an asshole, you're kidding yourself! Look at me! It makes me feel bad when you spout off that slobber about people being good and loving you. Perico came so I'd feed him, that's for sure! He's here at five in the evening, real punctual. Sometimes I'm not even home yet when I see him leaning on the wall, waiting for me. It didn't hurt me to give him a tortilla. What I mind is that he takes advantage of me . . .

One day Perico brought his bed and moved in here. If he had any shame, he'd say: "I'll get up early and go see what work I can find." But none of that. He sleeps in, What time does he open his eyes and wipe the sleep out of them? What time does he leave? Who knows. I'd leave for work and he'd bathe. He bathes every day. Can you believe it? He started that bad habit in Acapulco. He also changes his shirt once a week, but this week he wore three; he changed every piece of clothing and then went out. So it's not going great here. My *comadres* must have told him I had money, because one night when he was asleep, drunk, he started talking:

—No, I'm tired of looking . . . She doesn't have anything . . .

Who's he talking about? Well, it surely has to be me. As if I had such a pea brain. This one wants to suck me dry of something I don't even have . . . One day I said to him:

—I'm still short for the rent payment!

He acted as if I hadn't said anything. It went in one ear and out the other. Most people would've said:

—Listen, I'll help you out . . . I'll bring you money tomorrow for the rent.

But him, nothing. Sometimes he'll say:

—I'm going to sell frames tomorrow.

It may be true or not. They told me that he hooked up with a woman they call La Lagarta, the lizard, who gives as good as she gets, one of the whores from around here. God only knows. He never has money on him. But he has to drink milk, eat bread; at least three pesos of bread a day, because he doesn't eat regular bread; just sweet bread, buns, biscuits, the stuff that doesn't fill you up and costs more. I'd stuff a dozen rolls with beans for him, but no. And he also doesn't like machine-made tortillas, the ones that don't rise no matter how long they're on the comal. He says they're no good, that they grind the dough with corncob and all. I don't know how he ended up being so picky. It's probably my fault.

Men really take advantage of everyone; they're driven by what's convenient for them. Men used to take care of women; they brought home everything they earned. The wife took out money for expenses and what was left over was put away. And all the children had two sets of clothes. Now it doesn't do a woman any good to save, because he takes it away from her.

That's why I say that men nowadays only want to get whatever they can out of you. No one respects their wife or takes care of her. The more they can use her, the better. Any day now I may not be able to do anything, and I can't say: "My boy will look after me." No way. I'd be better off leaving. What am I good for now? I can't wash his clothes or boil his beans. When I can't go on anymore, I'll grab my bag and I'll go out to the hill so the vultures can eat me, since I know there isn't a hole in the ground for me in the cemetery. I've liked those birds ever since I was a little thing. That's why I talk about them so much. Tomorrow or the next day I could be their food, and I want to be eaten in the fields. It seems like they're already circling lower each time around. They're about the size of a turkey, just as black, with a red head. The young ones are real shiny, like hot tar. They're the ones that clean the villages after epidemics—after the peasants, the horses, the soldiers, and the animals die. The vultures gobble it all down. And there's nothing left, not even whispers! I wish the vultures could swallow the evil when they pick our skeletons clean, but that always stays on Earth.

Things are predestined to happen at a certain time. No one in my family knew the Obra Espiritual. Not a single one of them knew about it. They didn't take the blindfold off their eyes, so they banged into each other, and they never got anywhere. Of all the people in my family, I'm also the only one who's traveled all over. My father never saw what I saw. I've covered all these roads because it's written that I was supposed to walk a lot. I've been to a lot of places my father never went to. He'd just walk a little ways and end up on the battlefield. My husband said that he wasn't going to leave me alive on this earth, but God didn't concede that to him. That's why I say that things are already written and that God determines them. You have nothing to say about it and you can't speed up the hands of time. Here I am whining, with my tongue hanging out like a hanged man. I'm dying but I'm still standing, like a rotting tree. Only God knows for how long.

Not dying on time is hard. When I'm not well, I don't open my door all day; I spend entire days locked up. I might boil tea or *atole* or make something for myself, but I don't go out to raise hell with anyone and no one comes to my door. One day I'll be all twisted up inside here, and my door will be locked. That's why I ask God to let me die there on the top of a hill. If God would grant me that, I'd only need to make the effort to get there. But since God doesn't give wings to poisonous scorpions, who knows if it'll happen. I've asked Him, but if not, then let His will be done. I really want to die over where I used to wander around. Please let God remember me, because I'd like to stay under a tree way over there! Then the vultures can surround me and that'll be the end of it. You'll come ask for me and I'd be over there, happy, flying in the vultures' bellies. Otherwise, the neighbors come in to watch you die, to see if you're making faces, because most people come to laugh at the person who's dying. That's the way life goes. People die so others can laugh. They make fun of your condition; your legs could be sticking out straight, or be all twisted, with your mouth open and your eyes popping out. Tell me if dying like that isn't hard. That's why I lock myself in. Casimira, the owner, will have to break down the door to get me out once I'm stiff and starting to smell. They'll drag me out, but to have them come in here and look at me and say this, that, and the other thing, nope, no one . . . no way . . . Just me and God. That's why I don't want to die in the city, but out there, in a ravine like my father, who died in an open field under a tree. So I hope God will grant me permission to walk. It'd be good to know when you're going to die. I ask God to tell me so I can get ready and walk to wherever He takes me, and become food for the animals in the fields, the coyotes, like my husband, Pedro. It's not that I don't want to be buried, but who is there to bury me? They'd say:

—Thank God, this old breed has finally kicked the bucket.

I don't think people are good. Truthfully, I don't. Only Jesus Christ was, and I didn't meet Him. And my father, but I never really knew if he loved me or not. How can you really think the people here on Earth are good?

Now fuck off! Go away and let me sleep.

One day when you come by I'm not going to be here anymore; there'll just be pure air. There won't be anyone to tell you where I've gone, and you'll think everything has been a lie. We're not really here anyway. It's all lies. They tell lies on the radio, the neighbors lie, and it's a lie that you'll miss me. What the hell is there to miss? You don't need me anymore. They won't miss me at the workshop either. Who will there be to miss me? I'm not even going to say goodbye.

JESUSA